Praise For *The Perfect Stage Crew*

"*The Perfect Stage Crew* should be required reading for anyone launching their first stage production . . . or their second . . . or their third. . . ."

—Phil Trumbo, Emmy Award–winning
Creative Director, Amaze Entertainment

"John Kaluta's endlessly instructive book covers all the nuts-and-bolts basics so that you can concentrate on your artistic vision. I wish I'd had this when I started out."

—Joel Goss, Award-winning Writer and Director

"John's unique concepts in encouraging creativity have impressed me throughout the years. His text supports the idea that if you can conceive it, you can achieve it!"

—"Kinetic Eric," Owner, Kinetic Artistry, Inc.

The Perfect Stage Crew

The Compleat Technical Guide

for High School,

College,

and Community Theater

John Kaluta

ALLWORTH PRESS
NEW YORK

12   11   10   09   08   7   6   5   4   3

Published by Allworth Press
An imprint of Allworth Communications, Inc.
10 East 23rd Street, New York, NY 10010

Cover design by Derek Bacchus
Interior design and page composition/typography by SR Desktop Services, Ridge, NY

Library of Congress Cataloging-in-Publication Data
Kaluta, John.
    The perfect stage crew: the compleat technical guide for high school,
college, and community theater / John Kaluta.
        p.   cm.
    Includes bibliographical references and index.
    ISBN-10: 1-58115-315-5
    ISBN-13: 978-1-58115-315-6
    1. Theaters—Stage-setting and scenery.   2. Stage management.   I. Title.

PN2091.S8K25   2003
792.02'5–dc22
                                                        2003020912

Table of Contents

To . . .

all my students,
all my teachers.

PREFACE

It's All About the Show . . .

Theater is magical. With small budgets and an amateur production staff, pulling off good community theater can be quite a trick. Good theater in a high school is the closest thing to real magic you may ever see on earth. That's not to say it isn't a lot of hard work, and it doesn't mean good things will happen without a bit of effort. The magical part is the result of planning, teamwork, stick-to-it-iveness, and perhaps a little luck. It's magical when things turn out better than expected. And, when things go wrong and catastrophe looms, the magic comes out in the extra efforts by cast and crew. Mostly the crew. Then again, I'm partial to the efforts of the stage crew; I ran the crew at Montgomery Blair High School in Silver Spring, Maryland, for more than nine years.

I'd like to share some stories, some techniques that I *know* work, and some advice. Using the advice and techniques I've described here, almost anyone can put together a well-running high school or community theater stage crew that does unexpectedly good work. It takes time, skill, and dedication, but the payoff is, well, magical.

You don't have to read the whole book; you don't even have to read the book in order. Just read enough to get inspired, then get in the theater, with *your* crew, and make some magic of your own.

SOME DETAILS

Since I work full-time in a public high school, most of my examples come with an education perspective or slant. The advice is perfectly applicable to community theater groups, church groups, even Scout groups working to put on a show. You may actually have it easier in some respects since the school bureaucracy can put a few blocks in your road, if you know what I'm sayin'. . . .

You might, as you're reading, take a moment to change the wording of some of my examples. Where I say "The superintendent of schools . . . " you might say, "The bishop . . . " or "The community services manager . . . " or whatever. You'll quickly see that the lessons written for a high-school crew apply equally well outside of the school environment, and vice versa.

I CHANGED ALL OF THE NAMES

When I started out writing this book (it began as a short note to my successor), I wasn't going to use any names. When the note approached fourteen pages in length, I changed my mind completely. "Hey, I'll write a book!" thought I, and here it is. My successor got a copy free, though Lord knows he doesn't need it. I included an occasional story about something that happened in the past, so names crept in. That's when I changed the names. I have two reasons for this: One, I'm not sure all of these students want their name mentioned in my book, and two, it'll be great fun for them to try to figure out who I really mean. Since I had over thirty kids a year on stage crew, I had to search around for the right fake names. Once in a while a real name slipped in.

CREATIVE ITALICS

I'm a teacher, but I'm not an English teacher. So I've used italics and grammar in a personal, creative way to indicate emphasis and to change the stress or point of a sentence. My editor has fixed most of these, but if you catch a poorly written phrase just let it go. I'm very sensitive about my writing, so please don't write in with corrections unless you just hafta. Just read the line again, with a different inflection, like they taught you in drama class. When confused, try reading passages aloud. This is best done in public, in a muttering voice. At least people will leave you alone. If you read the book over and over again, everything will eventually make sense.

Actually, that might not be true. You're going to have to read it, then try the technique a few times, *then* maybe it'll make sense. Make sure you practice these techniques, even the simplest ones, before you try to show the crew kids how to do them. For instance, mix up some paint yourself (following my instructions) before you try to teach the kids how. This will prevent many embarrassing accidents. And try to think things through before you start them. There are, no doubt, plenty of techniques that work perfectly for me that will work differently for you. If you try something and it flops, redo it another way.

One more thing. The book is written to you as if you were going to actually do every little thing in it. We both know this isn't really the case. You will train and assign others, usually beginners, to actually do the tasks described. You have to know what to do in order to train them, so the book is addressed to you. Think of it as the "royal you," meaning you, your helpers, your crew, somebody else instead of you, youse guys, y'all— y'know what I mean?

By the way, if I mention a brand name, it's simply because I like that brand. Nobody paid me nothin' for the plug. And there may be better brands—I'm not perfect. Just look at my grammar, for heaven's sake.

CHAPTERS

Things have been arranged in chapters, in approximate chronological order, and are listed like cues. You will occasionally pick up a little tidbit about one thing while you are reading about another. And at the end of several chapters you'll find a couple of hints and tricks that don't really seem to fit into that chapter. This is a gentle reminder that you can't forget about painting while you're working on lights, and vice versa. I placed these items in this manner to match the approximate chronological order for a show. Some of these smaller hints are listed as edit cues, such as "Cue 3.9—Audition Posters." The truth is you'll be trying to juggle almost all facets of the production at once anyway, so there is no true chronological order, at least not in every detail. It's your book, so feel free to dog-ear pages you find important. There is an index, if you need it.

PICTURES

A lot of stage crew books have lots of pictures. Go buy those. Of course, it's pictures of monkey wrenches, and we all know what a monkey wrench looks like. So, not too many pictures in here. Saves you money on the price of the book. Where you really need a picture you'll find one, courtesy of me or my brother Mike. I'll throw in a couple of AutoCAD drawings where I can.

PERFECTION

Some people have suggested that you can never have a perfect stage crew, and they are right. The job of creating a perfect stage crew will never be compleat. There will always be room for improvement, and something will always go wrong. Do not despair. Reach for perfection, settle for 90 percent (see below).

90 PERCENT

If you don't understand percentages, just rip this page out of the book and throw it away. If you do, set your standards to 150 percent of what you think can be done. Trust me—150 percent. Firmly establish in your mind that every facet of your production is going to improve by 50 percent over your expectations. Shoot for the moon! Get excited. *Intend* to impress. Your shows are going to become great! Got it? Good. Now you have two things left to do. Remember what I just told you . . . and *forget* it!

I'd like all of you to think back to your wonderful high school years. If you'll be honest with me, and yourself, you'll probably recall that it was very difficult to show you or teach you anything. Today's kids are just the same. Your job is to show them what to do, then let them do it; *their* job is to not listen so well. So you'll show them again. And again. Eventually they'll get the idea. But it'll be a rare day that you get exactly what you ask for. And an extremely rare day when you get it on time (more on this later). The thing to shoot for isn't perfection, it's the stage crew equivalent of an "A." That's 90 percent.

One hundred fifty percent? Ninety percent? Allow me to explain. If your predecessor produced mediocre shows, well, that's about 70 percent. As in a "C." If you try to push production values to 150 percent you'll work yourself into a home. It's not gonna happen. So, in scenic painting, the lines end up a little crooked, 90 percent; the windowpanes on a set piece are uneven, 90 percent; the fake rifles look a little too fake, 90 percent; a couple of light cues aren't perfect, 90 percent. See, 90 percent is an "A," and "A" means excellent. There's a trick to this, of course.

You must never, never (*never*) admit to anyone (*anyone*) that you'd ever possibly settle for less than perfection. You must constantly push the kids to do better and better work. In effect, you must never be satisfied. That's the "150 percent" part. But in reality you have to say "that'll serve" from time to time; the skill is in knowing when. That's something I might not be able to teach you. But if you look for it, if you are aware that time is marching on and that last stair tread is just gonna hafta be a little crooked—well, 90 percent. This has to remain our little secret.

What you'll find, as the weeks and months roll by, is that the kids can do far, far better work than they or you possibly imagined (more on this later). So set the bar impossibly high, privately and secretly settle for 90 percent of the bar, and your shows will be incredible. When you notice your predecessor was only getting 90 percent of the 70 percent of what you're asking for (and getting), that's when you'll know you are on the right track.

The same thing is true in community theater. You'll be working with beginners as well as more experienced colleagues; push them for more than they think they can do. Strive for perfection. Once you establish a high level of quality, *then* you can lower the bar a bit.

Commit this page to memory, then tear it out of the book and throw it away. You must never, ever admit to anyone that you're pulling this dirty little trick. If you do, you too will get 90 percent of 70 percent from the kids, or even less.

If you do the math, 90 percent of 150 percent is still 135 percent. So your shows are going to blow the audience away.

FALSE LIMITS

Another way of putting this percentage thing is to recall the many, many times you found yourself doing something *well* that you never thought you'd be able to do *at all.* Our kids are just at that stage of life. Left to their own devices they'll put out mediocre work and think it's great. Good coaches, and good teachers, know this and push, push, push the kids to do more. They'll feel you pushing and might resent it a little, but you are doing them good; the show will get better, and they will have been a part of a life experience that is extraordinary, which means it wasn't ordinary, which means you did good. Push, push, push; just have a sensitivity as to when to lighten up a little. Get it?

There's a false limit and a real limit in every endeavor. Push past the false limits and your shows will be incredible. Trying to push past a real limit invites disaster. Stay awake.

SLOGAN

All good stage crews should have a slogan. Ours was, "The stage crew does whatever it takes to ensure the success of the production." I like it. You may use it, no extra charge.

SOME BAD NEWS

It's always harder (much, much, *much* harder) to *teach* stage production than to *do* it. You will, from time to time, end up doing something the crew should be doing. Because it must get done, and they can't, won't, or haven't done it. Whenever and wherever you can you're supposed to have the children do it—*they're the ones in school.* Just count on things taking as much as five times longer to complete than if you did them yourself.

Here's an example. Putting up posters around the school would take me about an hour, and they would be straight, and placed well, and they would stay up. It's going to take a crew of three kids *two* hours to do the same job half as well. At least until they learn how to do it. Persevere. Your job isn't to do it; it's to teach the kids how to do it. Accept that and you're halfway home.

By the way, if you are in a middle school you'll have to do more, as in cutting wood and ladder work; just try to set things up so the kids can do as much as they safely can.

COMMUNITY THEATER

Almost everything in this book is useful for or can be adapted to college or community theater. As anyone involved in community theater can tell you, you will still have to teach stagecraft techniques to the help. Luckily for you they'll be out of high school, they might listen better, and of course, may already know a thing or two about what they are doing. And, as most community theaters are non-profit, you can get away with a couple of things that a commercial establishment would have to do differently. In that regard, what you do is very similar to what happens at the nearby high school. Remember, expectations run a little higher for community theater productions, so redouble your efforts—especially when you recognize weak spots.

TEACHING TECHNICAL THEATER

If you need to get a show up and running and you've never done it before, then you've bought the right book. If you already know what you are doing and are just looking for new techniques and approaches to improve your work, again, you have the right book. If you intend to *teach* technical theater, well now, you may need to pick up a couple more books. The truth is, we're going to short-circuit some of the time-honored conventions of technical theater—in order to get the job done. For example, there is a way to calculate how much light falls on any particular spot on stage long before you climb a ladder and aim the light. We are going to skip right to hanging the light. Why? Because I doubt you have the time and budget to do everything by the book. And because you probably can't radically change the lighting positions anyway. And, if you're at all like me, you are going to have to *see* the light shining right down on the stage as you develop your light plot. Let me be clear. In this book you will be taught methods that work—shortcuts—not every technical thing. You're doing the job of a dozen people on Broadway; you haven't got the time or money to do things their way. In effect, we'll cheat. If it's a comfort to you, there's precious little in this book that actually contradicts accepted practice; we're just going to accelerate the process so we don't get bogged down. Which means we'll break a few rules where it really doesn't matter. OK? OK.

YOU ARE NOT THE DIRECTOR, YOU ARE NOT THE PRODUCER

Another important thing to remember when producing shows is that you are not the director. You're probably not really the producer, either; real producers raise money to finance shows. You're just the stage crew guy. Or the stage crew dame. Let's not be pedantic, for all love. Anyhow, you're not the director, *hee hee hee*, unless it just so happens that you *are*. That is, you may be doing the whole show by yourself. If so, please take your vitamins. The hints in this book are mostly for the stage crew guy (dame) or the director's assistant, the director's boyfriend (girlfriend), the person helping the director. There's not a lot about directing in here, except in the backward sense of having everything well thought out and working and completed on time, that sort of thing. No technique drills. No character development, warm-ups, or improvs. Just crew stuff.

You see, I was never a director. Some people say I thought I was, but I wasn't. My job was to do everything the director didn't want to do. If you are the director perhaps you should give this book to your boyfriend or girlfriend with that look that says, "Pleeeease?" Because running a stage crew is a huge job.

I did do one little bit of directing on the sly. This is a secret, so don't tell. We were doing a play version of *The Sting*—a pretty good show, by the way—and I made a suggestion during rehearsals to Peg, the leading lady. Just a little hint about how to say a line, no big deal. In a prescient moment I added, "Now this is just between you and me; if the director doesn't like it you can never ever tell him it was my idea." She agreed, and tried it; and she thought it was great, and I thought it was great, but the director did not think it was so good. He loudly and forcefully told her to do it the way he had said. I remember him yelling, "Who told you to do that? I never told you to do that!" I watched her turn white. I imagine I turned white too as I had never seen him so mad. But, with all of that pressure on her, she didn't tell on me. Peg. Cool kid. Fake name.

Later I learned a little tact.

RULES

In my classroom, I only have one rule: Follow the instructor's directions at all times. Works for me. The best and only rule on stage is for the entire cast and crew to do whatever the director says. And remember, you are just the director's little helper. So even *you* have to follow the director's instructions. You have to put a bit of faith behind this. The director knows best. We know in real life this isn't always true, but . . .

BREAKING THE RULES

As the years go by, an unwritten set of rules develops, modified by circumstances and enforced as well as possible. I'm thinking of things like, "Don't put your book bags in the back of the house," "No food backstage," that sort of thing. If you want to write all of these little rules down, go right ahead, I won't stop you. We installed the "no book bags" rule when some kid swiped all of the calculators out of the book bags. But please remember that the rules exist to make things run more smoothly. Try to be sensitive to situations where the rules aren't actually helping you; then change the rule instead of breaking it.

BREAKING THE LAW

Fortunately for me, I never had to "bust" a crew kid, except for petty thievery. Apparently they were clever enough to hide most of their illicit activities from me, or maybe they just kept it off campus; I don't know. If you make it clear that misbehavior won't be tolerated you'll have less of a problem with this. But beware. If something serious happens, you must deal with it appropriately. We did have to send a couple of kids up to the principal; he was perfectly fair to the kids, in my opinion—though the parents didn't think so. The worst penalty, of course, is being kicked off of crew, and a couple of kids got it. Whatever you do, don't ever say or imply that it's OK to break the law, even if someone points out that you just did.

CUE 1

REAdy

You can start stage crew work without a director, without a venue, and without a show, but things won't seem real until the entire staff is on board and a few things have been decided. This book covers pretty much everything except directing, costumes, and music, but your assignment may be just sets, or just sound, or maybe everything. I'm going to proceed on the assumption that you are working with a director and that someone else is handling the costumes, the music, the dance steps, and the singing. Assembling the staff is a job in itself, and if someone gets sick you may just have to take over volunteer assistant dance coordinator duties as well as the traditional stage crew duties. Let's keep the choreographer healthy; that way you can keep your mind on your job instead of everyone else's job. In a nutshell, your job is to instruct the stage crew on the technical aspects of the production; in reality, you'll be involved with *every* aspect of the production, the glove on the director's hand.

DECIDING ON THE SHOW

It's not really your job to decide on the show, it's the director's. And the director is always under a lot of pressure to pick a show that the kids will like, a big show so a lot of kids can participate, a popular show so you won't lose money, a cheap show. . . . Let's just admit that the director has pressures. You don't really want to make things harder by even suggesting shows. No, no, no, what you want is . . . *veto power.* Veto power means you get to say no to a show, for any reason whatsoever, and it should stick. Needless to say, the choral director and band director should have veto power over musicals—the same as you.

1

Our principal (actually it was an assistant principal) thought he had veto power over our newest director and screwed up his face when she decided to do Shakespeare for the second time in three years. I'm not a big Shakespeare scholar, but our director is. Guess who won that battle? It helped that she'd just returned from London, acting at the Globe. The concern was that it's sometimes difficult to win the student audience over to Shakespeare. Try one of the comedies—*Much Ado*, or *Midsummer*—and remind everybody involved that it's a comedy. . . . When Flute refuses to play Thisby (a woman) it's because, "I have a beard coming." That's a joke! Y'know . . . woman/beard. Get it? A joke. People are always surprised to learn that (done right) Shakespeare's comedies are actually pretty funny.

I don't recall actually vetoing any shows, except maybe while we were still in the musing stage. I did get to pick a show, though, once. It was my first director's last show before retiring. We started our career together with a screaming argument, and then, five years later, he asks, "What show would you pick?"

"*Fiddler*," I said, "for two reasons. First, because I've always wanted to do it, and second, I've always wanted to do it with you as the director." He chose *Fiddler*. I figured it was a compliment to me. If you do *Fiddler*, figure out a way to make Frumah Sarah really fly. Be careful, but do it.

ONE-WEEK RUN/TWO-WEEK RUN

Once you've decided on a show and gotten permission from the publishing company to actually produce it, you'll have to decide how many performances you can pull off. For several years we did three-day runs, and I was actually pretty happy, as there was only one weekend of pure panic and dread. But the truth is, I've come around to feel that you should have a two-week run—that is, Thursday, Friday, and Saturday of the first week, and Friday and Saturday nights the next week, with a Sunday matinee. At least for the musicals. You'll find the musicals generally are more work all around, so the longer run might be more easily justified. And a two-week run can turn a financial loss into a profit, as the only extra expense is the royalty.

Opening on a Thursday does not guarantee a full house—rather the contrary—but the best part is the buzz the next day at school. Kids who saw the show will talk it up (presuming it's good) and more kids'll come the remaining days. Try a student discount on opening night to pack the house. Closing on a Sunday matinee gives more time for set cleanup—called a strike party. Try to get *everything* done since no one will want to come to a stage crew meeting the day after a show is over.

You'll have to check with all adults involved and be cautious about overexposing yourself. As the years go by, you can vary the number of performances. When you finally get to do *Annie* and *Guys & Dolls,* you should schedule as many performance dates as you can.

A Saturday night closing can be great too; most parents will allow the kids to stay late at school to strike the set. You'll have to buy the refreshments unless you can talk a parent into doing it.

DOUBLE CASTING

If you decide on a two-week run, the director may be tempted to double cast major parts. This is a very noble idea. It allows more kids to have starring roles and also attracts a few new customers the second weekend. But it's not worth it. It encourages student rivalries and is hell on the director, not to mention the costumer. To top it off, the kids will rarely work together to make both performances better; instead they may actually (consciously or unconsciously) work to hurt the performance that they don't star in. If you have that many kids, then put on another (different) show, or let the drama club do it.

UNDERSTUDIES/CHANGES

You do have to be prepared in case somebody falls out or quits the show. Luckily for you it's more the director's problem; you just make suggestions and lend support. Mostly my suggestions were to put some kid from stage crew on stage. Many of them want to act but hold back, probably just due to shyness. We put Alan on as a judge, Cindy on as a waiter, everyone on as "The Mob" in *A Tale of Two Cities,* and a few kids in a few other places. I always encouraged the kids to try out—for the play, for cheerleading, for sports (I lost a good carpenter to the soccer team), but when a crisis hits, you promote from within. So an actor or stagehand gets pushed up, just like in the movies. Magic.

The truth is, a kid would have to be pretty darn sick to leave a show. We considered putting a "ringer" in the pit to sing Prince Charming's song in *Into the Woods,* but the (incredibly sick) kid did it, and the other Prince harmonized to lift him through the tougher sections. From on stage. Nobody noticed except the people who were coming back to see the show a second time, and his effort earned him extra applause. Magic, magic, magic. Life memories of the best kind.

If you see trouble brewing, pull a kid early and get the replacement in there. I think we did that once.

RESERVING SPACE

In almost every case, the location of a show has to serve other masters. In a school, the orchestra, choir, and even the school photographer will put demands on theater space. In community theater, there can be as many as three shows in production at the same time. This leads to quite a few problems, most of which can be solved with a great big padlock. Lock up every single item that you can't stand to have damaged, stolen, or used up. Lock up the tape if you expect to have any when you need it. Lock up the extension cords, or be prepared to buy more (perhaps you can attach them to a pipe with plastic cable ties). Lock up everything the other groups have no right to. They'll use your water and even your makeup, which is gross (all the actors should buy their own, but they never do). Outside groups may rent your space, right in the middle of your production. The superintendent of schools may come in to make a budget presentation. It stinks. You'll have to work with the director and reserve the space. Use this opportunity to begin a comprehensive calendar of the next few months of your life. (Don't forget to schedule in time to pay your bills.) Someone in the office will have an arcane, cryptic form that you have to fill out in triplicate; be sure to get three copies. There is no question that the first time you reserve space you'll do it wrong; for instance, you may skip the box that means you want the heat on, and the show is in December. In Pennsylvania . . . *oops*. Try to coordinate the school calendar, the community calendar, your social and religious obligations, account for possible bad weather . . . trust me, you'll overlook something. But—and here is the most important lesson in the book (fancy that, page 4)—the better you plan, and try to figure out things ahead of time, the fewer your problems. And the smaller your problems. And easier to solve. So . . . think ahead. Don't worry, *think*.

And find some alternate work locations for when you get kicked out of the theater.

REHEARSAL SPACE

Occasionally you will have the luxury of a long stretch of uninterrupted time available to you in the theater and the associated workspaces—the costume shop, the scene shop, makeup rooms—make the best of it. Since the crew will need a lot of extra time and space, try to get some of the rehearsals placed elsewhere, especially in the beginning, when blocking isn't quite so important. Directors want to block pretty early, though, so make the most of any early time you get. Turn all of your lighting technicians and painters into carpenters. They won't like it, but the jobs have to be done in their proper order. And it's not really fair to any group to dawdle. You've got time, you've got the theater (because you reserved it), you've got labor . . . GO! The actors can run lines in the drama room, or practice dance steps in the wrestling room (unused out of season). Beg a bit of time to rough in the major, major pieces. And *do* it—don't let the time slip away. You're going to be extremely busy later in the production, and the director will never give up the theater again if you don't take advantage of your week or two and at least get the stairs built and the bigger set pieces started. Plus, it gives the kids a thrill to see the set taking shape. (A great trick is to save some major painting until the night before the first tech rehearsal and stay late. Saturday morning, everyone comes in to find the set miraculously transformed—what a boost to the show. But we're getting ahead of ourselves.) The thrill is when the actors come in and see a *set,* not a shambles of unbuilt sticks.

One little detail. If you have to build elsewhere and move the production in later, you have to measure everything, including door widths and heights, and build to fit. And budget a little extra time for the move.

EQUIPMENT INVENTORY

If you are just starting out, you'll need to take account of all of the junk in the place, and you'll have to determine if it works or not. Inspect everything and sort it out as best as you can. Put all of the tools in one place; test the staplers, saws, sewing machines, etc. Put old props away in some logical fashion. You won't be able to reorganize the entire theater, especially if your predecessors were slobs, but you do need to get down a layer or two just to see what you have. Write down things like the blade size for the circular saw, the model number of the sewing machine, all that stuff. Use a permanent binder of some kind, something that will last the year through. Eventually you'll have to reorganize the binder. Think of that as a good sign. Little drawings of how things are hooked up go in the binder, notes about repairs made, dimensions you know you'll need later, a wish list . . .

In effect this little book becomes a substitute brain, remembering things you have no room for in your head. At the beginning of each workday, at the conclusion of each workday, every day during rehearsal, Sunday nights, and every day at lunch you're going to take a peek in this little book and try to get a task done. Of course, the master calendar is in the book. Post copies of it on the callboard. Usually you end up adding to the list, but be of good cheer—I found that the list getting longer was a sign that things were going well.

A fun task when you are tired and aren't actually going to *do* anything is to rewrite the lists in the book in priority order. You're just kidding yourself, of course, but it's cathartic, and you can pretend you actually accomplished something.

After a time, you'll have a pretty good idea of what you've got to work with, what you need, and what you want. You'll have a list of things that don't work and problems to solve. If you don't write it all down, you're going to forget something important.

ORGANIZING THINGS

I'm going to presume that the place is a mess and it's your first day. Your predecessor left you a huge pile of junk, including about half of the set from the last show. You can't find any tools, the paint cans are open and all dried up, the lumber rack is a total shambles (actually, that never changes), and if you had had any sense, you wouldn't have taken on this job. Too late—you signed the contract. Poke around a little. Eventually you'll see something that's worth keeping. Let joy fill your heart. Look around, and decide where you want to put it. You don't want to move things more than once, well, twice probably, but not a lot. Don't actually move the thing, just mentally note the best place for the paints (behind lock and key), the tools (same), the wood, the flats . . . everything. You may end up moving things to a poor location, but the truth is, just getting everything organized (and the trash thrown out) is an incredible first step. It's a step you'll want to be ready to take when you call your first stage crew meeting in September.

Try to think ahead as far as where things should go. At my old school, I felt strongly that the props room was too close to the stage entrance (in the wings). There was always a bottleneck of actors right in a bad place. I made the props room the paint room and moved the props room farther offstage, where they had room for a table and a wall to hang costumes on.

We didn't need the paints during the run of the show (except when we did), so actors could use part of the paint room for quick changes as the dressing rooms were in a really bad place (upstairs).

It worked great. The kids didn't like me changing things around, and let me know in many not-so-subtle ways, but the new layout worked better, especially as the tools were also put in a place closer to the wood. Just try to imagine how things will move on and off stage, where you want to set up the paints (near a sink)—brilliant! Figure out where you can fit the larger set pieces. Be flexible. Then call your first stage crew meeting.

STAGE CREW

If things are really bad, just start ordering people around, doing every-thing your way. Make it clear that you're the boss and that this place is going to present a quite different appearance from now on. If things aren't so bad, let the elected officers run the proceedings. That is, if the club even has elected officers. (We did—though being an officer was no guarantee of getting a choice job for any show.) What I mean here is if things aren't in good order, your job is to put them in good order; conversely, if the crew is running pretty well and things just need a little tidying up, then just instruct the crew on how you want things and let them handle it. As things get better and better, the crew will take over more and more duties as a matter of routine. From time to time you will have to reestablish cer-tain routines—mostly concerning food and taking out the trash—but a well-oiled crew runs itself.

The crew will let you know when they are ready to assume com-mand, so to speak, and you won't have to be so bossy. A few years into my gig at Blair, Claudia and several other crew members approached me with the notion of doing some set design themselves and a tactful request for more decision-making power. They knew how to paint, they knew how to build, and they wanted to try their hand at designing a set. Turns out they thought I'd be mad or upset—in truth I was thrilled—but they were ready. They didn't just *think* they were ready (big difference), they *were* ready. So I began incorporating their ideas into the set designs. As the years went by, first Claudia, then Julie, then Sonny, and then Edna gradu-ated, and suddenly there were fewer set ideas coming from the kids. Be ready to recognize this ebb and flow of creativity, talent, and desire. Encourage the *flow* whenever you can. Cope with the ebb. Did I get that right? Of course I did; I sail on tall ships in my spare time. Anyhow, teach; then get out of the way. In many ways Claudia's crew represented the pinnacle of stage crew talent at Montgomery Blair High School, taking over many of the jobs that most crews don't touch.

TOOLS

Have the crew gather up all of the tools that have been strewn about all over creation. You'll have to supplement the meager stage crew tool chest with tools from home and buy needed tools as money becomes available. Dollar-store tape measures are fine, and dollar-store paintbrushes and rollers are sometimes pretty good too. Sometimes. You will probably have to refurbish cords, plugs, and saws, and you'll need to pick up some blades, drills, and extension cords, but before too long you'll have a pretty nice tool kit—that is, if you can keep things from being stolen.

It may or may not be your kids doing the stealing, but face it, something is eventually going to get stolen. Buy some locks, use 'em, but don't take it too hard when something turns up missing. I had some clamps stolen before I had them out of their wrapper, and some work lights stolen by a member of my lighting crew. Bad boy (I caught him). Some of my kids were thieves. If any of you are reading this (you know who you are), I still need my cable cutters back.

Here is a list of tools that you will need and may not have:

- ➤ Crescent wrench (get several)
- ➤ Glue gun
- ➤ Staple gun
- ➤ Staple hammer
- ➤ Portable electric jig saw
- ➤ Electric paint mixer tool (2 sizes)
- ➤ A level with a laser in it (very cool)
- ➤ Battery-operated screw gun
- ➤ Chop saw (not the sliding kind)

My favorite power tools are Makita, though we used DeWalt a lot. The coolest screw gun is the Skil with the baby hammer drill built in. I bought three, one got stolen. But the Skil needs a power cord, and wireless (battery operated) makes the work go faster. Don't use a wireless drill for mixing paint, though; they're just not tough enough. By the way, most screw guns are just slow-running drills, so you don't need to buy drills at all. The wireless baby circular saws are good, and in my estimation they are safe enough for kids—a big concern.

(When you buy tools, or anything for the show, save the receipts. Eventually you'll turn them in to someone for a reimbursement, and you might not get the sales tax back, so get a tax-exempt number if you qualify. That way you won't have to pay sales tax in the first place. And shop the discount stores or you'll run your production company broke. Better take a moment and find out if you have a spending limit, too.)

We had one little accident with a power tool. Rita tried to brush some sawdust away from a jigsaw line, and the saw hadn't finished winding down yet. I thought she'd need a hospital trip, but she didn't. Very scary. Read and follow the written safety instructions that come with every power tool. The most important rule (besides "keep away from the blade") is to always let the tool stop before reaching in there.

THROWING THINGS AWAY

Theater people are natural pack rats. I'm not really convinced this is a good thing, but I was glad I had that old console radio when I needed it for *Annie*. If you have the room you could make a case for keeping just about everything. They kept the piano from *Casablanca*. Howsomever, chances are pretty good you don't have the room, and some of the stuff you want to keep will become a burden to you. (Don't keep any couches, they encourage laziness; don't keep beds, they—well, just don't keep beds). So you sort of have to decide what stays, and what goes. If its usefulness is unquestioned, it stays. If it's badly broken, it goes. If it's valuable, it stays, if it's easily replaced, it goes. If it's a big chandelier, it stays—what were you thinking? Almost any kind of cloth stays, unless it's real small. Lumber stays until it is less than eighteen inches long, then it gets sliced into paint stirrers. Pipes (like plumbing pipes) always stay.

Get the boxes the computers came in and load 'em up with the trash. Well, we got computers.

GETTING RID OF TRASH

Not to sound petty or anything, but our custodians just didn't get it when it came to stage work. I'd get complaints when the kids were actually being very good, and no help when I really needed it. At the old school the guy would want to clean up the hallway right after school. My feeling was he should have cleaned it after 5:00, when most of the kids left. He was there until 11:00 anyway. And the crew kids got blamed even if some other kids made the mess, which bothered me. I'm just sensitive that way. And at the end of a show there's always a huge mess, which would sit a while (quite a while) before the custodians would take it away. Nine times out of ten I'd put it in my van and haul it away myself. I realize they don't get paid much, but neither did I.

Eventually it became habit, and the crew kids would box up the trash, I'd haul it away, and everything would be fine; then came complaints about someone's soda can in the hall. "Hey, I'm hauling *boxes* of trash away, and that's your job, so stop whining about a couple of tin cans," I wanted to scream, but didn't. I did whine to the principal once, when I bought a new van. I wanted to be sure he knew the kids were doing a pretty good job cleaning up after themselves, so the complaints wouldn't hurt us. They didn't. Try to build a cooperative working relationship with the custodial staff, then you might not have to haul away the trash yourself.

Last complaint. I couldn't help but notice the football team never cleaned the stadium after the football games; my crew cleaned the auditorium before *and* after most shows. Parents helped, which was nice.

SWEEPING/MOPPING

There is a wrong way to sweep, and the kids will do it. Also, the best time to sweep is just before you leave, because you are going to raise a lot of dust. Not so good just before rehearsal. So make sweeping up a ritual part of getting ready to leave. If you have a regular old push broom you should start at center stage and work the dirt offstage, all the way to the exit, the scenery shop, and the dressing rooms. And you can't just push the broom—you'll drop too much dirt. You have to go over the same spot two or three times.

Then you can break out the kind of broom that looks like a dust mop. That kind of broom you just push and push, and don't lift it until you are done. Then mop. No soap needed, just rinse a lot and change the water a lot. Most times I just gave up and swept myself because the kids put such a halfhearted effort into it. If I yelled a lot it would help a little. And we never mopped until the costumes came out. Then we mopped every day. Actors can mop, and sweep . . . and they should.

CALENDAR

One of the easiest ways to stay organized is to write a calendar with every stupid little thing on it. This is not a job for a kid. Most important is to back-time the calendar; that is, to work backwards from the show dates and to coordinate the calendar with nearby school and community events. It's nice to know that the basketball championships are scheduled for the same day as your show (hint—reschedule the show). Look out for things like SATs and big field trips, music competitions, and outside groups using the theater. If it's all on your calendar, you won't be surprised quite as often, though you'll still get surprised. If you have teaser performances or previews—and you should—make sure they are on the school master calendar as well. Most people use a big box calendar from Staples, and they work fine. I sometimes typed the calendar down a sheet (several sheets) of paper; it looked somewhat like a checklist. Most of our shows were on a forty-school-day calendar; that's eight weeks of school. My work stretched before and after this of course, but the printed calendar was usually about forty days. Biblical in a way, don't you think?

Coordinate the crew calendar closely with the director's rehearsal calendar so you both have enough stage time to get your work done. Typically the rehearsal would go from 3:00–5:00, while stage crew went from 2:00–7:00. I always liked to go late on Fridays, 2:00–9:00, and have the kids bring dinner money. List everything on the calendar. When you put something on the calendar, like "Program Art Due," say, two weeks before the show, you have a great reminder when that day passes. So you can start screaming about program art and maybe get it before the show actually begins. Be sure to schedule several days for cleanup and think of an enticement for the kids, 'cause they won't wanna come. Keep the master calendar (your copy) in your little notebook.

CALL BOARD

A special bulletin board for all things drama is a must. Ideally the board would be in an open, accessible location, and would carry drama-related information only. It would be decorated, updated, and maintained by students. A copy of any reference material needed would be posted. Photos, posters, and sign-up sheets would be prominent. Show posters from other schools would share space with in-house publicity. It would be near the auditorium or theater.

Well, do the best you can.

CUE 1.9 STOCKING UP

We're about to get going here, so you are going to have to start collecting some supplies. First we'll deal with all of the kinds of tape needed in the theater. You'll need to stock a year's supply of several sizes and types of tape. Regular old masking tape is fine for painting purposes, but that's about it. The blue, low-stick tape is useful when putting up posters where people are nervous about peeling the paint off of the walls; it's too expensive to use anywhere else. In addition to masking tape you'll need to get some *spike tape*, and some *gaffer's tape*. Gaffer's tape is 2" wide and is used to hold just about everything in the theater. Get white and black. Get several rolls. Keep it locked up, as it's pretty expensive. The coolest thing about "gaff tape" is it doesn't get gunky too fast. But eventually it will get gunky, so if you are taping cables into coils to be put away, run the tape sticky side out. That way the stored cables won't get tape gunk all over them. (If things do get gunked up, you can clean up with some WD-40 on a rag.) Use the white tape on the sound mixer (and maybe the light board) so you can label everything. Spike tape is ½" gaffer's tape. Get a variety of colors, maybe ten rolls a year. This tape gets stuck on the stage floor to show the crew where to put things. You can write which spike mark means what right on the spike tape (use a Sharpie) but you usually don't have to. Don't scrimp and put masking tape on the floor. I said don't . . . *don't*. Really, DON'T!

Pick up one roll of *glow tape*. This is for spike marks in the dark. Use it only when props must be placed during a blackout. Please only use a little bit. If your stage floor looks like an airline runway when the lights are out, you are overdoing it. If you have the kind of theater where the stage floor can be seen by the audience, you have to minimize the taping and spike marks. Don't use masking tape on the stage floor—it's too hard to peel up.

While you should never put masking tape on the floor (did I mention that?), you should have an enormous amount of masking tape available . . . for painting. Some first-aid tape is nice. Don't rob the first-aid kit—pick up extra tape at the grocery store. There is special tape available at theatrical supply shops that will hold lavaliere (radio) mics in place—on the actor's head, that is—and the tape will take makeup. Buy it when you need it.

Yes, you should lay in a supply of good old duct tape. Just remember that it doesn't "last"—it gets gooey (gunky) pretty quick. Use it for any temporary taping job—that is, a couple of days instead of the run of the show. Scotch Magic Transparent Tape also comes in handy.

Tape and staples—you need an infinite supply of infinite sizes and types.

Speaking of tape, run by Costco and pick up a load of cassette tapes, VHS tapes, digital recording tapes, and any other audio- or videotapes you need to get you through the show. And your batteries. Keep 'em in the fridge—the batteries, not the tapes. The cool temperatures slow down the chemical reactions that sap batteries of their strength. I heard on the radio this does not actually work, but at least you'll know where to find them.

CUE 2

GET SET

While a tremendous amount of time and energy can be spent on detailed plans, it is sometimes acceptable to build a set from the simplest of sketches, a floor plan. This is a drawing from a bird's-eye view that shows the relative size and placement of all pieces of a set. Use extra pages as pieces are moved. The simplest sketches can work, but they must be somewhat close to scale. Scale means that the measurements on the sketch have some relation to the real thing as built. Perhaps it's a 4' × 8' platform; the sketch should be approximately 1" × 2". Remember (') is *feet*, and (") is *inches*—didn't you see *Spinal Tap*? No need to break out the rulers yet, just get hold of some ¼" grid paper, the kind you used in math class. Each block on the grid paper counts as one square foot, the same size as most floor tiles. This scale will give a nice single-sheet drawing for most performance spaces. A ½" scale drawing will show much more detail, but it will end up so large you'll have to roll it up, and you won't be able to make copies without a trip to Kinko's. Sketch away.

THE FLOOR PLAN

Well, perhaps a few minutes of preparation are in order. To really get things in scale you'll need to know the size of your performance space. If a previous sponsor has left you any well-made drawings, that is the place to start. Find an architect's scale if the drawings are not ¼" to the foot. Go into the performance space with two long tape measures. Bring along a roll of ½" spike tape, *not masking tape*. Start measuring, well, everything. Check the previous drawing—if you have one—though you can never trust someone else's drawing, even the original school plans. Ours were off just enough to cause trouble, and I had the architect's blueprint! Transfer all the measurements to your ¼" grid paper.

That grid paper is going to get crowded, as you need to know the proscenium opening width, how much stage there is downstage of the curtain (towards the audience), how much stage there is upstage of the curtain, the relative position of all curtain legs, the position of the "electrics" (where the lights are hung), the position of any pipes or battens that can hold scenery, the backstage or wing space . . . that's enough for the moment.

Since you have the tape measure handy, find center stage. Generally, it's one-half the distance across the proscenium opening. In some unusual space you may have to arbitrarily call one spot center stage, even if it's not mathematically perfect. Mark this with the spike tape. To be thorough you should lay a nice tapeline down the center of the stage from front to back, using your geometry, or your geometry teacher, to make sure it doesn't waver from the centerline. No geometry teacher handy? OK, get two tape measures, two helpers, and do it this way. Each helper is to hold their tape measure at the inside corner of the proscenium opening, closest to the curtain. (Curtain open, by the way.) Pull both tapes to center stage. Where they meet, where the readings are equal, that's center stage. Mark this spot with a pencil or pen, or chalk. In a large high-school auditorium the measurement will be in the neighborhood of twenty feet. Now hold both tapes and back up way back towards the back wall, as far as you can. If you're skilled, or lucky, you'll be standing about five feet away from the back wall, and both tape measures will have the same reading, probably less than forty feet. Mark this spot. If you can get away with it, drive a little screw down into the floor here, so you'll never have to measure for the centerline again.

Lay in the tapeline with the spike tape. You now have one great reference line for planning. Don't leave before laying another tapeline, just behind the closed act curtain. It should be placed about a foot upstage of the closed curtain, as it's not there to show the location of the curtain, but to show where someone must stand not to be hit by the curtain as it closes. This "spike" line should run all the way across the stage. No need to measure, just follow the floorboards and keep the line straight. Now you can tell the cast to "toe the line, there" and know that they won't get popped by the closing curtain. Please don't close the curtain slowly. Please don't open the curtain slowly. Please have your crew practice with the curtains. I see we're off topic.

Place these two important reference lines on your ¼" grid paper drawing. Before you leave, sneak one more screw into the floor, right where the two lines cross. No one will notice, and you will be able to find CS long after the tape has been removed. Other folks will have you use a layout line called the "plaster line" stretching straight across the proscenium from wall to wall. The truth is this line is almost useless for design as it's on the wrong side of the curtain when the curtain is closed. You may as well take note of the plaster line—it's probably about three feet downstage from our much more useful "I'm standing far enough upstage of the curtain that I won't get hit" line. Then, when a classically trained visitor drops by, he can line everything up his way.

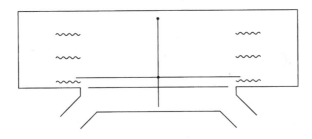

Stage Measurements

You'll probably have to redraw your little grid sheet—do a good job—in black ink, and you can make Xerox copies for years to come. You'll have to find the best Xerox in the store, and you'll need to play with the contrast buttons, but you should run off a lifetime supply while you have the chance, at least fifty copies. As the years go by you will add to this simplest of plans—the location of electric sockets, microphone and headset inputs, the orchestra pit, and the lighting locations in the house—and you'll have to learn to make scale drawings. Try to find a copy of AutoCAD for your computer, and learn it in your spare time. Ah, the power of the computer. Use layers. Use colors. Go crazy.

Until that time we'll have to make do with sketches. Rely on the grid paper. You can make little cutouts and place them, and move them, and have yourself a time. You can also make three-dimensional models out of Play-Doh, or Styrofoam, or clay. Models are great; just don't forget to put your eyes level with the audience's eye level to get the proper viewpoint.

SET DESIGN

A great set can help turn a mediocre production into a fine show, and of course a crappy set will do the opposite. I saw a show at my old high school (I think Sandra Bullock was in the show) where the set actually began to fall apart during opening night. And from time to time disaster has struck the Blair Players. But not very often. A set design that is attractive, strong, and portable is within the means of any self-respecting stage crew. Students can and should have a say in the set design, but for a variety of reasons they generally cannot produce a complete, workable design in the time allotted.

You've got to begin by knowing the show. A script, any stills you can find, a rental video of the show (or any similar show), and a bunch of impressionist art books to consult should set you up nicely. Your scenic painting will mimic the impressionist style, so start an art library early. Watch a video of the show to steal some set ideas and to firmly establish the time period of the piece. Remember, these folks had an almost unlimited budget (especially compared to you), but watch the video carefully and you'll usually find at least a couple of inspiring sets or scenes. Find the pause button on your remote; DVD players and fancy VCRs can click through a scene frame by frame. Read the script carefully and think about the most necessary set pieces. Decide what has *got* to be there, and where you can scrimp. For instance, if you were ever allowed to do *Miss Saigon* (fat chance), the helicopter has *got* to be there. You mean you were thinking of cutting it? You are in the wrong business. Certainly things can be cut, and no one is expecting Broadway quality in a high school, but you've got to produce the essentials to produce a good show.

In *Guys & Dolls,* for instance, the two scenes that have got to be great are New York itself, and the sewer scene. Put your first and best design efforts into these essential scenes first, then fill in around the edges. If you are starting from a blank slate, with no ideas, go to the auditorium, sit about a third of the way back, and stare at the stage until inspiration strikes. This could take hours, but usually doesn't. Imagine entrances and exits, then mark them down on a sketchpad, either a *plan view* (from up high, like your floor plan), an *elevation* (the audience view), or both. Don't bother trying to draw in three dimensions; simple blocky plans will be fine. Just get the basic sizes and shapes down on paper. If there have to be trees or buildings, you can get a good idea of their true size because you can compare them to your measured floor plan. If you have a "normal" auditorium, you can go up about sixteen feet, possibly a little less. Remember, a lot of the set will be painted to *look* like something, it does not have to *be* real.

While the director decides the blocking, a creative set design will make it easier. Decide where the doors or windows actually have to work (a *practical* set piece) and where you can fake 'em. In *The King & I* we had a huge palace with two levels. As it worked out, all the high entrances were from the center or from stage right. What do you think was behind the (painted, fake) railing on stage left? That's right, *nothing*! In *Hello, Dolly!* there pretty much has to be a trap door. If you are not blessed with a basement and a trap door, you're going to have to put a second level in. Ours was twenty-four inches high, which was too low. Make yours a little higher. I suppose you could play the scene behind a closet door, but it just wouldn't be the same.

Use the "natural" limitations of your stage to enclose your set; for instance, don't build or put anything across the curtain line if you intend to use the curtain. Lower the second story of a set if the talent can't be seen from the back of the house. It's much easier to lower things on paper, or in your imagination; after you build the thing it will be too late.

Try to design things to do double, or even triple, duty. Playgoers know about this trick, but no one seems to care. For instance, the cashier station can be changed into the librarian's desk just by removing the cash register. Then the whole thing can be turned around to show a new painted side—a newsstand, perhaps. Removing a tablecloth changes the restaurant table in scene one to the diner table in scene three. You can also make big pieces work this way by rotating them on a pin or putting the entire thing on wheels. We had a cool house for *Fiddler* that rotated and opened up on loose pin hinges. It was in three pieces and could open up every whichaway. The exterior set of one location can rotate to show the interior of that same location, or go off and come back on as a new location. You can also change locations just by changing the curtains and props, or just the lights. I saw a great trick in a comedy where a Christmas tree was decorated with red balls and lights on one side, then swung around to show silver ornaments and tinsel for another scene. Very cute.

So, you've begun learning the details of the show, cribbed some ideas from any available photos or videos, and decided (with the director) where you can scrimp and where you can't. Perhaps you've combined or changed scene locations (Ernestina Money can be inside the restaurant, not outside—one less piece to build), you have a pretty good idea of your budget and time constraints, you've considered how the pieces will move on and off for set changes, and you have the vaguest of sketches before you. I've completed good shows with less. But it's best to formalize the set design, using scale drawings. Track down an *architect's scale* and meet me in the next section.

THE ARCHITECT'S SCALE

Some people have a lot of difficulty with the concept of scale. In the briefest possible terms, "scale" is any convenient reduction or enlargement of any measured thing. In theater we're almost always reducing the drawings. Just for grins let's make up an example. In any daily paper you should be able to find a picture of a car. The car in the photograph is probably six inches long. Real cars are over twelve feet long. The *scale,* in this example, is six inches equals twelve feet. That's 6"=12'. Or 1"=2'. Or 1"=24". Or 1:24. Model railroaders have an actual name for this scale, but I'm not going to tell it to you. The concept is I draw it small, by some measured ratio, then build it to size.

One of the reasons people get confused is that the set piece itself may be a reduction from real life. The best example of that is the Empire State Building we built for *Guys & Dolls.* It was designed to be twelve feet tall. The real thing is huge, *but that doesn't enter into the scale we're talking about.* I needed to represent on paper the twelve-foot model we were going to build. I could have drawn a twelve-inch tall drawing, a *scale* of one inch to the foot. But I didn't. It wouldn't match my floor plan, a ¼" scale.

So for simplicity, let's stick with the ¼" scale we've used previously. See, that way, the mini–Empire State Building can be copied onto cardboard, cut out, and placed upright on the floor plan we made earlier, and we can see what it will look like for real.

Look carefully at the architect's scale. It really helps here if you have one in your hand as you read along. All an architect's scale really is is a whole bunch of *different* scales squeezed onto *one* ruler. Some scales go backwards. There is more than one scale along each ruler edge. Too many numbers. Hold on a minute, Tex, and I'll explain everything. Stare at the thing until you find the ¼" scale. Using this scale means a quarter of an inch is going to represent a foot. Just like the grid paper. Every inch equals four feet. These drawings end up pretty small, so only use this scale for the largest items in your set design— houses, buildings, palaces, backdrops, rolling pieces, that kind of thing.

As you hold the scale, the little mark that says "¼" is either on the right or the left end of the scale. If you can't find the number "¼" you are not holding an architect's scale. You've managed to find an *engineer's* scale or some sort of metric scale; you probably want to go back to the store and try again. Found it? Good. If the number is on the left, you read it pretty much like any ruler, except the numbers represent *feet,* not inches. The little tiny lines on the wrong side of the "0" actually represent inches; in ¼" scale they count as one inch each. The important thing to remember is you gotta start at the *zero,* not the very end of the ruler. Real rulers don't show the zero, so this takes a bit of getting used to. That is, normal rulers *end* at the zero; on an architect's scale there is a little extra space at each end. Just line things up at the zero mark, and you'll be fine. You can shimmy the ruler a little to the left or right for inches measurements when you need to. Ignore the second set of numbers, the ones that run the other way.

If the "¼" is on the right-hand end of the scale it just means everything is backwards. You still read the scale in feet. You still gotta start at the zero. The little lines at the wrong end of the scale still represent inches. And, most of all, you still have to ignore the numbers reading the other way. I don't use an architect's scale as much as I used to, so now I cover the wrong numbers with a skinny piece of tape. You have my permission to do the same. The whole scheme was dreamed up to save space on an architect's desk, and we're not really architects (thank God). By the way, the other sides of the architect's scale will eventually come in handy. Especially ½. And 1.

On most architect's scales, the ¼" scale starts on the right.

HERE'S SOME HELP

I've provided a ¼" training scale on the back edge of this book. The printers got a little mad because this means they have to cut the book covers *very* carefully. Check the back cover. There's a ¼" architect's scale there all by itself. So there are no confusing double scales to worry about. It appears to run backwards; the truth is, you get used to that pretty fast. The black lines represent feet. For instance, the black line between the 10 and the 8 would be *nine* feet. I put the extra lines in since a real architect's scale has these lines; you can ignore them. Find the small lines at the very end of the scale. They represent *inches* in scale, and count as one inch each. So, if you have a really sharp pencil you can draw in scale with an accuracy of about an inch, which is plenty good for most stagecraft. Let's measure something. Pull out a credit card—they are all the same size. On the ¼" scale, your credit card should measure thirteen feet six inches by eight feet six inches, which is ridiculous, but we're just practicing. A dollar bill should measure twenty-four feet six inches by ten feet five inches or so. Better? Good.

DID YOU SAY "METRIC?"

I will write a metric chapter the day *Home Depot* starts stocking metric building supplies. I do teach metric in my classes, though—I even found some metric rulers that don't include an inches scale at all. But here in the U.S. we're sort of stuck on the English system of measurement, lumber still comes by the foot, plumbing still comes by the inch. So, you wouldn't be able to find one-centimeter-thick Masonite even if you wanted it. If you are dead set on using the metric system go right ahead, but I'll warn you that American kids have a hard time with the term *millimeters.* They think that a millimeter is a millionth of something. Call 'em minimeters—maybe then it'll catch on.

DRAW SOMETHING

It's not cheating to locate a photograph of the Empire State Building and shrink it or enlarge it on a copier until it's three inches tall (for a twelve-foot model in ¼" scale); as a matter of fact, it works quite well. You'll still need the scale to pull measurements off of the photo or the copy, and a perfect miniature of the Empire State Building might not actually look that great on stage (it would be too skinny), but it's not cheating. Too many people skip this whole process and start slapping paint on a poorly thought-out set with little regard for proportion or perspective. You can tell this happened when you look at their sets and see a lot of crooked lines that are supposed to be straight.

I SAID DRAW

Draw your "Practice Empire State Building Version 1" onto copier paper (regular old paper), using the scale to get the measurements right. Use a T-square and triangles if you have them, or chuck it all and buy a copy of AutoCAD for your computer. You'll still need to use the scale, so let's learn how it's done. Draw, using the scale, a mini–Empire State Building eight feet wide and twelve feet tall. The proportions aren't perfect—there's some foreshortening involved—but keep these major dimensions unless you just can't stand it. Consult your photos and your floor plan and knock it out. Adding some lower buildings "in front" will make for more realism. Once you finish your drawing (it's pretty small, isn't it?), you *can* use the scale to determine true size measurements for cutting things out. Meaning you needn't write down all the dimensions. Just lay the ¼" scale next to the unknown measurement and read the size in feet right on the "ruler." This saves time. Purists, and building contractors, aren't supposed to do this, but c'mon, we're not making Chippendale furniture here.

When it comes time to build the thing, anyone with a scale and a tape measure can transfer the measurements to thin plywood and cut it out. Read off each measurement, with the scale, and chalk it down full size onto the plywood. With the ¼" scale, your largest measurements will be accurate to two inches or better if you are careful. If your design is extremely detailed, with windows, signs, etc., you can try a little trick I've described below.

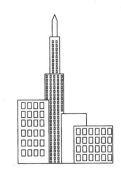

Empire State Building (8 × 12)

TO THE COPIER ROOM

The trick is to go get a transparency made. Ink in your drawing if you have to to get a good copy, roll over to the workroom or media center or Kinko's, and make a transparency of your drawing. It's pretty easy to do, but if you've never done it get someone to show you how. You'll be doing this a lot, so lay in a supply of transparency sheets, and learn the procedure by rote. You don't want to be blamed for melting the wrong kind of transparency master onto the copier's platen. Take notes. My box of transparency masters has my notes written right on it: which side up, speed and heat settings (for the Thermofax style), all that stuff. Check out an overhead projector, roll down to the workshop, and start cutting out your Empire State model.

THE SET UP

Two full-size plywood sheets, ¼" thick (⅛" if you can get it), go flat on the wall like an upside-down *T*. These sheets come eight feet long and four feet wide, so your construction will be twelve feet tall. Tape them up with duct tape; real gaffer tape is too expensive for this. Set up the overhead projector and move it and the transparency until the bottom and the top of the image perfectly match the edges of the plywood on the wall. Now you see why it had to be eight feet by twelve feet. If it were seven feet, you'd just be cutting off stock and throwing it away. If it were thirteen feet, you'd be adding material to the top or bottom. Planning ahead really helps out sometimes. Draw the thing in with chalk (make the cut lines one color and the paint lines another), take it down, and cut it out.

Reassemble with some 1 × 4s behind it and stand it up. You can paint it while it's leaning against the wall or lying on the floor. Use masking tape and several shades of gray if your design is conservative; use primary colors if you're going for that zany, avant-garde thing.

THE TRUTH HURTS

Time for a little honesty. I never built an Empire State model the way I just described. Mine was three-dimensional, hollow, lit from the inside, with cut-out windows and reflectors in a light-tight box. I also drew it in *perspective,* to look more lifelike. And we built it twelve feet tall, but it looked too short, so we added two feet. Add to the bottom. Plus we stuck an antenna on top, a dowel rod painted black. And it was on wheels. And we had the Roxy and the Astor Hotel on two other "wagons" as well. Our Empire State Building turned out fifteen feet tall. But Rome wasn't built in a day. Keep your first designs simple, rely on scenic painting (it really is incredible when it works), and get some experience before you try to turn your Empire State Building into a Taj Mahal.

ANOTHER WAY

It could be that you have a flat or an old piece of scenery that looks very much like the Empire State Building already. Jump on that and design to fit. Design levels to fit the stairs that are already built. Include an arch in the design if you've just obtained an arch from the British Embassy Players (like us!). Incorporate the custodian's scaffold or the choir risers if they are available. Use anything at your disposal to improve the set design. My front door, the one on my house, ended up on stage for *Guys & Dolls.* For three and a half weeks I had only the storm door keeping out the rain and the burglars. The door still says "Welcome Sinners" on it, which puzzles the pizza delivery guy. True!

YETTA NOTHER WAY

You *could* stick with the ¼" grid paper, and never use the architect's scale at all. I submit to you that that is unwise unless you find a supply of ½" grid paper too, and 1" grid paper, and any other size you'll eventually need. See, you can cheese the example from above on ¼" grid paper, but if you do, you are skirting the issue. The example is simple on purpose. Eventually you'll want to design something smaller, larger, or somewhat more complex, and the grid paper may not serve the purpose anymore. So you'll use the ¾ scale, or the ⅜ scale, because you know how. But if it's just not coming, draw everything out on the ¼" grid paper and get the plan done.

OUCH. MORE TRUTH (THE TRUTH HURTS II)

In order to really look good, your set designs, particularly the large pieces and the scenic drops, are going to have to incorporate perspective drawing techniques. Michelangelo was among the first to master the techniques involved in showing apparent distance in drawings and paintings. M.C. Escher was the guy that turned it into optical illusion. If you have absolutely no experience with perspective, we'll take it slow. If you've made a few perspective drawings, the theater is a great place to show off your stuff. The scenic drops in particular are huge, and you can go to three-point perspective, or radically move the horizon or vanishing points, and get incredible designs.

As usual, however, we're more interested in getting it done the first time. So you'll not see a lot about three-point perspective here. It exists, and after you've mastered what's in these pages you may go crazy and try it. We'll take these perspective skills in order of complexity. By the way, you can't just read the next few sections and expect them to make sense. You have to actually *do* the exercises. But, lucky you, you can put the architect's scale away for a while; these first few exercises have absolutely no measuring. Here we go. Don't just stare at the illustrations, pick up a pencil and *go!*

ZERO-POINT PERSPECTIVE

I don't think zero-point perspective exists. Maybe on *Star Trek*.

ONE-POINT PERSPECTIVE

Use one-point perspective for interiors.

TWO-POINT PERSPECTIVE

Use two-point perspective for large interiors (palaces and the like) and exteriors.

THREE-POINT PERSPECTIVE

Didn't you read the intro? We're not going into three-point perspective today.

ONE-POINT PERSPECTIVE

While I stated above that one-point perspective is best suited for interiors, the best example of one-point perspective is actually in the great outdoors. Imagine a railroad track going straight away from you forever. Picture in your mind the way the rails seem to connect in the distance. They appear to meet at the horizon. As a matter of fact, they appear to vanish at the horizon. A road parallel to the railroad track would also vanish at the horizon, at the very same point as the tracks! That point is called a *vanishing point.* The basic vanishing points are always on the horizon; special vanishing points may lie above it, perhaps even below it.

On some scrap paper, you can quickly doodle a one-point perspective drawing. I suggest you invest in a 6H pencil, as you're probably going to want to erase a lot. (6H pencils make a really light line—easy to erase. Get 'em at an art store.) You may sketch in the horizon (let's make it horizontal, OK?), then place a point in the dead center of the horizon line. Yes, you *could* move it left or right, but work with me here: Put the vanishing point in the center *this time.* Draw in one set of railroad tracks. Remember, they are straight, and meet at the horizon. They actually touch in the picture. For the railroad ties put in a couple of horizontal lines, box in the ends, back, back ... again ... again ... WAIT A

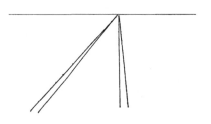

Railroad Tracks

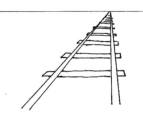

Tracks and Ties

MINUTE! Each railroad tie should be getting smaller, and they should be getting closer together. "Why?" you ask? Because your field of vision gets bigger with distance. "Huh?" you say? Because the ends of the railroad ties also have to vanish. "Hmm," I hear. As you get "farther away," you lose contrast and detail—so near the end you can just scribble, but the scribble has to vanish too.

GO BACK
Let's go back to the first few railroad ties. Being closer, we should be able to see some detail, like the thickness of the first few ties. Turn each tie into a long skinny box with thickness. You may have to start over as the concepts become clearer.

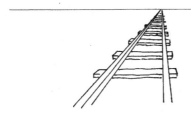

Detail on Railroad Ties

AN IMPORTANT HINT
At this stage of your drawing, almost all of the lines should be aimed either across the page or to the vanishing point. That is, either horizontal or vanishing. Let's add some telephone poles alongside the tracks. A *construction line,* a guideline meant to be erased later, will be a big help here. It's a vanishing line that lines up with the top of each telephone pole. Erase it later, after you sketch in the perfectly vertical poles. Remember, the poles are supposed to stick straight up. They are not horizontal, or vanishing. They'll get shorter as they recede into the distance, and they'll get closer together, but they *won't* tilt. Vertical lines stay vertical. Always. Use a triangle or a T-square; keep the vertical lines vertical. Even in two-point perspective, where there aren't *any* horizontal lines except the horizon—even there, the vertical lines are vertical.

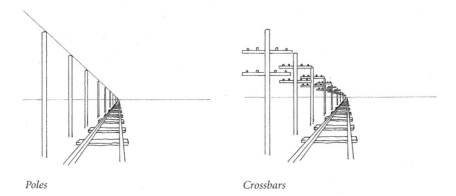

Poles

Crossbars

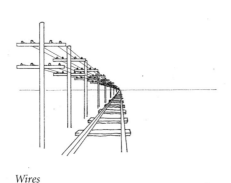

Wires

Erase the construction line and add the classic crossbars to each telephone pole. They are horizontal lines; don't you dare draw them as vanishing lines. Now the wires. They droop between each pole, but they should eventually make their way to the vanishing point. The same vanishing point.

VERY GOOD

Throw this embarrassingly poor sketch away and try it again.

THAT'S BETTER

Find a big old sheet of paper, a ruler, and a pin. Not a pen, a pin. Stick the pin through the vanishing point into your wife's antique roll-top desk. Strike that. Stick the pin through the vanishing point into a piece of cardboard or a drawing board. Use the ruler (ignore the measurements) to get better vanishing lines. Keep the horizontals perfectly horizontal. Keep the verticals perfectly vertical. A T-square and triangle from the art classroom really help here. Let's see . . . the railroad tracks, a road and sidewalk, a line of telephone poles, and a bike path all leading to the same . . .

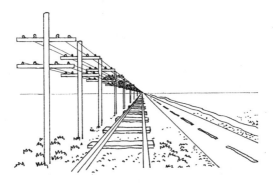

Better

FINAL EXAM

Try an interior. Start with a modest rectangle in the center of the page. This represents the back wall. The vanishing point should be somewhere inside that rectangle, even though it represents a point far away. The wall isn't glass, so no vanishing lines actually go all the way to the vanishing point anymore—they just head that way until they meet the back wall. Line up your ruler with the vanishing point, and with each corner in turn (stick the pin in the vanishing point). Draw from the wall (the corner) towards you. Look like an interior? A larger outside rectangle will help. Add doors and windows to the side walls. Add tiles to the floor. Color them in. Please remember that verticals stay vertical. Put a picture on a side wall. The side walls are in perspective. The back wall isn't. The fourth wall isn't there—it is the proscenium opening of your theater. Fourth wall, get it?

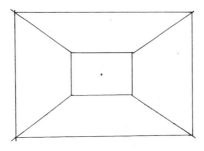

Interior

The fourth wall is actor's shorthand for "the audience." Archie Bunker's TV was also the fourth wall. It's not really there. I don't have to explain this any further, do I?

CUSSING OR CRUISING

Some people pick up perspective drawing relatively quickly, adding a picture window to the simple interior saying things like, "Him and his 'fourth wall.' Look, I got a fourth wall right here."

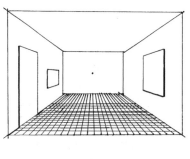

Plain

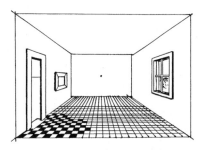

Fancy

Other, normal people have to work at it a while. There are some great books and a few good Web sites (search for "perspective"), but it's the practice that does it.

There are also the folks who'll quit right about here. Don't be one of them—it's just starting to get fun.

TWO-POINT PERSPECTIVE

First, a little review of Euclidean geometry. Parallel lines never meet. They stay, um, parallel. In one-point perspective we broke that rule, and parallel lines met at the horizon. We had verticals, horizontals, and vanishing lines. The verticals and horizontals followed the rules of geometry, and the vanishing lines *looked* like they did, giving the illusion of distance. In two-point perspective, we're just going to move the first vanishing point over to the left. Way over. Edge of the page. It's kind of like rotating our view. The new part is we're adding a second vanishing point, way over on the right. This'll be for the horizontal lines. Oops, they won't be horizontal anymore, they're *vanishing right*. Better get two pins.

If you're setting up a fresh drawing sheet, and you should be, lay in the horizon *very* lightly. Firmly establish in your mind that the horizon is the *only* horizontal line you will draw. Period. All other lines are going to vanish *left,* or vanish *right,* to the pins you have stuck in at each end of the horizon. Vertical lines will, of course, stay vertical. I told you so.

The easiest two-point perspective drawing is a mid-1970s office building. You know, the big boxes. We'll use a lot of construction lines in this one. Remember, they get erased later. Start with one vanishing line towards you from the left, and another from the right. Try to make them intersect somewhere in the middle of the page, below the horizon. A big, shallow *V.* Put up a vertical line at this intersection. This line must go straight up and down. Make it go above the horizon. Put a tiny little dot at the very top of this line. Concentrate on that dot. Totally ignore the original horizon line. The truth is, the horizon line interferes with the optical illusion you are trying to achieve. Ignore it or go ahead and erase it if it's bothering you.

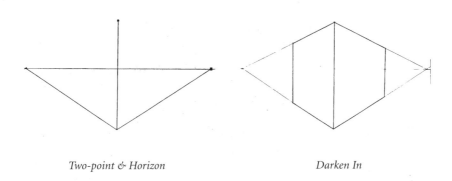

Two-point & Horizon   *Darken In*

OK, back to the dot. Vanish a line from the high center dot to the left (use the left-hand pin and a ruler). Good. Now another to the right. If you add two vertical lines in appropriate places you'll get a big box, with some extra lines sliding off into infinity. You can darken in the box a little. Let's pretend it's four stories tall. Mark off where the windows should go— together now, let's all do the right side first.

You are going to make some marks on that first vertical line you drew. The one that looks closest to you. Squint a little and try to visualize a four-story building, with windows. Windows are about half a story tall.

Hmm. Put little dots or tick marks where you think the windows would go. Right there on the frontmost vertical line. Now vanish each tick mark to the right. Good. Now, lay in some verticals (an even number, of course). You've got a mess a little like a checkerboard. Some of those boxes are your windows, some are just construction lines that you need to erase. (I told you to buy a 6H pencil, didn't I?) Darken in the windows. Erase the construction lines. Let's try to do better on the left-hand side, vanishing, thinner, smaller as we get farther away . . .

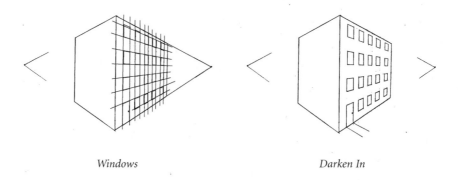

Windows   Darken In

WELL . . .

I think we all have a greater respect for Michelangelo now, don't we? Keep up with the practice. If you are getting upset, put a parking lot next to your building. It's easy, because there are no verticals. All parking lot lines will vanish right, or vanish left. Isn't this fun?

If your building looks funny, you may be misjudging the scale; just practice more. You could be drawing the verticals crooked. Try a T-square, running up and down the page. (Again, the purists will cringe, but they already know how to draw in perspective, so we can ignore them.) The "T" part of the T-square has to run along the top edge of your drawing board, or the kitchen table if you're working in the kitchen. Use this trick for vertical lines only. Keep the faith, and practice.

FINAL EXAM

Redo the Empire State Building in perspective. As far as scale is concerned, just make sure the total height and the total width are right. The bottom of the Empire State Building should rest on the horizon line. This will help give the illusion of great height. Use the architect's scale to get eight feet wide, and twelve or maybe fifteen feet tall. Then put the scale away. I mean it. There is a way to measure in perspective, and there is also a theory as to how to place the vanishing points, and there's even a way to show light and shadow. But you've got enough already to help you muddle through, especially if you cheat and get some photos to crib off of.

MISTAKES

Easy mistakes include not keeping verticals vertical and forgetting what is "in front" of what. My worst mistake was putting the horizon too high (twice!) in my set designs. To really look real, the horizon has to be very near the floor when everything's done.

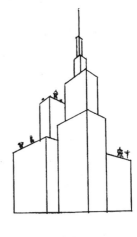

Perspective on stage works best with big objects, like painted drops. Some people have even built three-dimensional perspective objects, like trains. *Me?* No way. Well, a little bit, sometimes. And I've even experimented with three-point perspective, which is beyond the scope of this book.

Ta Da

THREE-POINT PERSPECTIVE

I hear some of your grumbling about three-point perspective. OK, just for you, here's a hint about three-point perspective. In three-point perspective, the verticals *aren't*. They vanish at the zenith or the ground, or underground, each at their own vanishing point. If you'd like to see this technique in use, buzz on over to New York and see *The Producers*. Have fun.

SET DESIGN REVISITED

A set that is built like a one-point perspective is called a "box set." They are usually built with three sides. But you, you . . . *you* could paint it all on a big drop in one-point perspective. Try it for a one-act play, or for a big scene in a musical.

DESIGN LESSONS

Try to fit the design to the show. Musicals will have a lot of moving pieces, while dramas are usually a little more static. I usually stuck with very realistic sets; if you try something way out there you run an increased risk of hurting your show, especially in the beginning of your set-design career. Go from photos (there are a lot of theater books that show old sets from many shows), and use movies to get design inspiration. I have been known to stop my car to photograph "scenic" houses, views, even streetlamps and signs. If your sketching skills are poor, sketch *more,* but also look for photos, and remember, some plays have set plans in the back. Your director will have set ideas and even demands (*I want a bridge in this scene . . .*), and of course the crew will have some suggestions—remarkably good suggestions sometimes. Use every resource you have.

If you are really stuck, use one old set piece for one scene, use a perspective drop for another scene, shoot some gobos (see cue 10) for another scene, borrow a set piece from another production company for another scene, and put up flats for one more scene. There you go.

Seriously, just start going to more shows—you'll quickly amass enough set ideas to see you through several shows. In this business you're sort of allowed to crib a good idea from someone else's show. Back to work.

FLATS

This is probably the perfect time to sort through your inventory of flats, those huge, painted canvas-on-a-frame things. Just looking at the flats can give you some ideas about a backdrop or set design. Flats are used to mask entrances and exits and to assemble (jigsaw-puzzle fashion) into set pieces. See what you have and build a complete set as the years go by. Don't throw away old flats that are beat up or even broken. They can be patched, and the patches can be patched, and a broken piece can be carefully replaced. When painted using good scene painting techniques, the repairs and seams hardly show at all. Flats can be combined with three-dimensional set pieces pretty easily, and extra parts (like church steeples) can be screwed on later. Use 'em; they're very versatile, if somewhat old-fashioned.

If possible, design your set so the seam on a flat really is a seam, or edge, or picture frame or something. This helps complete the illusion of reality. Then, of course, you paint 'em up. If you use latex paint, once every fifteen coats or so you'll have to replace the muslin, which is no big deal. You'll find books that advise stretching the muslin in place and trimming it right on the front, on the *face* of the flat. I much prefer flipping the thing over onto the muslin and attaching the fabric on the back, with weak Elmer's glue and staples. Seems to last longer. You have to water the glue down a little bit, since someday you'll probably want to remove the fabric.

When it comes time to stand the flats up, you can use stage braces or 1 × 4s, or (sometimes) they'll stay up by themselves if they are screwed together. In the old days, flats were lashed together, with rope. We can get away with screws, hinges, and the like since we're not taking everything apart every night while touring the country. . . .

BUILDING FLATS

If you have to *build* some flats you have a big decision to make. You can make them just like they are supposed to be made, following your best sample or a textbook, or you can build something called a *TV flat,* which is sort of an updated design. If you have lots of storage space, go for the TV flat. The difference is that the wooden frame is turned on its edge, and usually the frame is faced with ⅛" or ¼" plywood (use ⅛"). Then the whole thing is covered with muslin, giving a nicer painting surface, a step you can skip if you are broke.

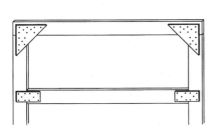

Flat Construction

TV Flat

Whatever you choose to build, don't just slap a flat together. They are supposed to become part of your scenery stock, to be repainted and reused show after show after show. You have to buy top-grade softwood to build good flats. Take extra time to be sure they are *square* (all corners are 90 degrees). Assemble with pilot holes, screws, and glue. The plywood can be glued and nailed. One nice thing about a TV flat is you don't need corner gussets for strength; you have the plywood. Build a variety of sizes. Long skinny ones come in handy for high-hanging signs. When you are at the top of your form in flat building, make a few with window and door openings, then make the window and door frames separately. That way, the flat won't move when you slam the door. Very clever, these technical theater people.

HOW TO MAKE DUTCHMAN

When using flats side by side in a semipermanent fashion (for instance, a box set), you'll probably want to cover the seams. Actually you can cover the edges of anything with this technique, and patch holes, hiding a multitude of sins. Mix up a coffee can full of weak Elmer's glue (two parts glue with about one part water added), spread it around like paint on the seams, and dip scraps of muslin in the can and slap them over the seams. It's a messy papier-mâché–type technique that covers gaps, giving a smoother appearance if done well. It's called *dutching*, as in, "Dutch up the edge of that platform." It can cover rough edges, and even, on a large scale, fill in a window opening that you don't need.

Dutching is not going to smooth over really poor construction. And it adds no strength at all, so don't depend on it for anything like that. In a perfect application, the long strip of muslin, about five inches wide, will be smoothed over two flats that are already pretty smooth themselves and aren't warped with respect to each other. That is, if the flats are crooked, the dutched seam is still going to show. If not done well, the dutching will look like a bad Bondo job on a car. The installer will take pains to smooth out the muslin as much as possible, allowing no folds, especially at the edges of the scrap muslin. A somewhat stiff paintbrush helps a lot here. And, of course, no one disturbs the thing until it's dry. (We dutched the edges of most of our platforms and wagons so they'd take paint better.) Let everything dry, then marvel at the smooth uniformity of your set surface.

CUE 2.8 SYNOPSIS OF THE PLAY

Take a break from all of this design work and reread the play. The stage crew has to learn the rudiments of the play before the actors are even cast in their parts. They don't need every detail, just a bit about what's coming so all the building and painting makes sense. For instance, we made two eighteen-inch dice for *Guys & Dolls*. I'm sure someone thought they were for the show; they were actually for the outdoor sign. The crew knew they were for the outdoor sign because they knew a little about the show, because . . . well, you see. Write a synopsis and distribute it to cast and crew. Later the synopsis can be reused by the publicity group, and you can send it out to coworkers before the teaser assemblies or previews.

CUE 2.9 THINKING AHEAD

Even though it's early, begin thinking about lighting design. You are going to have three-dimensional set pieces, painted drops, entrances, and exits. As they are designed and built, think about creative ways to light them up. One little point—you usually light the talent, not the set. But if you are building a staircase that leads on and off, you are going to have to light it. At this stage, just take note of pipe locations and try not to design or build any important thing where there's not a lighting pipe somewhere in front so you can easily set lights later.

Cue 3 Go.

Scene Painting Workshop

One place where I can save you an enormous amount of heartache is right here with the scene painting workshop. When you start work, you will have a large amount of time, an enthusiastic and energetic crew, and pretty much nothing to do. Oh, you'll have to collect props, build sets, and everything else. What I'm trying to say is the whole process starts slowly. So you have a bit of extra time. Contrast this with the week before opening. Enthusiasm and excitement might be very high, but everyone is tired. Light and sound cues need to be set, set repairs made, rehearsals take more and more time, nerves are a little frayed. Do you really want to *begin* teaching scenic painting at this late date?

Better to get some practice in early. Then the true scenic painting runs altogether more smoothly, with precious little intervention from you. The kids'll know what a *scumble* is, since you showed them back when. So let's collect a bunch of painting supplies and begin. Invite all your student artists and stage crew members and teach the rudiments of scenic painting.

UM, WHAT IS SCENIC PAINTING?

Scenic painting is a little like *faux finishing*; information is available at Home Depot and similar stores. It also utilizes *trump l'oeil*, which is French for "scenic painting." Actually it's French for "fool the eye," and that's exactly what you are trying to do. Add perspective drawing on a grand scale and you've just about got a handle on it.

PAINTBRUSHES

If you can develop a way to keep the paintbrushes clean, go ahead and buy real nice paintbrushes. There are special ones available for theater. But if you live in the real world, you'll be better off buying paintbrushes on sale, or even from the dollar store. Then you won't feel so bad when they are ruined. At the very minimum, keep a bucket of clean water handy so you can toss a brush in there and prevent it from drying out. We did this when we had a theater with no sink (and you wonder why I give architects a hard time—no sink in a theater!). Here is a short list of things that can be used as paintbrushes:

- ➤ Paintbrushes (sorry)
- ➤ Hand-sized whisk brooms (plastic or natural)
- ➤ Paint rollers
- ➤ Fingers
- ➤ Sea sponges
- ➤ Cellulose sponges
- ➤ Plastic trash bags crumpled up (really)
- ➤ Long wooden barbecue sauce brushes with an angled head
- ➤ Dust mops
- ➤ Those plastic things oranges sometimes come in
- ➤ Chore-Boys (and Chore-Girls)
- ➤ Feathers
- ➤ Feather dusters (v. cool)
- ➤ Carpet scraps
- ➤ Masonry brushes (near the bricks at Home Depot)
- ➤ Any broom-like device in the cleaning aisle at Kmart

Try to build or find some kind of contraption to keep all of these brush-type items organized.

INTERIOR FLAT LATEX PAINT

You can buy your paint at any old hardware store, or Home Depot. You don't need to invest in theatrical scenic paint. This is, of course, a heresy in this business, the second, I think, of several in the book. I'm running a horrible risk trying to publish a theater book that does not push theatrical scenic paint. But the truth is, the stuff stinks. Parse that; my *considered opinion* is, the stuff stinks.

THE PROS AND (MOSTLY) CONS OF THEATRICAL SCENIC PAINT

A) It's expensive; don't listen when they say you can stretch it with water.

B) It's expensive; once you open a can it'll spoil, which smells really bad (the stuff is milk-based). You'll end up pitching almost-full gallons.

C) It will always blend. This is kind of cool actually, except you forget you're working with beginners. Try to overcoat something and the bottom coat mixes in. Which means you have to buy:

D) Glaze overcoat, another expense.

E) You have to scrub the old stuff off.

F) That's gross, extremely messy.

G) The time will come when you have to use some smelly spoiled-milk paint, and you'll use it, and the smell *never goes away*.

H) Never.

I) I mean *never*.

J) You can't keep an open can until the next show, which is months away.

K) The manufacturers know all of this, and also sell acrylic paints.

L) Fool me once . . .

M) They're expensive.

N) They don't stretch as much as they say, same as the milk stuff.

O) With the exception of a few, really brilliant colors, you can get the same selection in interior flat latex at Home Depot.

P) Cheaper.

Q) Really, really cheaper.

R) Especially since you don't need the twenty-year stuff.

S) Get the house brand (America's Finest around here).

T) And stretch it with water.

U) Buy some black and white to mix shades.

V) Get large empty coffee cans.

W) With lids.

X) Top them off with a little Lysol.

Y) I'm padding the list here to get a complete alphabet. Bear with me.

Z) And the latex paint will do just about everything you need, and dry quickly, and clean up with water, and not smell. I think you get the point.

My predecessor ran up a $600 tab for theater paint alone (my girlfriend told me), and I had to throw it all away. Latex paint, on the other hand, gets a little skin over it, and the stuff below stays fine for years; just peel away the dried paint and add a little water. I won't tell you what the kids call the latex skin. Oh, all right. They called them "paint condoms," even though I tried to stop them. Anyhow, I bought "oops" paint at Home Depot for as little as one dollar a gallon, and no theatrical paint is that economical. I also got some great donations from house painters; try to network and see all the cool stuff you can get free. Speaking of free, lay claim to the coffee cans from the teacher's lounge, and any other location. You'll need 'em to hold mixed shades and new colors.

MY CHALLENGE

As I have, perhaps unfairly, slammed the theatrical paint industry (who also sell this kind of book . . . *uh-oh*), I feel I should give them equal time, or at least a chance to redeem themselves. If any manufacturer of scenic paint would care to work with me to find my average paint expenses for a show and then provide, free of charge, a financially equivalent amount of theatrical scenic paint, I will use it, following manufacturer's directions to the letter, and, if it works out better, I will appear in an ad for that brand of theatrical scenic paint free of charge. You can't say fairer than that. Until then, *interior flat latex.*

PAINT CLOTHES

Try your best to have the kids bring in some ratty old clothes for painting. Plus, clean out your own closet. Heck, go shopping, and donate your old wardrobe to the theater. The nicer stuff can become costumes, and the junky stuff can become paint clothes. Remember to save some paint clothes for yourself. Time and time again kids will begin painting while wearing school clothes, inevitably they get paint on themselves, and you might have a very upset parent to deal with. Our biggest problem with paint clothes was finding a convenient place to put them. Near the paints is good; near the dressing rooms acceptable. Our second biggest problem was the crew kids wanting to wear the paint clothes to school. You can let them as long as they bring 'em back. After a show, you might find the paint clothes closet a little thin and empty looking, because kids have decided to keep their paint clothes as a souvenir. Fine. There are always more available at Goodwill.

HOW TO MAKE PRIMER

Don't buy primer. Primer is just weak paint with a stronger binder. Instead, just collect all of your half-empty paints (not black or white) and pour them into a five-gallon bucket. All latex, right? Add some water and stir with the electric paint mixer tool, connected to a powerful electric drill. The kids love the electric paint mixer tool. They only cost a dollar each. Well, the big one is more, but the little one's a dollar or two. Buy them both. But, be careful with the electric paint mixer tool. It'll splash paint everywhere very effectively. Goggles and paint clothes are a must here. Add a bit of water (and some Lysol if you are going to store the primer) and blend carefully with the electric paint mixer tool. This brown or green yuck is a perfectly good primer. It's best to mix primer at the conclusion of a show and seal it up; then you can rinse out the old paint cans and store them for the next show. Then wash up.

Make friends with a plumber, because your sink's gonna get clogged no matter what you do. But put a screen of tight hardware cloth or an air conditioner or furnace filter over the drain, and you may postpone the inevitable for a few years.

COME BACK HERE LATER

Promise me you'll come back to this section after you've built your set. I want to put all of the information about painting in one place, and it seems appropriate to put in here even though you have to build the set before you can paint it. Practice scene painting early. Because you have to train your painters. Early. Like I said, you usually have a little bit of extra time in the beginning of a show, and you'll have *no* time to stop and train near opening night. Use the spare time available at the beginning of a show to practice, practice, practice, and to train your painters. Then, when the set is built, boom, go! There's magic for you.

HERE WE GO

Let's start the scene painting workshop with something simple—say, a cabinet door. Make a practice "door" for everybody out of scrap plywood. I suggest they be seventeen inches by twenty four and that you stand them vertically. It does not matter how thick they are, just that you have one for everybody involved.

Choosing colors can be tricky. But most cabinets are brown, so mix up a batch of brown, or buy some dark brown, flat latex paint from

Home Depot. Get the absolute cheapest and darkest they have; remember, in the theater the paint only has to last a month or two. If you have no paint at all, pick up some black and white as well. Buy *interior* flat latex; they'll probably have to mix the brown and black colors for you. Always buy latex paint. Usually you want flat paint (except when you really want it shiny—rare on stage). Exterior paint is fine, except it costs more . . . got it? Good.

You now have enough paints to get you through the scene painting workshop. The other things that will come in handy are brushes—lots of brushes (four-inch wide is good, and smaller), rollers and trays (mostly just for priming things), the junky plywood cut into the shape of a small door, chalklines, masking tape, sidewalk chalk (try Toys "R" Us), rulers, a flat wooden office door (watch out on trash days), coffee cans, and liquid laundry detergent bottles filled with water. If the plywood and the door have some garish painting on them, give them a quick coat of some primer (any old paint will do). Otherwise just set up the stuff, turn on the work lights, and let's go.

FOR THOSE WHO HAVE NEVER USED A CHALKLINE

A *chalkline* is a specialty tool for carpenters. It does four things (five, if you count spilling colored chalk dust everywhere). It looks like a fishing reel—you can unreel the string inside, pull it tight against a layout piece, and snap a layout line by plucking the string against the workpiece. The powdered chalk dust on the string transfers to the layout. You can also hang it off of a nail to get perfect verticals, just like a plumb bob. You can hold a pencil at one end and scribe circles and arcs of any size (and you will, if we can ever get you to Cue 4). It also makes a great toy, so you will have to stop folks from playing with it almost every day. Hey, you! Stop playing with the chalkline and start mixing paint!

EVERYONE PAINT A CABINET DOOR

It's best if *you* begin doing things at a scene painting workshop, then turn it over to the kids. First you have to mix up your paint. Fill up two new coffee cans with white until they are just under two-thirds full. For the brown shades you'll need to pour out a little less than one-eighth of your brown paint into one coffee can, and about one-third into another. A common mistake here is to slop too much paint out, which will prevent you from getting the shades you want. Sandi, my stage crew president, reminded me you are supposed to add dark paints to the white slowly, and mix as you go until you find the shade you want. Good idea. Save the last bit of paint in the original can. You can add some water to stretch out the paints and save money. When these are stirred, you'll have three brown tones, commonly called light, medium, and dark. Using three wide brushes, paint your cabinet door brown, mostly medium, with streaks of dark and light thrown in. Then use a fourth brush to blend the colors— just don't blend out the different shades completely. The idea here is to give the surface a variegated appearance that won't look flat under the powerful stage lights. Many beginners will blend the three distinct tones into one by brushing too much; be on guard for this and prevent it when you can. Keep the fourth brush as dry as possible and don't overdo the blending. This whole procedure should take less than five minutes.

EMPHASIS HERE

I need to emphasize the importance of this blending, or *scumbling,* technique. Slap three different shades of paint on the back of one of the practice pieces. Take the fourth brush and mix the three colors with, oh, say, five strokes. That's probably right. Now keep blending. See how you eventually even out the color? That's bad. Don't do that. You can blend like this in streaks, random splotches, and curves or circles. At this stage it doesn't matter too much, but generally you follow the shape of the thing you are trying to paint: random and circular for clouds, streaks for fences, etc. Whenever you are doing scenic painting, make sure everything on stage is a scumble or blend of some kind. And avoid pure white, in painting and in costumes. It's just too bright.

ATTACK THE DOOR

While the cabinet doors are drying—and they must dry—attack the big door. Here you get to "wet blend" on a larger scale. In addition, you can try your hand at fooling the eye. Paint the upper left of the door mostly light brown, and the bottom right mostly dark. Continue the wet blend as usual, taking pains to keep an exaggerated spectrum of brown. You can throw in a very little black near the bottom of the door, then blend it in as well. Latex paint actually dries pretty quickly, so work fast. It won't really look like much at this stage, but don't get discouraged. Set this aside and go back to the smaller plywood pieces, which should be dry. If they're not, call a ten minute break.

BACK TO THE CABINET DOORS

The next step is to paint in some detail that will make the brown wood look like a cabinet door. Let's try a simple raised panel, like the one on many desks. A raised panel is actually sunken, then raised, and in normal circumstances will cast small shadows under every part that drops in (so to speak), and little highlights will show on every raised surface. It's the placement of the (imaginary) light that determines which surface is which.

So let's pretend that the light is coming in high over your left shoulder. Here comes the sunken part. Break out the masking tape and, if necessary, the rulers. Tape a nice box on your plywood door, say, three inches in from every edge. If you are the meticulous type, and have cut every door the same size—say, seventeen by twenty-four inches vertical—you could actually use these in a show. Sit every kid down facing the same way with their little door in front of them. Determine where the shadows will fall if the light is coming in over the left shoulder. Everyone should get the same answer. Since the inside of the door is sunken in, and the light is coming in high left, the top edge and the left edge will be in shadow. They gotta be painted black.

The Look

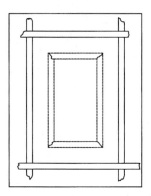

How It's Done

Now comes the hateful part. If you just paint a solid black stripe down the left side and across the top (inside the taped box, of course), you won't get a very convincing shadow. It's time to teach the "starved brush" technique. Dip a one-inch paintbrush in the black paint and daub it off onto a scrap piece of wood (or the stage floor) until it is almost dry. Then daub it along the inside edges of the tape so the paint is not solid, except perhaps at the tape edge itself. Change brushes and put in the highlights using white. You can use pure white here, just this once. But not too much! Starved brush, daubing. You're not done. Tape another box inside the first for the raised part of the panel, one or two inches smaller than the first box. Again the light comes over the left shoulder, but this time the surface is supposed to be raised. The *outside* edge of the tape will go white on the top, and on the left. Starved brush, and these lines are smaller. Don't forget the last shadows in black, looking like a backwards *L*.

Finish off the thing by adding highlights and shadow to the very real three-dimensional edge of the plywood door (highlight top and left, shadow bottom and right). Here you don't have to use the starved brush; just keep the paint off of the front of the door. Then peel off the tape. Don't wait for the paint to dry—peel off the tape while the paint is wet. Always. You'll thank me if your kids remember that one detail.

THE MOMENT OF TRUTH

You'll want to line all of these pieces up on stage facing the audience. Lean them against a box or something. Make this a powerful lesson by having the kids turn away from their work and move out into the house. They can stand in the aisle, about halfway back. Turn on the stage lights, then let the kids turn around. The distance and the stage lighting combine to pop these flat paintings into three-dimensional cabinet doors, and it will be clear to everybody which ones are good and which ones are great. Everyone will want to try it again, so set them loose on the painted door with a complicated Colonial pattern from a photograph. They'll need the chalkline for this. It'll probably turn out wrong, but the enthusiasm and practice are the real goals today anyway. Congratulations. You now have a scene painting crew.

ONE LITTLE TIP

Whenever you use tape—and you'll use a mile of it—place the tape so the paint will lie on the sharp edge of whatever you are painting. The sharp edge is the corner, and the paint is the shadow. This allows the shadow to fade away naturally. Again, a variegated appearance is desired. The shadows can get fatter and skinnier, even darker and lighter, but the sharp edge will always be constant. The same is true for highlights.

This means when two sharp edges meet you'll have to tape and paint, remove the tape, let the paint dry, retape on the other side of the same edge (covering your work), *then* paint the second edge a second color or tone. If you don't do this, you'll get a line where the tape was. Just buy lots and lots of tape. Try the dollar store, but if the tape does not work well, ditch it and pay retail.

Using tape of several thicknesses (½" to 3") is a great way to make stripes and fake wallpaper. Lay down a base coat; a two-tone "scumble" would be fine. Then tape in a pattern (be meticulous here), overpaint with one or two different tones of color, and remove the tape while the paint is wet. The base color shows through where the tape was, and the overcoat gives a great appearance. Don't worry about small "bleeds" under the tape. The audience is much too far away to see them.

MORE PRACTICE

Fake crown molding, which can be any color, and rocks, like a rock wall, are great scene painting skill builders. When some vandals hit the school with graffiti, I "volunteered" the stage crew to paint it out. What the principal expected was a gray wall like before; what he got was a rock wall that looked so good he stopped his car and got out to see if it was real. As he walked towards it he wondered when the maintenance department had come by and put up stone. The job was so good even the vandals left it alone.

HOW DID THE DOOR COME OUT?

If all went well, the door should look particularly striking and real; that is the effect of the wet blend. The lower, darker corner should seem further away under stage lights. Set the door up at an angle to the audience to exaggerate this effect. Put it up facing the wrong way and it'll look funny. Trust your eyes. Temporarily place the door upside down to really see the power of this effect.

SUBSTITUTE

Now that you have a handle on the techniques, it's time to try a little substitution. Use rolled-up plastic bags instead of brushes. Roll up a big ol' trash bag, dip it in the paint, and then roll it across a piece of plywood.

What a cool effect. Bunched-up newspapers work too. Sponges give great texture and can be cut out in semi-rubber stamp fashion. You are allowed to do pretty much anything that looks cool from far away. This is hard on beginners—they'll usually be quite conservative in their painting techniques. The sooner you change that pattern, the better.

WOOD GRAINING TOOL

Theater supply houses sell a couple of different kinds of wood graining tools. I particularly like the ones that look like round rubber stamps. Get a lesson on how to use 'em, and pick up a couple for a show. I designed a show with wainscot paneling, and I was clever enough to have the dimensions of the paneling match the size of the graining tool (the graining *combs* aren't quite as cool; maybe I just couldn't get the hang of using them). We ran a little graining production house on the stage apron for a couple of days and made about sixty feet of very convincing wood-grained wainscot paneling for *You Can't Take It With You.* Then, of course, we had to do the doors and door jambs. In the end it looked better than real paneling, since the theater lights would wash out the wood grain of real paneling.

The short lesson on the wood graining tool (in case you already own one): Undercoat the "panel" with a medium or light brown. This does not need to be a scumble or blend; just slap the paint on with a roller. After this dries, lay on a much darker overcoat, then quickly run the graining tool along the wet paint (in a straight line). Rock the graining tool a bit—the rubber grooves rub the paint away to reveal the undercoat—very cool. As you move the graining tool, you'll see a little painted edge on each side of the "grain." Leave it; it shows as the panel edge. For a really cool effect, come in later (with tape) and lay in some white highlights wherever they should go. Sit and think about it for a minute or two; getting these highlights wrong will ruin the 3-D effect you've worked so hard to achieve.

A COOL OPTION

Before graining, slap a very few long streaks of powerful bright color on your undercoat. Red, purple, green, and orange. The streaks should follow the direction of the grain. After they dry, grain as usual. The brilliant colors show through to give a contrasting look, breaking up the space. As usual, don't judge this effect close up; sit in the house and look at the finished product under stage lights. It usually looks great. If you overdid it or don't like it, you can always paint over the offending spots.

THE FEATHER DUSTER

Another neat way to get a two-tone appearance is to overcoat the painted piece with a feather duster lightly dipped in a contrasting paint. You can swirl and slap the feather duster around, making streaks and dots to great effect. Purists pay extra for ostrich-feather feather dusters, but the artificial-feather feather dusters work fine for this, and are cheaper too.

STENCILS

Stencils are great if you can build them tough enough to last. Try thin plastic, like the cover of an old plastic notebook, or overhead transparency material. Cut out the design (carefully) with an X-Acto and daub the paint on with a bunched-up old rag or sponge. Take your time with the X-Acto. Have fun. When using the stencil, be careful to place it well. If it's crooked or off-center, it won't look so good. Try a two-tone, with two different stencils. Just be sure to budget a lot of time . . .

By the way, you don't need to completely fill in a stencil, as you might imagine you would. It's quite all right to let some of the undercoat show through. While you are standing there daubing, you won't want to allow this; fight that feeling and daub sparingly. Also, move around as you do this sort of work. You are bound to get tired, or change your technique as you go. It's best if you don't stencil or paint in any sort of rigid left-to-right kind of order because the mistakes will show. If several people are working with stencils (or paints), move them around from time to time so their individual styles don't show. Or give one job to one person only, for consistency. You . . . you're the highlight girl. You're the stencil guy. Last tip, never turn your back on the set painters for more than five minutes. Avoids surprises.

FAUX FINISHING

As faux finishing is getting kind of trendy, keep an eye out for unique painting supplies. I once saw a paint roller that could roll two colors at once. Any device like this is worth having. Someone is selling patterned rollers, pick a few up—the floral patterns are particularly nice. Don't buy the expensive paint, though.

MORE ON THE STARVED BRUSH

Kids have a hard time with scenic painting until they get the hang of it (another reason we started early). I kept a lot of impressionist art books around, since the effect you want on stage is very similar to the effect these painters put into their work. You can buy these books in the bargain bins of major bookstores and save a bundle. The scumbling comes pretty easy, and the wet blend; it's the starved brush that kids don't understand. Everything they've ever painted (and all housepainting) consists of covering the work with a nice even coat of paint. That's just what we're trying to avoid with the starved brush technique. Show them how to dip in for just a smidge of paint, and to brush off the first big glob onto a board, or an unpainted area, or the stage floor. Brushing off the first big glob of paint is the one single thing that will improve scenic painting the most. Then paint away, letting the undercoat show through. Don't cover the old color. Less is more in this regard. Then step back to judge the effect. One should never judge scenic painting from close up; the audience is at least thirty feet away. The blending, graining, and spattering techniques, combined with distance, give the illusion that the painted object is real, even if it doesn't look real at all when you are up close.

SPATTER TECHNIQUE

This incredibly messy technique makes your sets look better—a lot better—so use it. The idea is to lay the painted flats down and sprinkle them with contrasting colors of paint, which serves to break up the visual field, magically making the scenes look better. You can spatter black and blue on pastels, for instance. Remember, the pastel should already be some kind of blend; nothing looks worse on a stage than a monotone wall. Spatter tiny drops of black over the work. You'll have to paint over the inevitable big drips and spills, and there you go. Don't pick it up too soon, as the spatters will run.

I saw Evan, my coworker from the museum industry, spatter with an old toothbrush once. He was making a repair to a previously painted museum wall (in the Smithsonian) using this weird, emulsified paint. He'd dip in the toothbrush, then flick the paint onto the wall, or seam, or whatever. You'll do the same with a larger brush. Did you keep the practice doors from the scene painting workshop? They'll do for practice, and you'll need to practice. Mix a bit of water in the paint so it's a little runny, dip in a big fat brush, stand over the work in your best paint clothes, and flick the brush like a whip, or tap it against your free hand or a block of wood. Move around so no one can see any direction to these spatters. Messy, messy, messy, but a fun and truly effective technique.

You can also spatter (I think the more descriptive term is *sprinkle*—too bad it's not manly enough) with a modified pesticide or stain sprayer. It's a little tough to get this to work with latex paint (you have to water it down a lot), but if you get it right, this job is over in a snap, except for the drying. Worth a try.

Do spattering last.

WASHING THE BRUSHES

No one wants to sweep, mop, or wash brushes. Your veteran crew members will try to force these tasks onto the beginners; don't let them, as it'll just make the beginners quit. You are going to be stocking the paint closet with dozens of brushes, from four inches wide (and even wider) to the ones about as big as a pencil. Smaller just can't be seen, so don't bother. If the brushes get clogged with paint they're ruined, so be sure to get them cleaned daily. This was a problem for me, as I'm a bit of a slob, so in the worst case just get them in water, and you can rinse them the next day. At the old school we had no sink, so there was a recurring problem with this. Ah, but now we're in the new school. After cleaning, we would hang the brushes in the paint closet. I think a better place would be in a rack near the sink; that way it's easier to get them hung up. Easier to steal, too, so watch out.

If you need it, there is a brush softener available. It'll soften dried-on latex paint and you'll be able to use a brush that would otherwise have to be thrown out. I always did this job at home since the process is quite nasty.

GIANT DROPS

I hope you have a giant drop somewhere. I mean a huge canvas, twenty by fifty feet or so, that can be tied to a batten or against the back wall. If you do, your scenic painters can work on it as the rest of the set is being designed and built. Decide early where to hang the thing—way upstage as a backdrop for everything, or close to the audience so you can run a scene change behind it. It's best if you can fly it in and out of the scene (during a blackout), but a little ingenuity can substitute if you don't have a fly gallery. For instance, you could untie it and drop it to the floor during intermission.

Giant drops are great. It can be a little impractical to use our transparency technique on something this big, but you can draw a scene, in perspective, on the big drop just the same. Measure your big drop and make a scale drawing, a perfect replica of the measured sizes. Stick with ¼" scale and knock out a lovely perspective scene. A palace, say, for *The King & I*. Or a generic medieval town. The Bastille. Whatever. Now you've just got to do it again in full size, on your big canvas drop. This is quite a trick. Using your small perspective drawing as a guide, you duplicate everything on the big drop, also in perspective.

> ➤ Stretch the whole thing out flat.
> ➤ Keep the horizon near or at the bottom of the drop.
> ➤ Put the vanishing points at the edge of the drop.
> ➤ Lay in two screws instead of pins.
> ➤ Use chalklines instead of rulers.
> ➤ Buy extra chalkdust (chalkline chalk).
> ➤ Double-check the verticals when you hang the thing up (use a plumb bob).

The scenic painting should begin with the canvas spread out on the floor, but it can be finished after being tied up, using a scaffold or the basket ladder. Whatever you do, don't let the paint dry while the drop is still on the floor. The drop will stick to the floor if the paint bleeds even a little bit. Needless to say, you will want to start this on a day when you have lots and lots of time, and no one in the way. Stretch and snap chalklines on the drop in perfect measured alignment with your scale perspective drawing. Tape the lines with masking tape and slap a coat of paint on the drop to give a rough idea of the major shapes. Use a couple of different paint techniques as described above. Peel off the tape while the paint is wet (always). Blue in the sky. Remember your scumble and wet blend techniques. Add clouds. Yes, they are a wet blend too—three shades of pale gray (pale, paler, and palest gray; don't use pure white).

FOOTPRINTS

When you paint a drop on the floor, no matter how careful you are, someone will step in the wet paint, putting a beautiful footprint smack in the middle of your painted drop. You won't be able to avoid this. Just look at the drops carefully, *carefully,* for footprints and paint 'em out. Some kids like to paint secret messages into the scenery. If these are small no one will see them; if they show, paint 'em out. Well done.

NO BIG DROP?

There's no reason you can't paint the back wall of the theater for a back-drop, even if it has plumbing or columns in the way. If you have a traveling back curtain, you can open and close it as needed, covering the painted scene. If you don't, you just aim the lights a little more carefully so you can dim the background out when you don't need it.

IF YOUR DROP HAS HOLES—BIRDY NET

At theatrical supply houses, you can buy this scenery netting stuff that covers any open space in a painted drop with a wide-open woven mesh cloth. This can fill gaps in trees, for instance, allowing you to see through painted drops and keep the branches hanging up there normally. Kind of like a very open scrim, except there's no way to put an image on the front, except my secret way, which I will tell you in a moment. First though, don't buy the real stuff unless you have to, or until they lower the price. It's made for Broadway, and you'll pay dearly for its semipermanent strength. Instead, go to Home Depot and get a roll of fruit tree protective netting, the kind that keeps the birds away. This stuff works great as a sort of poor man's scenery netting. Let's suppose you want to see someone peeking through the branches of a painted tree on a drop. You can cut away the space, but the drop will flop out of shape. What you do is stick this stuff on the back of the opening in the painted drop, gluing it in place with strips of dutching (see "How to Make Dutchman," page 36). After everything dries, hang up the drop as usual. Hole filled, tree limbs stay in place. I used real scenery netting to hold parts of a Buddhist temple together in *The King & I*. At the time, I promised myself I'd find a cheaper replacement. My buddy Juan (his real name) tipped me off to the bird netting, which we used in *Guys & Dolls*.

TWO TRICKS USING BIRDY NET

You can hang this stuff almost anywhere, off of almost anything; it will hold up almost any light object, and it's almost impossible for the audience to see. Wonderful stuff. The simple trick is to hang decorations off of it; it'll look like the things are floating in space. Pretty cool. The *really* cool trick is to put an image on the stuff. If you build a huge open frame and staple the birdy netting behind it, you can make a very impressive sign, cartoon, or silhouette. The way we did it was to build a pretty tough, light frame out of 1 × 3s that had the proportions of the borders of a three-panel comic strip, about eight feet tall and twenty-four feet long. We attached our birdy netting with staples (from the back) and flew it up till it rested on the floor, about five feet in front of our cyclorama. We had an enlarged comic strip to go by. Instead of drawing or painting on the birdy net, we just laid in what we wanted with masking tape. It won't want to stick, so you should have the crew attach tape from both sides of the net. Then paint the tape and the frame black. Don't use electrician's tape—it's too expensive.

There's not much image there (it'll look like a line drawing), so to allow the audience to see this contraption you have to light the cyclorama or the back wall behind it. You are shooting for a silhouette effect here. When the thing is finished, have the crew fly it up a bit off of the floor, and light up the cyc behind it; it'll look like the cyc has a comic strip painted on it. Quick, easy, and cheap, and a very impressive look when done well. This works for skylines, too; just try to hide or omit the frame.

SCRIM

A *scrim* is a giant drop that you can see through. Or not, depending on the light. They are made to be painted, showing the audience a scene; then the area behind the scrim is lit, showing a see-through hazy scene upstage. Perfect for Granny's House in *Into the Woods*. Unfortunately for us, the scrim material (it's called sharkstooth scrim) is so expensive you probably won't ever want to paint it. Even if you buy the proper paints, you'll never be able to fully rinse out the scene, ruining the entire scrim for any other purpose. So we never painted our full stage scrims, using lights to decorate them instead.

But you will probably be able to afford a smaller piece, window- or house-sized. Attach it to some kind of frame and you can have a cool scrim effect on a somewhat smaller scale. Just remember, any paint you apply will *not* transmit light, so you can't fill in the holes in the scrim. Just water down your paint a bit. They sell special dyes, but you probably don't want to mess with them.

What you do is paint the scrim, using all of the classic stage painting techniques, while the scrim lies on a bunch of newspapers or rests on the stage floor. The paper will absorb the excess paint; the bare stage floor will just get painted. If you daub and blot (again with newspaper) you can lay in a pretty cool scene. Then pick up the scrim before the paint dries, and there you go. Light from the front will show the front scene (you'll have to experiment with the lights), light the area behind and the scrim becomes see-through. We had a pretty convincing Granny's House. I made one little mistake, which I suppose I should warn you about. After attaching the scrim to a house-like frame and covering the edges with bark from a cedar tree, I decided to spray-paint the layout of the house directly on the scrim. Spray paint is dead opaque, but I didn't realize that would be a problem. It was a great effect, showing the silhouette of the house perfectly. And of course it showed every mistake. And I could not get rid of the mistakes. They'd still show through when lit from behind. Oops. Reusing this scrim is out of the question, unless we need another Granny's House. Lesson learned. Stick with latex paint.

OK, clean up this mess and let's get this show on the road.

CUE 3.9 AUDITION POSTERS

Audition posters and PA announcements help get out the word that you are ready to cast for your play. In strict chronological order, *now* is the time to get them out. Be sure to include all of the important information on the play, the parts, the practice times, and locations . . . and try to do it in an unusual and eye-catching fashion. The concept is to find and inform not the kids who will be there anyway, but the kid(s) who probably wouldn't know about auditions or normally bother to try out. The drama kids are gonna show—you want to find and attract the latent talent hidden in the general school population. And they will need extra encouragement to come. I would occasionally personally invite a student singer or dancer to come try out, hinting that a part was perfect for him . . . but of course this is difficult.

One good *bad* example was the case of the dancing waiters in our production of *Hello, Dolly!* The audition posters begged for break dancers, and I personally tapped a few kids to try to get them in the show. I had seen them practicing their moves after school right outside the theater, and I knew they'd be a big hit as dancing waiters if I could just get them to audition. The scene was hilarious, the dancing waiters did a fine job, but the break dancers never auditioned. In the back of my mind I couldn't help musing how much funnier the scene could have been if I had managed to convince a couple of them to try out. Another time, our audition poster asked for student rappers, to punch up the first song in *The Music Man*. I was thrilled when they showed; talented student rappers would have been a great touch because that first song has the rhythm of an old steam train (chugga chugga chugga). Perfect. Unfortunately, they sort of misunderstood what the audition was for (they didn't want to sing someone else's lyrics) and again passed on auditioning.

This doesn't mean that audition posters are ineffective. We did find several talented kids who were not enrolled in the drama classes. The posters and school announcements (and their friends) had convinced them to try out. In accordance with the best of theater tradition, one of these walk-ons was cast as the lead in our production of *Hello, Dolly!* Magical—almost makes you cry. Besides, the break dancers *swear* they are going to try out this year.

The audition posters can also help start the buzz about the play. Our audition posters for *Annie* were cribbed from a library collection of Little Orphan Annie comic strips. I changed the word balloons to give information about the show. I don't recall them bringing in a lot of unknown talent to the auditions, but I do remember a huge audience for the show. Part of the credit goes to the early publicity generated by clever audition posters. Our posters for *Fiddler* had quotes from the play. So many great lines. . . .

Put up audition posters everywhere students hang out.

TAKE DOWN AUDITION POSTERS

Take down the posters when auditions are over. This little task is usually forgotten and makes you look bad.

CUE 4 *Go.*

Build the Thing Already

Your major set pieces are either going to stand still or roll. Some may fold up, some may be carried, and skinny pieces can "fly" if you have the setup, but most roll, or slide. If it stays up for the whole play, and can get covered or darkened, just go ahead and screw it down. The problem with something up there for the whole play is that people will be looking at the thing for almost two hours. Make sure it looks good. The big pain with rolling pieces is that they don't stop; that is, it's hard to anchor them once you've rolled them on (there is hardware available to help you fasten them down). The trouble with sliding pieces is that they *don't* roll; that is, they are heavy and hard to move. Use your best judgment and invest in some big casters, three-inch minimum. Use a lot of casters, since one or more will probably break. This was a problem with our little train in *Hello, Dolly!* Somewhere along the line we rolled it up and down the main hallway of the school, with far too many kids riding it (sort of like a costume parade). Anyhow, the casters broke, necessitating a quick repair. Don't bother to buy the casters with little brakes, they're designed to stop a garden cart, not a wagon with an eight-foot-tall newsstand on it. Do buy the kind that don't spin, and the kind that do spin; both will come in handy. Try to get a whole lot the same size. Don't forget carriage bolts, nuts, washers, and lag screws. As the weeks go by you'll spend a lot of time in hardware stores. If they are far away you'll quickly learn to think things out and buy extras of everything you think you'll ever need. If you live way out in the sticks, there's always mail order.

If you have an unlimited budget, there are some great things available from Rose Brand (*www.rosebrand.com*).

SET CONSTRUCTION

Chances are you'll spend most of your stage crew time building sets and unbuilding them. That said, there is remarkably little to tell you. The sets must be strong. The sets must be light. The sets must stay up by themselves. You'll use 2 × 4s except when you can get away with 1 × 4s. So let's build a set.

SCREWS

Assemble your set with screws and screw guns. We had the best success with Deck-Mate deck screws. These have a proprietary bit that comes in the box with the screws, and it doesn't "cam-out" (strip) like Phillips screws sometimes do. You're going to have to stock several sizes, up to 3½", and sometimes you'll have to drill pilot holes so the wood doesn't split. Caution the long-haired among your stage crew to tie their hair back when driving screws. Ouch.

SCREW GUNS

The best screw guns are the battery-operated electric drill type. The kids beat our DeWalts to heck, but they did the job until they broke. Whatever you buy, buy them all the same; that way you can swap batteries easily. I was happiest with the 18-volt models, though 12 will do. Buy the drills that have a slow-speed selector, and *don't* buy the ones that need a chuck key.

Many crew kids will find it tough to drive a 3" screw into lumber, and you will use a lot of these when you build a set. If you set up one drill with a ⅛" twist bit, and another with the screwdriver bit, the puniest little brother of the puniest crew kid will have no problem driving these screws. They'll simply drill a pilot hole first. And if one person holds while the other assembles, things will go faster. I held for my buddy Mark in high school, and he drilled my finger (two stitches), so teach safety.

I WISH

I wish Deck-Mate made really short screws, with that head design I'm certain they'd be popular. And I wish those wide pan-head screws were more easily available. You can find 'em, and when you do, buy a lot, they come in handy. And if you find a brand of screws where the tips are really sharp, buy 'em (McFeely's). That way they'll punch through plywood without a pilot hole. And I wish those little contraptions that both drill pilot holes and drive screws were *just a little bit better*; generally they clog up with sawdust and slow things down.

You are also going to have to stock a lot of #2 Phillips bits for the screw guns, as well as the Deck-Mate proprietary bits. And you'll need some #1 Phillips and #3 Phillips bits too. Buy the long screw bits; they won't get lost so easily. Go ahead and splurge on a huge set of many little screwdriver bits, including the Torx type, and the little nutdriver bits. Keep 'em put away until the day you need 'em. Then you can thank me.

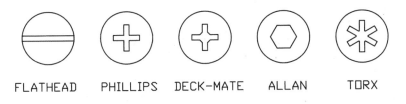

FLATHEAD   PHILLIPS   DECK-MATE   ALLAN   TORX

Screwheads

WRENCHES

As the years go on you'll find the need for a complete toolkit, but a surprising amount of work can be done with just a crescent wrench for the lights and a selection of pliers for everything else. When you are tightening things, take note of how big the nut or bolt actually is. Little teeny bolts do not need to be really, really tight. So easy does it. Larger bolts are larger, so you can put some moxie onto 'em and bear down a bit. Show a little judgment if you want to avoid busting the bolts, and your knuckles. Instead of nutdrivers, get the little nutdrivers you can chuck up in your electric screwdriver; again, being careful when tightening not to wring the head off of the screws. Eventually you'll need to pick up a complete socket set, too.

MAKE IT BIG

When you are making things for the theater, you have got to remember their purpose—to show something to the audience. Props, masks, and scenery pieces have got to be large enough to show, and, when needed, to impress. So think big. BIG. Look at some old painted pieces while standing at the back of the auditorium to see what I mean. Things on stage have got to be larger than life to make an impact on the audience. If someone carried a life-sized roasted turkey on stage it would look about the size of a Cornish game hen, so props have to be especially big. No one will be able to tell Tony has a knife unless it's big. Really big.

MAKE IT BIG, EXCEPT WHEN YOU SHOULD MAKE IT SMALL

Big, big, big. Everything on stage should be big, since your audience is about a hundred feet away. Except doors. If you ever have the chance, don't miss an opportunity to pick up or make some slightly undersized doors. Under-*height,* that is. And save 'em if you get 'em. Full-sized doors are a problem on stage as they force the second story of your set too high. This'll be a huge problem for the light guys. Also, a full-sized door sometimes looks too big in the scene. The audience is very forgiving if the players have to duck a teeny bit to get through a doorway; in fact, they probably won't even notice. I'd realize it's a little difficult to trim down a full-sized door, impossible with hollow-core units. Use factory-made doors until you have the time or desire to build a few nice, tough, reusable, slightly undersized doors, including the door jambs. If you are stuck with real doors, lower the second floor of your set until it almost touches the door jamb. This makes it just a little bit easier to light up kids on the second floor of a two-story set. As you might imagine, on a one-story set this problem magically disappears.

FLATS

Since you have already sorted out your flats (and maybe even repaired a few), you should have a pretty good idea about how and where to use them. Flats are good to fake in walls and buildings and to mask entrances. You can add extra pieces to a flat pretty easily, to escape the boxy look. Their portability makes them especially useful for short scenes.

PLATFORMS

We usually built our platforms out of 2 × 4s (on edge) and ¾" plywood. It's best to build a variety of sizes, and if the platform itself is supposed to last, you should use glue and screws to put it together. Attaching legs is no big deal; add some 1 × 4 cross-bracing if the thing is more than one foot tall. Platforms that roll are called *wagons.* Making them roll is pretty easy; it's making them stop that's a problem. Once you roll a wagon into place you have to dream up a way to keep it there. We've had pretty good success with big nails slipped into holes in the floor. An eight-inch spike will easily fit through a set piece and drop into a hole drilled into the stage floor. Two of these spikes will hold a wagon pretty well, unless you are dancing on it. 'Course, you'll hafta put holes in the floor . . .

COLUMNS

Columns are round, and sooner or later you'll end up painting columns onto flat stock. Until then you can use carpet rolls for skinny columns, and Sonotube, but Sonotube is expensive. We got a deal by purchasing damaged stock from a building supplier. Sonotube is great for fake pipes, too.

If your carpet tube columns look too skinny for the set, try putting them up in pairs, about six inches apart. Add some molding at the top and bottom for a better look. I have a photograph of a castle in Italy with this style column, and it looks great. If you try to *paint* columns onto flat stock, remember that they are supposed to *look* round. It's an optical illusion, of course; check out the back of a twenty-dollar bill with a magnifying glass for some ideas here.

PVC

Plumbers PVC pipe can be a godsend when you have to build something large, curved, and light. Just remember it's not very strong, and the solvents used to glue the PVC together should not be used by the kids. They can cut and test-fit everything; you should do the solvent welding. Thin PVC can be made into a pretty convincing pointed arch, with a corner connector at the apex.

A WORKING HAND PUMP

Because so many plays and musicals are set in the past, a period hand pump is a great investment for the prop closet. An added pipe and a large basin can improve things by making the pump a practical set piece; that is, it can actually pump water on stage. Just change the water once in a while. We put ours on hidden wheels in *Fiddler*; the extra work was worth it for the convenience. You can buy these pumps down in the holler at the general store, or from Harbor Freight Salvage Company (*www.harborfreight.com*).

SIGNS ON STAGE

One way to make signs is to start with a text box on a computer, made the same approximate shape as the sign you want. Experiment with fonts and sizes, burn a transparency, enlarge with the overhead projector, scribe it out, paint it in, and there you go. If you are good, you can warp the text in a pseudo-perspective fashion. Take the extra time to make painted signs look good—no one else does. Using computer fonts almost guarantees a good-looking sign; hand-lettering invites disaster.

LIGHT-UP SIGNS

There are two ways to make light-up signs. One, light translucent plastic from behind with Christmas tree lights (in a light-tight box). Two, build a wooden shadow box with fluorescent or "black" lights in front of the sign. If you try method one, you have to paint the signs onto clear plastic with translucent paint. If you try method two, you have to hide the fluorescent lights really well within the shadow box. Method one is easier. We built an "APPLAUSE" sign for *Annie* that looks just like the real thing. Light-tight box, lights behind the plastic, black letters on translucent white plastic. Worked too; everybody clapped. You can pay a local signmaker for vinyl letters if you have money to burn; otherwise, use the magic transparency/overhead technique to get the lettering right. If you try to make a shadow box, you'll need a frame to hide the fluorescent lights because they go in front of the sign. These work best using black light and ultraviolet paints.

ARCHITECTURAL REFERENCES

It's always nice to have a few architectural reference books laying around so your set designs look good. You can shamelessly crib off of these to help your designs. Old photographs of New York and Europe come in handy too.

BROKEN TAPE MEASURES

Whenever a tape measure breaks, open it up (carefully) and attach the tape measure part to the wall with adhesive caulk. Make sure it measures correctly from the floor, and you have a nice convenient measuring device for when you are holding a stick and you need to know how long it is. Put a couple near the lumber rack, near the saw, on a door jamb, along a table edge, whatever. The lesson here is that there may be some useful part of some broken thing, so save and use whatever comes in handy. Buy lots of tape measures.

THE DRAWER OF LAST RESORT

You are going to build an enormous collection of hardware for all of the things you assemble. Get some heavy-duty drawers and organize things as well as you can. All of the aircraft cable clamps should go in one drawer, all of the loose pin hinges in another—you get the idea. No matter how careful or meticulous you are, you will always have some random pieces of useful hardware and no place to put them. Label one drawer "The Drawer of Last Resort" and throw all your surplus hardware in it. Again and again you'll go to The Drawer of Last Resort for some little hardware item, and four times out of five you'll find something that will do the job. Lucky you.

NOTHING IS FREE

Once in a while, someone will offer you some free stuff for the theater. I always tried to accept these offers, and about half the time I'd actually get something useful for my trouble. I hear you asking, "What trouble could free stuff be?" You poor thing. You will have to go and pick the stuff up. You will have to pay for the rental truck. You will have to lift and carry it, and probably move something else, or fix something for the contributor—nothing is free. OK, once a house painter came by and gave us some latex house paint, unloading it himself, and he didn't even want a program mention in return, but, generally, nothing is free. And you won't know if it's useful to you until after you schlep all the way across town to get it. And you usually have to also take something you *don't* want. Like I said, nothing is free.

SOMETIMES YOU HAVE TO MAKE A GUILLOTINE

I put the section on making a guillotine right before the section on safety on purpose. When we made our fake guillotine for *A Tale of Two Cities*, I realized how easy it would be to make a real one, and the thought is chilling. If you've got to have one, make the entire blade assembly perfectly light and harmless, with no metal at all. Use "foamcore" and Styrofoam. Be careful. Face the guillotine away from the audience; with creative lighting it will look positively real. At the climax of the show, put in a blackout. Our little fake guillotine was so scary I wouldn't put my head in it, and I'm usually the first to test everything. My director had to take my place. It gives me shivers just typing this, and it's June. By the way, the French retired their guillotine in 1977. That's right, 1977.

Just as this book went to press, I got an e-mail from a fellow at a movie production company in England. They found a photo of our guillotine on the Web and wanted to use it in some sort of documentary film. I gave him a call. "Can you ship it over, mate?" he said, just before I explained we'd already taken it apart. They wanted our prop for their movie. True, true. I'll be telling that story till I die.

SAFETY

Stage accidents can be deadly. No room for jokes here; you must develop a method of completing your work that does not put anyone at risk. Power tools probably represent the greatest danger, followed by the possibility of dropping something on somebody. Burns from the lights are always a concern, while falls from ladders and slips and trips can hospitalize. Time for a little truth in advertising. Running into something in the dark put me in the hospital for four stitches over my eye; happily, that was the worst thing that happened backstage. Among the students, Allison broke her arm; I said, "Don't jump onto the stage," and she said, "Ouch." A fall from a three-foot-tall platform put Suzy in a neck brace for a couple of days, no real damage done. Someone got popped by a marauding skateboarder, and Rita touched a jigsaw blade while it was still winding down. I think that's it. The jigsaw injury still bothers me, as we have a rule not to move or touch anything until the jigsaw stops. A very good rule. Suzy was acting dead in *A Tale of Two Cities* (and doing a fine job) and was actually dropped off of the three-foot platform, a little too realistically, so she had to go to the hospital. The doctor about fainted when she was describing her injury: "Well, I was on the guillotine, and afterward they dropped me!" And the skateboard thing happened while the kids were at dinner; I still don't know the whole story, but it cost Betty two stitches. Nine years, six stitches, one broken arm. Not a spotless safety record, but my brother got hurt more in sixth grade.

Develop a method to instill safety habits in the crew. First, you have to know how to do things safely. So if you really aren't comfortable with the jigsaw, for instance, find someone who, is to help out the crew and to teach you. To choose a ridiculous example, if you don't know which way to turn a nut to tighten it, you shouldn't be training kids to climb a ladder to hang lights. Get a competent adult assistant or co-sponsor to help. There is no shame in admitting (to yourself) that you don't know how to do something (never tell the kids). What *is* a shame is trying to bluff your way through it without even attempting to learn the proper procedures. If you aren't competent with portable electric power tools, you simply must find an adult who is, to make sure the job gets done well. And sign up for a woodworking or home-repair course.

My method, which some might call sloppy (I stand behind my safety record), is first to determine what tools you'll allow the crew to use. I decided the following power tools were safe for students' general use:

- Glue guns
- Drills and screw guns
- Jigsaws
- Electric staplers (we eventually gave up on these)
- The chop saw

We also had portable circular saws and a table saw. I did not allow students to use these, as I thought them too powerful and dangerous. Later I allowed the crew to use the battery-operated baby circular saw; it's smaller and the blade stops very quickly. My successor added a bandsaw, drill press, and air nailer—safe enough, except for the air nailer. Other sponsors allow more or less.

The next step is training the students to use the equipment. The essentials:

GLUE GUN
- Don't touch the glue. Don't touch the tip of the gun.
- Don't trust hot melt glue to be strong; it isn't.

DRILLS AND SCREW GUNS
- Long hair and loose clothing must be secured.
- Know where the drill bit is going to come out.
- Don't put anybody's hand near the spot where the drill bit is going to come out.
- The above rule is for screw guns too. The screw might be too long; keep clear.
- Drill pilot holes for screws where necessary.
- Don't use the drill unless I am there to watch you.

JIGSAWS

- ➤ Long hair rule applies.
- ➤ Cut only wood. Watch for screws, etc.
- ➤ Stay behind the saw.
- ➤ Keep both hands behind the saw, too, in case of slips.
- ➤ No pocket cuts; use a drill for a starter hole.
- ➤ Let the saw stop (at the end of a cut) before picking anything up.
- ➤ Don't use the jigsaw unless I am there to watch you.

Some students "pick up" the jigsaw skill very easily; some need more help and instruction. The saw will shake if you don't hold it securely, and so will the wood. That's the reason for the "hands behind the saw" rule. One hand is holding the saw, so that hand is automatically behind the blade; it's the other hand we're concerned with. This hand must hold the wood in a safe place, *not* in front of the blade. Some students don't quite understand this, so you must watch the beginners and stop their bad habits before they start. A student who can recite, "Keep your hands clear of the blade," and therefore passes a safety test, is still liable to put his hand right in harm's way without thinking about it. Watch the beginners until they pass the real-life safety test of experience.

THE CHOP SAW

I say "the" chop saw as a mark of respect. I did allow advanced students to use the chop saw to cut 1 × 4s and 2 × 4s to length. The essentials:

- ➤ Long hair rule applies.
- ➤ Hold the wood securely with one hand.
- ➤ That hand must never be in the danger zone (approximately 6" around the blade).
- ➤ Do not cut small pieces.
- ➤ Check for screws and nails.
- ➤ Make sure the saw stops before letting go of anything.
- ➤ Do not operate the chop saw unless I am there to watch you.

SAFETY GOGGLES

Must schools require students to wear safety goggles when operating any power tool. You could try to argue that an electric screwdriver does not pose much of a safety hazard, but it's a good rule and protects the school in the case of an accident. Jigsaws and drills are relatively safe, as power tools go, but I recommend you follow the official rules in this regard.

MANUFACTURER'S SAFETY RULES
Every power tool you buy will come with a detailed safety sheet. I suggest you post these on the tool cabinet, to be read by all.

FIRST AID
I had to take a first-aid class to get my degree, but most teachers don't. As you will be working hours and hours after the school nurse has gone home, the responsibility to care for minor cuts and scrapes, rope burns (ouch), and major crises falls to you. Most communities have first-aid training available; if you have *no* skills, you have to do something, so take the class. And buy *two* really good first-aid kits. One for everyday use, with Band-Aids and alcohol wipes, etc., and one for emergencies, never to be opened, except in an emergency. That way you can be certain the first-aid kit is fully stocked without inspecting it every week. Resist the temptation to break into the emergency kit when the everyday kit runs low. The emergency kit is for 911-type emergencies only. By the way, the little book Johnson & Johnson gives out with its first-aid kits can be quite helpful; read it ahead of time, one evening when you are "winding down" but not quite ready to go home. Be prepared.

STAIRCASING
Almost every set you build is going to need stairs. Stairs, though, are a problem. Even on expensive houses you can find poorly designed and shoddily built stairs, which are a true danger to all. Multiply the risk by putting the stairs on stage or backstage and having nervous people climbing them in the dark, and you have a recipe for disaster. Stairs simply must be built strong and well. And stage stairs are usually made a little extra-wide, maybe four feet wide, or wider. This causes problems with flexing and sag that you might not see at home, or on your outdoor deck, so prepare to think and work hard.

Make this effort a little easier by developing stock units; these can be saved and used again and again. Many of these units can have a standard *rise* and a standard *run,* making them easier to build and safer to climb. For our first staircase we'll do exactly that. Pick up stair treads, riser material, and stringers from Home Depot. This stuff is all pre-made to pretty much the right size, saving a lot of calculation and heartache. Of course, you'll have to design the rest of the set to fit the stairs . . .

WATCH YOUR STEP

In addition to building the stairs strong enough to last, there are three things to look out for: the lip, or overhang on each step (called the nosing), the first step, and the last step. At every theater I visit, I see "crew-built" stairs where someone forgot to include a slight overhang on each step. It's supposed to be about 1⅛". Lots of people include the overhang, but forget about the riser; then they stick the riser on, which pretty much takes away the overhang. Some people leave the nosing off on purpose, figuring these stairs are for temporary use. Big mistake. People have to climb these stairs with confidence, while preoccupied with saying lines or using props or remembering their blocking; they shouldn't have to worry about the stairs.

So spend a little time measuring things, and get the top and bottom step right.

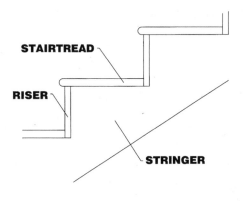

Stock Stairs

THE BOTTOM STEP

The first step up from the stage floor is different from the others. It's because you are building and measuring every other step from the *bottom* of the step, and the first step is measured from the *top* of the stage floor. You have to compensate for the thickness of the stair tread. Real softwood stair treads are one-inch true thickness, so you can measure wrong and be two inches off. This is what a contractor actually did to my mom's house, and no, I've never fixed it. Stair treads rest on *stringers,* and it's the stringer that you have to build right. If the stringer (the zigzag stair thingy) is built correctly, everything else will follow pretty well. On a simple staircase you'll need two stringers. They must match each other, and they must be cut in such a way that the first stair tread is the right height. You can find pre-made stringers at Home Depot. They have a 6¾" rise, so of course you'll have to custom fit the first step. Presuming the unit is going to sit right on the stage floor, and presuming you are using one-inch-thick stair treads (you'd better check), measure carefully and slice off the bottom of the stringer just perfect— one inch *less* than all of the others. On a factory-made

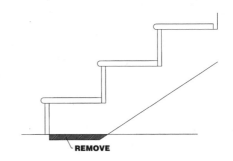

REMOVE

The Bottom Step

stringer it'll be 5¾". Usually this is not done for you, as house builders need the wood you are removing. When the stringer is *plumbed up*— meaning put up correctly so the stair treads are level—the first step will match the others. Good job. If you blow it, fix it, and don't curse yourself; it is easy to get confused—to subtract from the wrong line, to add instead of subtract, to hold the ruler wrong so you accidentally subtract twice, to forget you are using 2 × 10s for stair treads, which throws the calculation off—there are a thousand things that can go wrong. Just redo the mistaken piece. There's a cheat sheet of riser heights in the back of the book, so you can double and triple check all of your stair measurements.

THE TOP STEP

The highest step takes a bit of calculation too. If you are not careful in your figuring, you will end up with a staircase with exactly one too many steps. That is, you'll have a staircase that ends at the exact same level as the second floor of your set. That's fine, unless you forgot that that step takes up room, which means your staircase is 10⅛" out of place. What I mean is, the last step usually *is* the second floor, not a stair tread *connected* to the second floor. Perhaps we should walk carefully up our stairs at home, and you'll see what I mean.

First, check the bottom step to see if it was built right. If it isn't, you can smugly ascend your steps knowing that you are a superior being to the workman who installed your stairs. Just watch your step coming back down.

Are we at the top of the stairs? Good. Do you see that what you might call the top step actually isn't a step at all—it's the second floor of your house? And the second floor isn't made out of stair treads, it's made out of flooring. This can be a problem for you on stage, but it doesn't have to be. Nine times out of ten you just tack your completed staircase to the outside of your platform, no problem. Of course, the platform and the stairs have to be exactly the same height, but you knew that. In some cases, though, you are going to want to end your staircase exactly one step below the second floor. This is especially true when you are squeezed for space. Stairs take up an enormous amount of space. Take your time and chalk the entire thing out on the stage floor, full size. Then you'll be able to see that the run of the stairs is going to take the actors offstage and you need to make a change.

One more thing about the top step. It doesn't have a riser above it. So deduct ¾" for the nonexistent riser before you trim the "top" of the stringer. This insignificant little detail actually is quite important, so sit and stare at the top step until that last sentence makes sense.

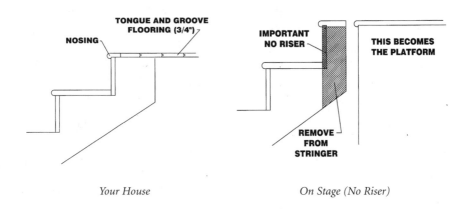

Your House   *On Stage (No Riser)*

When assembling the stairs, be dead certain that they are plumb; that is, be sure they aren't crooked. Plumb bobs and levels help here. Assemble everything with glue. Ready?

1. Install the bottom riser—it's skinnier than the others. Use glue and finishing nails and lots of helpers to hold things.

If you want the stair treads to overhang on the ends (and you do), you must shorten the risers about four inches. That is, the stair treads should be 4" longer than the risers. The top edge of each installed riser must be flush with the stringer, where the stair tread goes. No little gaps allowed. This is because the riser must support the stair tread.

2. Install the riser that goes under the top step.

Use glue and nails. This gives you a somewhat rigid staircase-like structure that you can stand up. But before you stand it up . . .

3. Measure and calculate carefully and install a 2 × 6 at the top of the staircase.

This piece goes inside the stair stringers under the topmost stair tread. With "dimension" lumber it would be 3" shorter than the risers. On an extra-wide staircase you'll have to notch the center stringer(s) to accept this piece. Also, if you are not careful to deduct for the nonexistent riser on the topmost step, you'll get a ¼" error here. Test-fit the top stair tread to see what I mean. You'll use this 2 × 6 to attach the staircase to something when you need to.

4. Stand the unit up.

5. Make sure the stairs are *plumb*—that is, the stair part must be level and the riser part must be vertical.

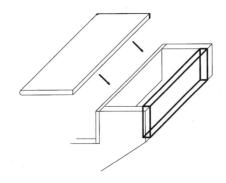

A 2 × 6 To Hold Up The Unit

6. Install vertical 2 × 4s every three or four steps or as needed for strength.

These must be out of the way, so screw them inside the stringers. And don't glue these on—you may want to change them later (higher or lower).

7. Install the rest of the risers.

8. Install stair treads cut to overhang the risers by 1⅛".
Glue and nail the stair treads, and nail the risers to the stair treads from the underside.

9. Add support, including skids, or wheels, on the bottom of the unit.

OPEN-FACED STAIRS

These are just stairs without risers, so you can see through them. They need an extra stringer in the middle so they won't flex too much. Note: If you have glued-on risers, the staircase will be very strong (like a shear wall), and you won't need cross-bracing. If you make open-faced stairs, they won't be as strong, so plan accordingly.

ALL DONE?

Take a moment and number the steps going up. Use paint. The stage floor is *step zero.* Where your feet go on step one paint a *1,* then continue up the stairs. Then your director can place everyone for the Busby Berkeley–type numbers: "You, get on step three, Dolly, stop at step eight for a kiss . . . "

CURVING STAIRCASE

I've built three actual curving staircases, and believe me, they *are* worth the trouble. When that curtain opens and your jaded high school audience sees a real, full-sized curving staircase, they will be spellbound. The railings are the hardest part. Let's try it.

Needless to say, you must measure everything a million times to get a curving staircase right. And you won't be able to use factory-made anything, except maybe risers. You are going to need a huge supply of ⅛"-thick plywood, at least fourteen sheets. The Luan type is fine. You're going to have to order it, but once you get your hands on it you'll buy some every year. The stuff is just great for flats (it can replace the muslin completely), any curved shape, almost any cutout; load up on the stuff. You'll have to run a Web search to find ⅛" plywood in your area—believe me, it's worth it. Now you have learned the two biggest secrets in stage crew: transparencies with overhead projectors for enlargements and signs, and ⅛"-thick Luan plywood for lightweight construction. You are also going to need a bunch of nice 1 × 4 furring strips (fifty or so, for temporary use), lots of screws, and gallons of glue. Elmer's glue is fine. One more thing. If you can afford some 1"-thick plywood for the stair treads, buy some (three sheets). You can live with ¾", but it changes the measurements and it's weaker . . . Ready? Here we go.

Paint the stage floor below your curving staircase a light gray. You are going to lay out and build the curving staircase right in place, on a wooden floor, since you have to put screws into the floor to temporarily hold everything together. Don't tell anyone you put screws into the stage floor; they'll never understand. For your first curving staircase, take the extra trouble to build it right in the exact location it's meant for. It does not *have to* be built in the exact location it's meant for, but if you can build it right on the spot, you'll be certain the layout is right. Very important. By the way, this is going to take at least a week. Start on a Thursday for good luck. Calculate the correct height, and the correct number of stairs. A curving staircase should end one step below the landing it is heading towards.

Our example is going to be four feet wide, nominal. *Nominal* means it comes out a little smaller. Decide on the number of steps by fudging the rise. This is critical; the rise can only vary from about 7" to 8¼". I once (twice, really) made steps with a 9" rise. It was a pair of 90" tall stairs for *Anything Goes,* and when I realized my mistake it was too late to change. A 9" rise is too much; people will slip. You should stick with the standard rise of 6¾" for your first time, as I will do for the example. Ready?

Here's a brief overview of the steps we'll take over the upcoming week:

- ➤ Sketch out what you *think* you want with chalk, on the floor, full size.
- ➤ Find the centerpoint of the curving staircase, somewhere on the stage floor.
- ➤ Scribe out accurate arcs for the curving stringers.
- ➤ Lay out the proper number of stair treads with a protractor.
- ➤ Install temporary support for the stringers using 1 × 4s.
- ➤ Laminate the stringers together using flexible ⅛" plywood, glue, and screws.
- ➤ Cut the zigzag on the stringers perfectly using a plumb bob and jigsaw.

➤ Fake in some extra support.

➤ Fit the risers.

➤ Fit the stair treads.

You can make the curving staircase any size; these directions will give you a pretty useful unit that won't take up too much space. To make things a little easier, we're going to presume the stairs top off at a square landing just off center stage (CS). We'll come down towards stage right, curving gently towards CS. At the bottom we'll be facing half-left. This is about 130 degrees of curve.

THURSDAY—WE BEGIN

Dig out a chalkline, a protractor, a calculator, a ruler or tape, a pencil, extra gray paint to cover mistakes, and some scratch paper. If you feel like practicing on a piece of paper before going full size, go right ahead—I suggest a one-inch scale. A practice layout might help firm things up in your mind. (Here's a thought: Any self-respecting geometry teacher would love to help you with this. Seek one out.) Let's put the centerpoint three feet directly downstage from the platform corner. The centerpoint is a reference point on the stage floor that you'll use first to help scribe all of the arcs and then as a mark for the protractor. Tap a big old nail about halfway into the stage floor, right at the centerpoint. This will make the layout go quicker.

Connect the chalkline to the centerpoint (on the nail) and pull it to the corner of the "second floor" platform. It doesn't matter if you haven't built the platform yet. Hold the chalkline real tight at the corner while holding a pencil in the same hand. Carefully scribe in the first reference arc. This should swing from the very corner of the second floor platform around to the bottom step, and a little beyond. The arc has a three-foot radius. The chalkline can be stretched out to make a serviceable compass. You could use trammel points if you have them, or a super-duper-huge compass (right), but most folks'll just tie the pencil onto the string and scribe away. You must hold the pencil on the chalkline (real tight) and swing the arc while holding the pencil point on the floor. Don't wiggle the pencil. The chalk in the chalkline is more of a nuisance at this point; if you like, you could use a regular old piece of string.

This first arc represents the inside edge of the stair treads. Draw another arc exactly four feet bigger in radius than the first arc. This represents the outside edge of the stair treads. If the layout or location of the stairs doesn't look right at this stage, you must redo. Really. If all is well you can now fake in the steps with the chalkline; in the example there are going to be thirteen of them. Use the protractor and the chalkline to snap a line every 10 degrees, from the second floor layout all the way around. Counterclockwise. Thirteen steps. The steps will look pretty small; trust me, they're OK.

These radial lines represent the outside of where the riser goes. You can check your accuracy by measuring the *chord* on the outermost circle. A chord is a straight line between two points on an arc. That means measure corner to corner at the widest part of each step; you should get about 14½", and they should all be the same.

With a pencil, you can lay in a parallel line exactly ¾" in from each of these chalklines. "In" is to the right if you are standing at the centerpoint. This skinny box represents the riser under each step. Number each imaginary step. The stage floor is step zero, the 94½"-high platform will be "lucky" step 14.

Scribe another arc 3½" inside the first arc. By "inside" I mean at 39½". One more at 56¼", and 59¾", one at 76½", and one at 80". Whew. You should see two arcs, then two arcs, then three arcs. Very good.

Now you are going to install a whole bunch of vertical 1 × 4s, fourteen in all. These will all be eight feet long, which seems wasteful, but isn't; they support the first stringer, and they will later be removed. You'll temporarily strengthen them with some cross-bracing, also to be removed. Put one of these 1 × 4 furring strips standing straight up right between the two smallest arcs, dead on the spot where the first riser is going to go. There

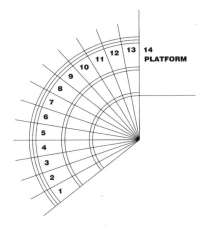

The Layout

should be a perfectly sized box waiting for you at each location. These furring strips must stand perfectly straight, so get out a level or a plumb bob, secure them to the floor and to each other, and add a few braces leading down and away from the future staircase. Try to plan ahead to keep the bracing out of your way, way above or way below where the stairs will actually go. The better you do here, the easier the rest of the job will be. Paint all of these furring strips red.

Vertical Support

You are going to need twelve slices of plywood exactly 14" wide, and 8' long. In order to save material in the long run, you should slice the twelve pieces out of twelve individual sheets of plywood. Set aside each 34" slice for later. That is, you want to end up with twelve 14"-wide pieces with twelve 34"-wide pieces left over. Then glue two of the skinny pieces together so they are 15' long. Leave some kind of weight on the glue joint, then go home and get some rest.

FRIDAY—LAMINATIONS

Ready to start fresh? The long plywood strip has to be trimmed and installed to perfectly fit the rise of the stairs. This means we need a layout line for each step, and we need to determine the proper angle for cutting the plywood so it will rest properly on the floor. Get a ruler and head back to the scene of the crime. Find the nicest, straightest 1×4 out of the ones you have left. You are going to make something called a *story pole* out of this 1×4.

Measuring carefully, mark the story pole for every riser height—5¾, 12½, 19¼", etc. See the riser cheat sheet in the back of the book for all of the measurements. Better cut the very top of the story pole at an angle so you don't accidentally turn the story pole upside down. Starting at the bottom step, use the story pole to mark the first vertical furring strip 5¾" above the stage floor. Go ahead and mark all the way around the stick. Mark the second furring strip at 12½". Mark the third furring strip at 19¼". What's going on here? You are laying out the rise of each step on the furring strips that belong to that step. Do it carefully, as it has got to be right, 6¾" up each time (except for the first step, of course). When you are finished, you lay the big piece of plywood against the furring strips, bend it to shape, and line it up perfectly with the high marks on the furring strips. It's going to be too long, which is a good thing since you have to trim the bottom to match the floor. Have some seven people or so hold this tight, perfectly lined up with the layout lines you just put on the furring strips. With the plywood piece lined up perfectly, you can see that you'll have to knock the bottom corner off of it so the plywood will properly touch the floor. That is, the plywood piece will have to be trimmed (with a saw) parallel to the floor.

It's not too hard to scribe a line along the plywood parallel to the floor, about eighteen inches off of the floor. You need a lot of hands to hold the plywood just so, but you can tape a pencil to a chair and scribe the line as easy as kiss my hand. Then everybody can let go a minute while you cut the plywood along this line. Save the extra piece—it has the proper angle for your next few cuts! After the trimming, the long plywood piece should rest on the floor and should again line up perfectly with the layout lines. You are just about on your way.

Screw this plywood piece to the furring strips, making certain all of the layout lines line up perfectly. I use the word "perfectly" loosely here; get it as close as you can. Use the teeny-tiniest screws you can find, #4 × ¾". Ignore the leftover plywood at the top of the stairs, and ignore the pointy end of the plywood down near the floor. All of this extra wood will be trimmed off later. Recheck everything, then check everything one more time. At this time, the installed skinny plywood piece should be firmly attached to all fourteen vertical furring strips and should actually evoke the future stringer it is to become. The only problem is it's way too skinny in the thickness department, so we have to add several more skinny sheets to it, with glue and screws, until it's ¾ of an inch thick. Six laminations total. You can call the laminations *layers* if you prefer.

Scribing the Line

If all has gone well, you should be able to accelerate things now. You have a leftover piece of plywood that gives you the correct angle to cut the next four pieces, giving a total of five (six counting the one already installed). It's a good idea to cut them each a different length—that way the laminations will "lap" better. Go ahead and cut two of the remaining skinny plywood pieces at this magic angle, about one-fourth of the way up on one and about one-third of the way up the other piece of plywood. This gives you five angled pieces that are different lengths. These pieces will be the beginning (bottom) of each succeeding layer on the staircase, until we pad out the ¾-inch thickness we need for strength.

Let's return to your perfectly lined-up "master" stringer secured to a rigid collection of furring strips. All that remains is to install five more layers of ⅛" plywood to the master stringer. You do this with screws and lots of Elmer's glue. You can extend the glue with a tiny amount of water so it doesn't dry too fast. Use a roller to spread glue on an angled piece of plywood *and* on the master stringer. This is goopy and gooey and a lot of fun. Slap the plywood piece in place at the bottom of the staircase and affix it with lots of screws. Point the screws out from the plywood towards the original centerpoint from long ago. Try your best to drive them all the way flush with the plywood. You'll trim the screw points off later with a Dremel Moto-Tool if they stick out on the other side. Put the screws along the bottom edge of each plywood strip, along the top edge of each strip, and in the middle too. You'll probably stick in a few that will later be right in the way; if so, you'll just cut through them with the jigsaw, no big deal. When the angled plywood strip ends, just butt a full-sized plywood strip up against it at the break point, no overlap. Try to get all six layers done in one day, and try to vary the break point between laminations. When all six laminations are on, you can blow some 1½" screws into the vertical sticks (for real strength) and some small screws from the other side, if you feel the need. Go home. Sleep.

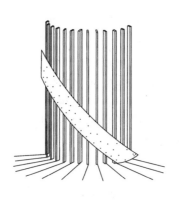

Let the Glue Dry

MONDAY—REV IT UP AND GO

It's time. You are master of the curving staircase and you are going to trim out the first stringer. That is, if the glue is dry. Transfer all of the layout lines to the last installed plywood piece. You need the layout lines on this side of the stairs to actually cut things out. They should run flat and level at 5¾, 12½, 19¼, 26, 32¼, all the way up to 86¾". The vertical part runs right along the *inside* of the red furring strips. Let's take a moment to make sure we get these lines in the right place.

The easiest way to get the vertical layout lines in the right place is to stand in among the support sticks and hold a pencil against the *right-hand side* of one of the (red) vertical furring strips. Hang a plumb bob off of the pencil, and there's your vertical line in the right place. Getting these right is very important. You can cheat and stand on the easy side, but don't blame me if you chop the stringer in the wrong place.

The story pole can be a big help putting in the horizontal lines. Line it up along each of the vertical lines (the ones you just drew) and mark the appropriate increments as you work your way up the stairs. Trace in the horizontal lines by connecting the dots. If you are following the layout example, these should be about 7½" long (the top one is 6¾"). Look carefully at the layout. It should have the classic zigzaggy shape of a normal stair stringer, rising from the floor step by step to the top step. When you cut away the waste with a jigsaw (with a brand new, sharp blade), you'll be left with a curving zigzaggy stair stringer. The red 1 × 4 furring strips will fall away, except where they are still secured to the stringer holding things up.

If you discover some gaps in your lamination, squirt in some glue and blow in a few more screws. Discard all of the cut-away wood. Step back and admire.

We're going to move to the second stringer. I suppose this step is just about the hardest part of the staircase. You have to measure carefully here to ensure that things will fit together well later. In addition, the parts we're installing end up *behind* the more visible parts of the staircase, so you can't line up things with the layout lines—you have to compensate for the thickness of each piece. We'll go step-by-step so you won't get confused. We're going to install furring strips as before, secured to the floor and

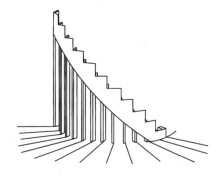

Curved Stringer Number One

to the first stringer. The only difference is that some of these pieces are *permanent*; it's easiest to make them to size ahead of time, then install them perfectly straight and level. Any error here will be magnified as we continue, so be careful to get these fourteen pieces just right.

Cut out fourteen 19½" braces. These are 1 × 4s that will connect the work you have already done to the new center stringer you are about to build. Use the chop saw and make sure these cuts come out at 90 degrees all around. Then cut out a vertical 1 × 4 for each step. These must be cut to the height of each step, one per step. Use the story pole to lay out a 5¾" piece, a 12½" piece, a 19¼" piece, all the way up to step 13, 86¾". Better number these, and make an extra stick for step 13. Mark and cut these out *one at a time* to avoid errors from the saw cuts. Lay these pieces on the stage floor and form them into an upside-down *L* shape, with the 19½" braces on *top*. Let me clarify this. The shape is exactly like a backward *7*, and the horizontal 19½" piece is on the top, and the vertical piece is on the left. You have to assemble these with screws and glue, and they absolutely must be *square*—90 degrees to each other. Start with the short ones. By the time you have finished the rest, the short ones will be ready to use.

When these vertical furring strips go up, the end of the upside-down *L* piece should line up with the outside corner of the stair stringer you cut out earlier today; you just screw it in with a couple of 2" screws. I suggest you drill pilot holes and use glue. The vertical part should land between the two center arcs scribed out on the floor. You'll be tempted to place the vertical stick right on the little layout box on the floor like you did before, but this would be a mistake. Instead, install the stick ¾" to the right of the little box. The horizontal pieces (the 19½" you just made) will not perfectly line up with your original layout marks either. Remember, those marks are for the *risers,* so these 19½" pieces will be hidden just behind. Check everything very carefully here; a small layout error will be magnified greatly at the next

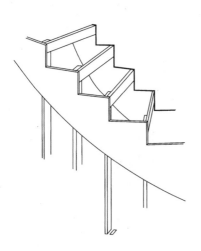

Setup For Middle Stringer

stage. If you place a plumb bob on the *riser* side of your support stick (the 19½" stick) the plumb bob should point at the pencil line directly below it. This proves that this support will be right behind the riser you are putting in later, which is good. Since we're starting with the bottom step, it should be pretty easy to tell if things are lining up right. (By the way, if you can remember this trick, you'll have no problem laying out the vertical cut lines later.) Screw everything down and add some extra temporary bracing if anything wiggles. Slice your leftover plywood into 16" strips (leaving you with twelve 18" strips for later), glue up a beginning piece as before. I'll see you tomorrow.

IF IT'S TUESDAY, IT MUST BE LAMINOS

Everything must be recalculated for this second stringer. The plywood is wider because the angle is different. Line up the plywood along each corner of each support stick and scribe a new trim line. If one of the support sticks is installed wrong, it'll stick out; look for this and make any corrections needed. Trim the new piece of plywood and install as before, adding glue on the new vertical furring strips for strength. There are supposed to be six laminations in this center section, same as before. Here you can screw the screws into the vertical piece of furring strip for added strength. Plus, you can use slightly longer screws since these pieces are permanent. The original (red) pieces from Thursday are going to be removed; these aren't. Get it? Somewhere along the line here you are going to catch on to the system. You are going to scribe fresh layout lines and trim out the second stringer just as before. It's bigger, but the rise is the same in every case, and should line up with the riser side of the little *L* braces perfectly. Get out the plumb bob and get those verticals perfect. The story pole will again help you set the horizontal lines. Take a good hard look at everything before cutting, then cut.

WEDNESDAY, THURSDAY, FRIDAY

You've got one more stringer to build, using the 18"-wide pieces of plywood leftover from last week. Unfortunately, you'll need more than twelve of these, so you have to slice up a few more sheets of plywood. Sixteen pieces should be plenty. Glue *three* of these strips into one really long 22' piece for the final push. You'll need fourteen more *L* braces, 19½" long, step by step, made with exactly the same technique as before; they'll go right beside the others. You'll blow in some 3" screws to hold these in place (don't forget the glue); it's best if you drill some pilot holes to guide these screws into the solid *L* brackets from Tuesday. Laminate, let dry, layout, trim. Should look pretty real now. If you are in a hurry, throw in the risers real quick. Put glue everywhere, especially on the 19½" support sticks, and use screws to assemble, not nails. Put the screws into the solid wood 1 × 4s, and just put a couple into the laminated stringers. And use pilot holes. Take your time with the stair treads. You'll be cutting them out of 1"-thick plywood; they are trapezoids that reach all the way across the width of a plywood sheet. Remember, they are supposed to stick out about 1⅛" from the riser; you may want to check each one as you go, since even the best of us make some kind of measurement error here and there. If you like, you can round the business edges of each stair tread with a router. The stair treads should be 1" thick; if you are making do with ¾" you'll probably want to put in a little more bracing underneath each step. Don't forget the glue, and you can blow in a few screws from the back of each riser, too. Wait three sentences before attaching the top step.

Time to put in some real support. Like you did with the straight stairs, you will want to glue in a nice 2 × 6 underneath the top step, for support. This takes a little persuasion with a saw, carefully cutting the middle stringer just so, but get it in there good, with screws and glue. Attach a couple of vertical 2 × 4s to this piece and knock away the red furring strips with a hammer. Trim away the others at the bottom and *voila*, a curving staircase. It will seem wobbly since it's not attached to anything, so you can temporarily attach a third support stick if you need to.

You'll have to grind away any of the screws that are sticking out of the wood with a Dremel Moto-Tool, but you are pretty much done—and buddy, if you can do this, you can do anything. Add the railings . . . done!

These stairs will stand up with no visible support if you remove the 2 × 4s and clamp the stairs or screw them to the high platform they lead to. We put ours on huge hinges to swing offstage when not needed.

SEND ME A PICTURE

Send me a picture of your finished curving staircase (care of the publisher) and I'll try to talk them into posting all of the photos on the company Web site. Won't that be fun!

A MORE VERSATILE AND PERHAPS EASIER WAY

I can almost hear some of you whistling in disbelief about the amount of work that goes into building a permanent curving staircase. One must remember that one is building for the ages; this is a set piece you are going to keep and use again year after year. Like everything else in this world, it can be done another way. I was helping out a woman named Elaine, who used to work over at Chantilly High School, in Fairfax, Virginia, and her crew had developed a different, more versatile, and perhaps even easier way to build a curving staircase. The cool thing about this method is you can "break" the stairs anywhere you want, add a landing or platform, and twist and turn each individual step. It's a way cool and very simple method. It's called *cheating*. (Not really.) Instead of building real, you simply assemble a complete set of rigid flats, three feet wide (or whatever), one for each step. The flat frames are made just like regular flats, then faced with ¼ or ⅛-inch plywood. Buy knot-free 1 × 4s and construct with small screws and glue. When you are done, you'll have a whole bunch of blank flats, one each for each future step you are going to build. Once they are put in place (you'll probably have to screw them to the floor), each flat gets a little extra brace, installed horizontally at the height of the next smaller step. It's just another 1 × 4 glued and screwed into place (across the flat) exactly 6¾" below the top edge of each flat.

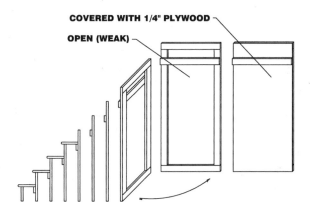

Flats As Stair Risers

What happens is you place these units vertically, in order, the way you want the steps to go. You aren't limited to evenly sized steps—you can spread these things out any which-a-way. They'll be very wobbly, so you'll have to brace everything up really well with 1 × 4s. Then add more

1 × 4s across from flat to flat, to support the stair treads (add lots of support). You don't need risers, since the flats serve the purpose of risers. Instead, you custom cut each stair tread. Remember the nosing (the 1⅛" overlap) and overlap the outside edges if you like. The proper technique would be to start at the top, lay down a sheet of plywood (again, I prefer 1"-thick here; you can live with ¾" if you add extra bracing), chalk out the step shape from underneath, cut it out, there you go. It's probably best not to nail any of the stair treads down until you've finished shaping every step. And you might want to round off the edge of the stair treads with a router, so folks don't trip. Then you can assemble with screws (no glue) from step one up. You can make a serpentine staircase with this method, with landings, and reuse the bracing next year in a different layout—very cool. I must admit I was a little jealous when I saw this easy technique. I still like my method but I'm gonna steal Elaine's method whenever I need a dramatic, twisting staircase. It does take a bit of extra labor to cover up all of the bracing; just cover it up and get some dramatic scenic paint on there to mask any sloppiness.

RAILINGS

You'll need a railing on almost every staircase you build. Backstage staircases (*escapes*) need strong 1 × 4 railings for safety. Onstage railings need to be as strong as possible and also need to look good. Straight stairs are no big problem; just measure carefully to get the slope right, and be extra-careful at the corners. For curving staircases, one technique is to cut away some of the stair tread and install balusters connected directly to the staircase itself. Make sure the balusters are all the same height. Then you can bend and attach 1" strips of thin plywood at the right height for the railing. These can be covered with dutching, making a pretty convincing railing. You can also run regular old garden hose up the balusters. Thin PVC pipe will work, although we had a bit of trouble with the PVC, so keep the plan simple.

CUE 4.5 DON'T FORGET TO . . .

As you are beginning the set there are a couple of other things to attend to, listed below.

AUDITIONS

When you are beginning the set, the director will no doubt be holding auditions. I never had a big part to play during this process. Out of respect for the kids, who were always quite nervous, I would make sure there were no students lurking about watching other students audition. I left everything else up to the directors. They had a great system to make the process run as smoothly as possible. The drama club kids would organize the audition lists, make sure everyone correctly filled out their paperwork, and control the door. The kids would come in to audition, hand their papers over, boom, done. If it was a musical, they'd pass on to the choral director, with a different sheet of paper. Afterwards the adults would get together and compare notes.

The kids have a great fear that, among other things, all of the best parts have been precast by the director. They know the drama kids get most of the parts and are well aware that there actually may be a better singer, dancer, or actor in the school who didn't get the part. My associates were as open minded as possible about this and were still accused of preferential treatment. If you are involved with the audition process, it would be wise to start developing a thick skin now.

I did happen to enter the room during an audition when two young men were competing for a lead role. It was particularly obvious to me who was a "natural," and he eventually did win the lead. The vitriolic hate spewed out by the "loser," who still got a great part, was amazing. To this day he believes he deserved the lead role; I guess that's part of what makes actors tick. The truth was, he didn't even deserve the part he got. And, while directors are human, and can make mistakes, this time our lad did do a great job and later made a movie called *The Fanatical Teachings of Julian Tau.* And another called *The Accountant.* More movies than I've been in, that's for sure.

I was in *Broadcast News,* but got edited out.

CHECK ELIGIBILITY

Most schools have an eligibility policy that does not allow students with bad grades to participate in extracurricular activities. I always find it amusing when someone points out that students who participate in after-school activities have higher grades than students who don't; that someone is confusing cause and effect. Make sure to check these eligibility lists or report cards very carefully if your school follows this policy. I'm not defending the policy, you understand, I'm just enforcing it. And have a care that the kids don't try to flimflam you about make-up work or a grade change. The registrar is the voice of authority in these matters. When you have to exclude someone, keep an eye on her, and help her with her make-up work so she can get back in good academic standing and back on crew. One of our coaches runs a special study hall for his kids just for this purpose.

There was a rumor at Blair that we had to kick off a kid for grades, and now she's a very famous actress, but I don't know if this is really true. It was a long time ago.

CALLBACK LIST

After the auditions, which mostly winnow out the students there are no parts for, come the callbacks. Here is where the roles are decided and offered to students. It always surprises me when a student turns down a role—who are you, Harrison Ford?

POST CAST LIST

The director posts the cast list on the callboard at the appropriate time. Your involvement up to this point may have been quite slight, but now you may be called upon to defend the director's choices. Defend them even if you don't agree with them. You must use this "teachable moment" to remind everyone that the director gets what the director wants. Lead by example. This is a recurring problem in the theater; almost everyone has ideas, sometimes great ideas, but a hierarchy must be firmly established. The director's choices will always be questioned—it's a part of theater—but, eventually what the director says, goes. This is true even when the director is wrong. Very tough lesson for the kids, and even for staff. But it must be so. I did hear of a student lighting designer who said *no* to a director once. Only once. Rest assured, it was not my kid.

SCRIPT

Try to get ahold of a complete script as soon as you can. Note that abridged scripts of many shows are floating around, and different printed sizes too. The words and page numbers are not going to match unless everybody uses the same printed version of the play. You (actually the director) are supposed to order enough scripts for everybody from the publishing company, and we always did, though they sometimes came a little late for my taste. For my convenience, I usually made a Xerox copy I could scribble in. I'm sure I broke plenty of copyright laws by copying the script onto notebook-sized paper. But it gave me a place to put my notes without writing in the (rented) scripts. I don't think they mind as long as they get their money.

ORDER SCRIPTS/MUSIC

The director usually handles ordering scripts and music from the publishing company. These are usually rentals and must be returned in a timely fashion to avoid a very expensive penalty. Numbering the books as they are given out, keeping track of who gets what, and making sure things are returned is the director's job. You may have to lend a hand here, but luckily I never had to.

MEASURING FOR COSTUMES

Strictly speaking, costumes aren't a part of stage crew; nevertheless, I've included a little costume cheat sheet in the back of the book. The costume crew will need this information to custom fit costumes for the cast, and every serious actor should carry this little card in his wallet. Why? Because he might just happen upon a casting call while on vacation, or while walking down the street, and casting agents want to know your glove size, among other things. You can also give a copy to your significant other for gift-buying purposes.

1ST READ-THROUGH

The cast is assembled for the first time and the read-through begins. In the meantime, you get the stage to start work. See how you have to be ready early? Trust me, you need this time; you can't dawdle while everyone else learns the show. And many directors need to see the real set to help them decide on their blocking. So get busy.

Cue 5 Go.

Fix the Lights

Face it; eventually you are going to have to wire something up. And, since there is usually little desire to actually burn the theater down (except in *The Producers*), you'd better make sure you wire things up correctly, and never overload a circuit. If you don't have a clue (be honest with yourself), find someone who does and get his help. Do not rely on students to wire something up without supervision. *Especially* if they think they know what they are doing. When you plug something into a wall socket or dimmer, it's going to be connected to 120 *Volts of Voltage* at perhaps 10 or 20 *Amps of Current*, consuming up to 2400 *Watts of Power*, and turning most of that into heat. This is much more power than a toaster oven, and way too much power to play around with. Let me say it another way . . .

If someone wires up something wrong it can produce more heat than a blowtorch *before* the circuit breaker snaps!

ELECTRICITY—THE SHORT COURSE

So, if we are going to wire up anything, we're going to do it right. We did a couple of shows with a lot of Christmas tree lights. Generally, I'm not in favor of having Christmas tree lights on stage except on Christmas trees, but these were behind translucent plastic and didn't show. They just lit up the painted signs in front of them. Stringing Christmas tree lights on stage just looks kind of tacky, "Oh look, Ethyl. They're using *Christmas tree lights.*" Hey, but if you need 'em, do what you gotta do. By the way, even these little lights get hot, so don't do anything stupid, OK? Try your best to avoid cutting or splicing anything, if you can help it. If you must splice something, use the proper size wire and cover the splice really well with electrical tape.

For instance, you may want three sets of Christmas tree lights to light up in different places at the same time. Instead of buying several extension cords (too expensive), you pick up a roll of two-conductor *zip cord* at Home Depot. It looks like extension cord but comes in hundred-foot rolls. Run the zip cord to each location, and there install a female end (a *socket*). Follow the wiring directions that come with the socket and properly wire up the end of these cords. Then plug in a string of Christmas tree lights. There is no "ground" wire in this sort of hookup. You then gather up several of these wires and collect them at a convenient spot near a wall socket, install a plug, and plug 'em in. By the way, you can't use zip cord for real theater lights—it's not tough enough.

If you want to plug these into your dimmer system, you're going to have to install a plug that matches the sockets on the dimmer system. We're covering the dimmer system later, but you had better take a look and find out what type of sockets your system uses now. Some are *Edison* style, just like the wall socket in your home; some are *stage pin sockets,* and some are *twist locks.* Stage pin sockets look a little like the electrical outlets in Europe; supposedly they handle the heavy electrical currents better. I don't like them, and I don't know anybody who does; if you are stuck with them there's pretty much nothing you can do except treat them nice so they don't break. Luckily, the wiring directions are molded right into the plugs; unluckily, you'll have to purchase them from a supply house since they are only used in theaters.

Twist locks are just what they say: They twist as they are plugged in so the plug won't fall out. You *can* buy these at Home Depot; just make sure you are getting the right-sized unit. Later you can get some heavier electrical cord and build some adapters if you've been stuck with non-Edison type sockets. That way you can plug a lighting unit into a wall socket when you need to.

IMPORTANT

Don't cut and splice the Christmas tree lights themselves, the green wires. It's not worth it; plus, you won't be able to reuse them after the show.

OK, back to the wiring. Zip cord has a *tracer* built into it so you can tell which side is which. It *does* matter, insofar as it would be nice to keep the deadly "hot" leads together. See, someone has figured out which side of a lamp socket, for instance, is more deadly, or dangerous, and they've purposely hooked that side of the plug to the "neutral" part on a plug. It's the fatter part of the plug, if you need to know, and is usually colored silver. The "neutral" represents zero volts and is connected to the earth itself, a true ground. The "ground" wire people are always breaking off of their extension cords is also connected to the ground. It is there so unwanted static charges and dangerous short circuits are sent to the ground instead of through you. It's best if you don't break the little gimmer off, as it's sort of like a seat belt against electrocution. Plugs that don't have a ground wire don't need them; plugs that do have a ground wire do.

Somewhere you must carefully gather these leads, strip the plastic off of the last inch or so, twist the proper wires together (including the one from your plug—you could solder them if you want), then tape the whole mess up nice and strong and safe. If you don't, the bare wire might touch the batten, for instance, which is metal, causing one of those short circuits and popping the circuit breaker, which is proof positive you did something wrong. At least, I've heard that kind of thing can happen. Don't cheat and use the yellow wire caps electricians use—those need to be in a circuit box to be safe, where they can't unravel.

Remember, don't splice the Christmas tree lights *themselves* together. You can plug in a few in a row; just don't cut 'em. And never permanently install Christmas tree lights anywhere. That's just begging for trouble with a capital "T." By the way, the really dinky lights just aren't tough enough to use on stage. If you use them, you can bank on them breaking sometime during the run. Buy the medium (C-7)-sized sets just after Christmas and lock 'em up in the safe until you need them.

Here's where we did use Christmas lights, in spite of all I just told you. We hung red ones in dark corners of the theater so we wouldn't brain ourselves during the run of the show. If an architect would simply incorporate some kind of ghost lighting backstage (like they have in the aisles), this wouldn't be necessary, but they are all idiots. We used them on the Christmas tree in *Annie*. We stuffed a boxful behind some signs painted on plastic. We stuck little teeny white ones through our cyclorama (from the back) to act as stars (the secret—don't stick them all through, just a few). We put them around some signs. All of these things are probably illegal, or against code, and some of them are just plain unsafe. Show a little judgment—if you'd not do it at home (thirty-seven strands of lights into one plug, for instance), don't do it on stage.

REAL LIGHTS

Let's hope that all of your *luminaires* (that's "theater lights") are in perfect working order and never need a moment's attention or repair of any kind. *Hee hee,* that was kind of funny. If you are rolling into a new assignment backstage, one of the first things to do is some kind of lighting inventory. It's extremely time-consuming and unpleasant, and you are almost bound to be upset when you find out now many of your theater lights need work. The best way is to pull every last stinking, dusty one of them down and get every part or whole unit out of storage, throw them all away and buy . . . No, wait. It can't be that bad. Sort them out by type, or by looks, and let's see what we can salvage.

Each unit will need a C-clamp, unless you have one of those awful lighting systems with the interlocking, bolt-like connectors, in which case I pity you. The C-clamps fit on pipes hung especially to take them. If you have a *counterbalanced* system (with weights offstage), taking all of the lights off at the same time is going to be a big problem, so you may want to work on them on the pipe, which can be lowered for this purpose. If you have a *winch* system (with cranks to raise and lower the electrics), just lower away and remove everything. If your pipes are *dead hung*, that is, if your lighting pipes are immovably bolted to the walls or ceiling—you have a lot of ladder work ahead of you. Try your best to find all of the lights, as you'll only want to do this once. Here we go:

- ➤ Sort
- ➤ Inspect
- ➤ Clean
- ➤ Repair
- ➤ Relamp
- ➤ Rehang (in the right place)

But first, a little more schoolwork.

ELECTRICAL POWER

One of the things you will have to do is put the proper-sized lamp into your theater light. There are code letters, and nicknames, and maximum ratings—a true pain in the . . . well, a true pain. There are a couple of simple things that can help you muddle through. Do not presume that the lamp taken out of a unit is the proper lamp. There's a good chance it isn't, at least until you straighten things out. Here are the two (only two!) rules for doing this right. You may end up breaking both rules, but here they are anyway.

ONE

Lamp similar lights the same.

TWO

Use the highest-power lamp allowed for the light.

BECAUSE

Lamping everything the same will help you get nice, even washes when you aim the lights side by side. Also, it won't take long before you get a handle on what each different kind of light will do. And it's easier to restock. And you can get quantity discounts. Betcha didn't know that "lamp" was a verb.

Use the highest-power lamp because *you can always dim them down.*

POWER

Electricity can get confusing because people (including me) write things like, "A 1000-Watt lamp will *consume* as much power as a hair dryer," and, in the same paragraph, "The lamp *produces* 1000 Watts of light." The trouble is in a lack of scientific precision coupled with, shall we say, creative liberties with the English language. We do need to know more about electricity than the man on the street, but if we stick with strict scientific precision you are never going to figure electricity out. Scientists are just a little too picky. So we'll play a little fast and loose with the definitions. You won't pass a physics test, but you will get your lights working.

Some common choices in lamp power are 500, 750, and 1000 Watts. (We capitalize our electrical units as a sign of respect.) Watts is *Power,* and it is what most people are really thinking of when they say "volts" or "current." The more power there is, the brighter something is going to be. And the hotter the fixture is going to get. The highest power reading light in your home is probably 250 Watts; even our smallest light will have twice that. So show a little respect.

Let's clear up this voltage, current, and power terminology. In a nice simple table lamp, you plug it in the wall socket, which means you are going to put 120 Volts across it; you've got no choice, as that's what comes from the power company. If you want a bright light, you buy maybe a 150-Watt lamp, or bulb; if that's too bright you might settle for a 60-Watt, or maybe a 75. If you figured a 75-Watt lamp will give you about half the light of a 150-Watt lamp, you figured right. This might seem odd, as they are both plugged into the same 120 Volts. Hmm. It's the current that is different. There's less current in the smaller bulb—therefore less power, less heat, and of course less light. Why less current? The 75-Watt bulb is made to restrict or *resist* current, probably by being made of thinner wire. Here's a succinct way of putting it:

> ➤ Voltage is the pushing and pulling force of electricity.
> ➤ Current is the actual movement of charge (when it's pushed and pulled).
> ➤ Resistance is inside the things that use electricity.
> ➤ There's even a little bit of resistance in the wires themselves.
> ➤ Resistance makes it harder for current to flow.
> ➤ Power (in simple circuits) is the mathematical product of voltage and current.

Simple enough. Let's remember, however, that we are playing around with high-voltage, high-current circuits. Multiply the two and you notice you get really high power. This could be a big problem when we start plugging these things in. Plus, things get really hot, so lay in a pair of gloves.

BREAKING RULE ONE

At the end of the day, all of your lights should have similar lamps in them. That's rule one. If you don't have a bunch of lamps the same size, or if you are "certain sure" that you want a hot spot in a wash, then go ahead and break rule one. If there is a dim area in spite of everything, go ahead and break rule one. If you just feel like it, go ahead, suit yourself, break rule one.

BREAKING RULE TWO

Rule two, as you recall, says to buy the highest-power lamp that is appropriate for the unit. There is a problem with this rule. It has to do with something called patching. *Patching* is setting up your light board controls to your dimmers and hooking up your dimmers to one or several numbered sockets where you actually plug in the lights. It's possible to hook up all the lights to one dimmer, which would be bad. You need to determine how much power your dimmers are rated for. That is, you need to determine when the circuit breaker is going to pop, then *not exceed that amount of power.* By the way, circuit breakers don't *blow,* they *snap,* or *pop.* And they can be reset after you've found and fixed the overload. Fuses blow. If your system has fuses, you really ought to upgrade. They removed the fused system from my school around 1970. I was in sixth grade.

The easy way to determine the rating of a dimmer is to look directly at the circuit breaker controlling it. Try the dimmer room and/or the patch panel. The chances are good that the breakers are all the same, and they probably say 20 on them, as in 20 Amperes of Current. The power company provides a constant 120 Volts of Voltage; 20 times 120, hey, you've got 2400-Watt dimmers. I will let you have the satisfaction of calculating the power if you have a 10-Amp breaker, but it's half as much . . . *oops.* Well it is.

AND I NEED TO KNOW THIS BECAUSE . . .

You need to know this to better determine what lamps to buy. For instance, if you expect to put four lamps on the same 2400-Watt dimmer, you've got to buy 600-Watt lamps. So you stock up on 500-Watt lamps (a little bit less, see, for safety), or assign a second dimmer; then you can use 1000-Watt lamps. Of course, you'll quickly run out of dimmer circuits, so be frugal, thoughtful, and creative. Lucky for you there are new, high-efficiency, 575-Watt lamps that put out a lot of extra light! Four of those will work on a 2400-Watt dimmer just fine.

TO REVIEW

You may break rule two if following it puts you in a bind as far as the dimmers are concerned. If you are hooking up some front light—say, a special color for one special scene—and you can only use two 1200-Watt dimmers (because you've run out), and you want four units patched in (to get a good spread), well, you can't use 1000-Watt lamps, even if they fit the fixture. You'll pop the breaker. On both dimmers. Pop. Pop. No light. The maximum power—that is, the current times 120 volts—is kind of like a speed limit that you can't break. So you break rule two instead, lamp the units with an appropriate, lower-power bulb. Lamp. Light bulb. (They're called *lamps.*)

PATCHING

Patching comes later. We haven't even sorted out all our stuff yet.

SORT

You are probably going to end up with four piles of lights. Heaven help you if you have a real mismatched set. Find the biggest—not the *longest,* the *biggest*—ones you've got. These are probably scoops, with a 16"-square contraption on them to hold a colored gel. Count 'em up; I hope you have twelve; otherwise, make do with what you've got. They go on the back pipe, pretty much behind all the action, and get aimed at the cyclo-rama or back wall. (By the way, you can paint scenes on the back wall; I don't know why more folks don't do this.) For general use, make four blue, four red, and four green, space them out in even sets, and hook 'em up so you can mix the colors in any combination.

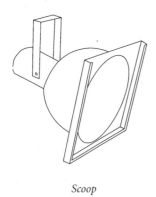

Scoop

I CAN'T RESIST

I can't resist breaking in here to see if you really get it about power. If you do have twelve scoops, and you want each one to get a 1000-Watt lamp, which would be nice, you'll need either twelve 1200-Watt dimmers or six 2400-Watt dimmers. Get it? You'll eventually be able to assign them to three separate sliders (channels), one for each color, but that comes later too.

FRESNELS

Now the smallest lights. These are prob-ably Fresnels. You can check by looking at the lens. If it has a bunch of circles on it, it's a Fresnel lens, and a Fresnel fix-ture. (Don't say "freznells" unless you want to be marked an amateur. Just pre-tend the "s" isn't there.) Most of the time there is one adjustment you can make on these, apart from aiming it. You can slide the lamp via a knob on the bottom to a *spot* or a *flood* position.

Fresnel

Usually you flood 'em. They go above the actors to give top light, side light, or front light. Fresnels generally have a short "throw," meaning you hang them pretty close to the action, right above the stage. It also means you need a lot of them.

They make really big Fresnels. I just doubt you have those.

ELLIPSOIDALS

Ellipsoidals are mini-spotlights, and some of them adjust the size of the spot and some of them don't. All of them can be *focused*—given a nice sharp edge or a fuzzy one on purpose, kind of like the Fresnels only better. They have several lenses inside. Most have shutters, metal blades that can be adjusted to *not* light a part of the normal spot. Meaning you can adjust the shutters and project a square instead of a circle. Or you can erase the "spill" of the light onto a set piece or curtain that should remain dark. The chances are good that the shutters are bent, broken, or missing, or, in the case of "EC" brand, incorrectly installed. These things can be fixed! Plus, ellipsoidals can be adjusted for maximum light output. This is called a *bench focus*. Plus, ellipsoidals can project patterns, called *gobos*, almost like a slide projector. Ellipsoidals are *cool*.

Separate your ellipsoidals into the kind that can zoom (more knobs), and the kind that can't (fewer knobs). The ones that can't zoom might have an *iris control* that changes the size of the spot, kind of a poor man's zoom. Don't throw away any leftover parts (never), especially things that look like an ellipsoidal that's missing most of its hardware. These are *barrels* and can be changed manually—that is, with a screwdriver—giving a smaller or bigger spot. Longer barrels give a smaller spot. Save the extra barrels.

New ellipsoidals are the coolest. The Altman Shakespeare can zoom over a pretty great range (it's when you need a nice tight spot that this

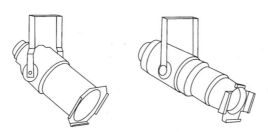

Ellipsoidals

comes in handy). Also, its pattern holder can rotate, and the gel frame too. It stays cooler than the old type, it uses more efficient lamps, it aims and focuses easier . . . it's just the cat's meow. You can even put a *gobo rotator* on it (don't ask) and have psychedelic light shows. Promise yourself now, as you're cleaning up your ratty old units, that you will save your pennies and buy your school a few of these absolutely great lights. Unless Source Fours are on sale. Then it's a tossup.

FOCUS/ZOOM

There are two knobs on the underside of an adjustable ellipsoidal. If you are behind the thing trying to adjust it, the knob farthest from you is the zoom. The closer knob controls the focus. You'll probably have to go back and forth between the two as you try to set the light perfectly. Hand-tighten these knobs—no need to wrench them into pieces.

PAR CANS

Par cans look a lot like Fresnels, except that they have no lens at all. They are used a lot in rock and roll, but not so much in theater. They are perfectly good, however, and you can use them like Fresnels, usually pretty close to the action. You have to buy the right *type* of lamp for a par can, as well as the right power. The lamps themselves come in "spot" and "flood." You see, the lens is inside the lamp itself, built right into the light bulb, saving a lot of trouble, especially on tour. Take your time buying lamps for par cans, there are about a million choices. You probably want floods.

The "par" in "par can" means "parabolic." No letters, please; technically it means "parabolic anodized reflector."

STRIP LIGHTS

If you turned a set of strip lights on its end and lit them up one by one, they'd look a lot like the lights you see at a drag strip. This is not why they are called strip lights. They are just a set of twelve or fifteen lights that are wired in sets of three, so they have three plugs hanging off of them. They also usually have three sockets hanging off of them, too, so you can string 'em along until you have reached the maximum power allowed for your dimmer. You usually load these up with 150-Watt indoor floodlamps (you can buy spots but I don't think you'll want to). You can buy the lamps on sale at Home Depot! If you are going to string up a whole bunch of these, perhaps you'd better settle for 100-Watt floodlamps. See rule number two above. But make them all the same in any case. See rule number one above.

Strip lights are the knockabout rough thugs of theater lighting. You'll end up building them into set pieces, laying them behind things pointing up, or back, or both, using them on the floor pointing up to augment the cyc lights (this is really cool), hanging them for top light if you don't have enough Fresnels, placing them as footlights when the situation calls for footlights, facing them towards the audience in discotheque fashion, and using them at a school dance since they won't pop the circuit breakers in the gym. Trust me, they'll come in handy. No lenses, just wipe off the worst of the dust. Some strip lights come wired in sets of four, some in sets of three.

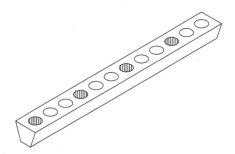

Strip Lights

CYC LIGHTS

Sometimes you'll find three or more scoops built into one, kind of like a huge, short strip light. These are *cyc lights* and take the place of scoops. The "cyc" in "cyc lights" means *cyclorama*—that's the back curtain.

SPOTLIGHTS

Spotlights (follow spots) are super-brilliant moveable units used to heat up the singer in a musical, and in a couple of other ways. Well, they are supposed to be brilliant. Most community theater and school spotlights are overdue for an overhaul. Some places even have the sparky old carbon-arc kind, which is probably not wise. Clean the lenses, replace the gels if you have to, use powdered graphite to lubricate the moving parts (not oil). A follow spot is supposed to swing around easily and stay where you put it when you let go. Replace washers and knobs. Make the best of what you've got.

Spotlights are unique in that each one needs an operator, a crew member whose only job is to run the light when it's needed. They aren't really part of the dimming system, but they are a huge part of the total lighting design, especially in musicals. Spend the extra time to fix 'em up nice.

Think a moment about the proper place for a spotlight. I used to like to have the actual spotlight beam show behind the actor; I still do. If you like that look, keep the spots in a lower location—at the back of the house, maybe. A friend showed me a technique where the spots shine down from on high (in the beams), the actor is brilliantly lit, and the stage stays relatively dark, giving great contrast. Good trick. Another great trick is to gently dim down the stage lights when the spots come on, and bring 'em back up at the conclusion of the song. Done subtly (with practice), this helps focus attention, and even cues the applause. Plenty of laughs and applause are stifled by poorly executed stage cues.

If your spot doesn't give out enough light, check it out thoroughly, then rent a better one (or two). Nothing is worse than a spotlight that doesn't spot or light.

MOVING LIGHTS

The chances are pretty good you don't actually own any of these newfangled moving lights. There are two kinds. The first are found in nightclubs and such, and sort of spin around and blink and look kind of like miniaturized carnival rides. These are great fun for school dances, and maybe for variety shows. We used some in *Charlie and the Chocolate Factory*. The second kind are programmable spotlights of some sort and can be set to move in unison, change color and size, and move independently. Some have mirrors and some move the entire lamp housing. They are way cool, and way expensive, and my advice is to leave them alone until such time as you have everything else under complete control; then maybe, *maybe*, I'll let you splurge and rent a few for a special event. They usually need a special controller anyhow. Back to the grind.

INSPECT

Turn the power off. And unplug everything. Everything. Check the cord on each unit. Is it asbestos? Scream, run, and hire somebody to replace all of the cords. Don't do it yourself, as there is a tiny chance you'll get very sick. Figure out how to open up the unit. Check the lamp. You'll probably have to push it down and twist it counterclockwise to remove it, kind of like a childproof cap. Regular screw bases don't do well in high-power lamps. The second kind of lamp you'll find a lot comes out sort of like a Rubik's Cube puzzle. In either case, don't get your grubby hands, or even your clean hands, on the glass part of the lamp. Use a clean cloth or gloves, for two reasons. One, the bulb could break. Two, the oil from your skin will stick to the lamp, just like it does to your glasses. That little bit of oil will burn (1000 Watts, remember), and the lamp will fail. Cleanliness, and not touching the glass—very important here. Inspect the lamp and the socket it came out of. Determine if the lamp is the right one—call someone, carry the fixture to the store if you have to. Stockpile all the lamps. You can clean them with isopropyl alcohol if you feel the need, but at least sort them out. Remember to read the part above about having the power off.

BILL'S DIAPER

My high-school buddy Bill (his real name) had a nephew, and Bill eventually got a used, clean baby diaper as a sort of whimsical souvenir. He used it to polish his guitar. Eventually I got it mixed up with another diaper that had no historical significance, which broke his heart. If only I had known. Anyhow, the diapers are good for holding these lamps, so find some if you can. I still have Bill's. Um, mine. Um, Bill's nephew's. Um, truth is, we don't know which one is which.

TESTING THE LIGHTS

You can test the lamps—the light bulbs, that is (cold, out of the socket)—with an *ohmmeter,* and you should. The physics teacher can show you how. No physics teacher? Where do you work, anyway? Just set the digital multimeter you bought (quick, run, go buy one) to read Ohms (the lowest scale is fine) and touch one lead to the side of the lamp base, and the other lead to the bottom. When testing the kind of lamp with two little pins, just connect up to each pin. Don't touch the metal parts. It's not going to shock you, but your fingers *can* mess up the reading. Oddly enough, the numbers don't actually matter in this test; if you see no change in the meter when testing a lamp, the lamp is bad. If you see any number at all, the lamp is good. Actually, in many cases you can just look at the lamp; if the filament (that's the inside wire) is broken, bad lamp. Set all of the bad lamps aside. You are going to throw them away after you test them a second time. Just being thorough, ma'am. Don't throw away lamps that *look* ugly and blackened but test good. They are still good. Well, they are still usable. Remember, just because a lamp doesn't light when you plug it in doesn't mean the lamp is no good. It could be the plug, or the wire, or the lamp socket (or the wall socket). Test all of the lamps.

AS LONG AS WE'RE BEING THOROUGH

I might as well point out right here that it's extremely difficult to change one of these lamps when it's burnt out, but still hot. People do it, though. They are usually smart enough to wear gloves, and usually dumb enough to leave the power on. We call this *temporary blindness* if it's not too severe, a *broken neck* if you fall off the ladder after getting shocked. If you're the lucky type you'll just get a couple of blisters on your fingers. Back to work.

CLEAN

Check the reflector; it's probably filthy. You can clean old fixtures, reflectors, and lenses with isopropyl alcohol. Put the alcohol on the rag, not the lens. Better check if you have any newer stuff—some lenses have coated optics, so follow the manufacturer's instructions. But the old junk, use isopropyl alcohol and lots of old towels. You sorta gotta clean the lenses . . . be careful . . . you are probably going to break one if you're not . . . *too late*! Yes, you will probably break something, a screw, a knob, even a lens. It happens. Persevere. Clean everything, unless it's too hard to get to, like some ellipsoidal reflectors I know.

If for some strange reason you are reluctant to apply the alcohol-soaked rag to some surface, perhaps it's your good sense warning you that damage will occur. If you think you shouldn't apply the isopropyl to a white reflector, for instance, because you think it'll damage the paint, well, you could be right. Test your theory out with a Q-Tip.

After everything dries, you'll probably see streaks on the lenses. Clean 'em again.

REPAIR

Look for loose stuff. Some scoops, most Fresnels, and all ellipsoidals have adjustments; see if they work and do what you can to set them all the same. Locate or purchase enough *gel frames,* one for each unit. Gel frames hold the color, and you need a complete set. In a pinch, you can clip a gel in place with a bulldog clip or one of those bendy brass paper clips, or even a wooden clothespin, but it's bad form and time consuming, too. Don't use any kind of tape on any kind of theater light. Bad wiring is a real fire hazard; rewire correctly. Replace stripped screws and missing knobs, rob the worst units of parts to repair the more promising ones. Never throw lamp parts away. Unless they're broken. What I mean is . . . well, use your best judgment. Don't throw anything away that might come in handy. What you want is an admittedly smaller collection of lights that actually work, that can be hung, aimed, and focused without a lot of cussing. Try to free stuck parts. Bang the shutters back into shape before reinserting them into the ellipsoidals. Clean as you go, but don't oil anything. The oil would burn; no, no, bad idea. Lay in a supply of safety cables and permanently attach one to each unit. Check the plug again— this is usually where the wiring fails.

RELAMP

Count up your working units, deduct for the working lamps you have on hand, and chalk up an order. An inventory sheet, even one created in Excel or FileMaker Pro, would not be out of place here. You are trying to get organized, dad-gum it; make a list or something.

Your theatrical lighting supply house, and most mail order companies, will help you buy the right lamps for your fixtures. The first time, you may want to either carry in or bring a picture of your fixtures. You have to be able to tell the vendor exactly what you have. Sometimes that is difficult. Don't rely on buying the lamp that came out of the unit; you could be just perpetuating an expensive error. Besides, the lights work better when they have the right lamp in them.

Your order is going to be complicated by the fact that there are better lamps out now. Some are brighter, more efficient, using less power, and giving off more light and less heat. Buy those. Some last longer. Buy those. A stickler will point out that the "color temperature" of these lamps is different. Try to stifle a yawn as you tell the guy to mind his own business, you've got more important things to worry about than color temperature. *Sheesh.* Who bothers with color temperature? Get a life, pal.

Buy the efficient, long-lasting lamps that are appropriate for your fixtures. You can mix them with the old lamps until the old lamps have all burned out. Just do it in a way that will give a nice pattern of light. For instance, your predecessor stocked 500-Watt lamps in the scoops, but you have learned that they are supposed to take 1000s, and the dimmers can handle it, no problem. Mix and match old and new in a creative way. The 500s can go in the red scoops, the new 1000s can go in the blue, and you can mix the green. It'll look funny, but not so bad if you go dim, bright, bright, dim. Plus, you can turn on a little blue whenever you have the green on. Plus, you can buy this gray gel (Rosco 97), sort of like a neutral density filter for the bright lights. That'll dim 'em down a bit. You can even assign the brighter lights to a different slider (channel) and keep them dimmer. Buy as many lamps as you need to get the show on the road. You should also stock up with some spares, as these powerful lamps blow out relatively quickly. Get as many as you can afford.

A BENCH FOCUS

While you've got all the ellipsoidals in perfect working order, you might as well *bench focus* them. This is just a procedure that aligns the lamp with the reflector. Like a tune-up for light output. It's surprising how much difference this can make in light output. Hang the light on some convenient pipe or clamp it in a vise in the workshop. Aim it at a white wall. Focus it perfectly. It is pointing straight at the wall, right? OK, move the little knob or screw on the very back of the lamp, the one that's connected to the lamp socket itself. Wiggle or slide the lamp around until the spot on the wall is at its most brilliant, perfect, and even in every way. Tighten down. Don't cuss too much when tightening down causes the lamp to move, ruining everything. Redo until perfect. Look carefully for more adjustment screws, sometimes found on the side of the unit. Perfect? Acceptable? Good. Set every other ellipsoidal up with a bench focus, then go get lunch, or dinner probably, as this'll take forever. But it's worth it.

MEASURE FOR GEL SIZE

When you've got a pretty complete inventory of your lighting units, take a moment to measure all of the square or rectangular frame holders, where the gel frames go. Measure in inches, and note all sizes. You'll need these numbers when you go to buy color.

REHANG (IN THE RIGHT PLACE)

You can take a few minutes, even without a show to "hang," and determine where all of these lights are going to go. The ellipsoidals are the best choice for front light, as they throw their beam long-distance. The ones with the short barrels should hang pretty close, as they spread out their spot pretty quickly. You need a lot of front light, so in your mind you can assign as many units as you have sockets up in "the beams." Some folks call the beams the *front of house.* The beams are lighting positions that are above the audience, directly "in front" of the stage. If you've got powerful enough dimmers you can even double up on the lights in the beams with a *two-fer,* a sort of double extension cord. The reason you want to get a lot of units up front is you are going to shoot them all over the stage, and stock them with two or even three different colors to help set the mood. Plus you'll probably have a couple of *specials* in there, aimed directly at a specific spot for a specific purpose; "*What light, through yonder window breaks . . .* "

If compromises have to be made, here is the order of importance as far as lights are concerned:

- ➤ Front light from the beams (ellipsoidals)
- ➤ Front light from the electrics (Fresnels)
- ➤ Top light (actually, it's usually high side light)
- ➤ Side and backlight
- ➤ Cyc lights (just get a lamp in there, any size or power)
- ➤ Specials

Hang the lights so the slot in the gel frame holder faces up. If you don't, the gel will fall out.

POSTPONE THINKING ABOUT SIDE LIGHT

Side light is actually pretty important, but it doesn't look that great if you don't have enough front light. What I mean is, you've got to let the audience see, then you can get fancy. Later there's more on side light.

When you're deciding, in a general way, what light goes where, try to group your lights into similar types. If you have ten "matched" ellipsoidals, they can be aimed five and five across the front (the *downstage*) areas. If you only have eight, well, four areas will have to do. I hope you have lots more so you can heat up the upstage areas with front light, too. *Upstage* is when an actor backs *up.* Get it? Some stages (not mine) are tilted so upstage really is up. Pick and choose and sort, leaving a couple of spares, and set up a nice front light wash with your ellipsoidals. As you hang each unit (later), take note of the gel frame holder, in the very fronty-front. Make sure the opening faces *up,* so your gel frames don't fall out. Some have clips, some can rotate; face the opening *up.*

FOR THE RECORD

A typical 575-Watt, incandescent stage lamp converts (not consumes) 575 Watts of electrical power into somewhere around 14,000 *Lumens* of light. About eleven hundred Candlepower. It depends on the quality of the lamp and the fixture, and the age of the lamp (newer is better). There's no such thing as "Watts of Light," even though everybody says it. Not all of the power becomes light. Most becomes heat. Some becomes magnetic field. Really. Some becomes sound. Lay your head up against a wooden telephone pole if you don't believe me. You won't hear phone calls—you'll hear a low buzz or hum. Comes from the electricity. True fact. Useless, but true.

SLAP A JELLY ON THE BABY

I read somewhere that they actually say this in Hollywood. It means to put some kind of color on some kind of light. You can buy colored gel at any theater arts store, and you cut it to size with scissors or a paper cutter. The gel fits in the gel frame, which slides in front of all the lights you've hung. It's a good thing to plan ahead and get a variety of useful colors for effect. There is an almost infinite selection of gel available from Rosco, and Lee, and I think GAM sells color gels, too (I use Rosco). The salesperson should be happy to help you select colors and calculate your total order if you know the number and sizes you need . . . and of course you do know this, since you did all the work last week.

If you just can't decide which colors to use, pick red, blue, and green for the cyc lights (or scoops), pick Rosco 02 and Rosco 60 for front light (I believe they are the bestsellers), and use Rosco 51 for top or side light, or use nothing on top. These give a pretty decent look and will get you through a few shows until you learn to trust your own color choices. Buy a couple of sheets of other colors to experiment with. And sort out the colors you already have. You can use them again and again. I had some flat file drawers from the drafting lab (look around). The accordion files from Staples are almost perfect for cut sheets. Pick up a white china marker and write the color number on each and every piece of gel. It won't show on stage, and the colors will be easier to sort that way.

As you experiment with color you'll learn that the *light transmission* of these gels makes a huge difference in how bright things are on stage. The richest colors are also the dimmest; you'll have to use your most powerful units to get any kind of brightness when you use these. But they look cool, so throw some in somewhere—a special effect or something.

Buy a selection of the various *diffusion* gels to experiment with. Diffusion is the saffron of gels.

DIFFUSION

I'm just mad about diffusion. That's an old people's joke. Show this page to a child of the sixties and he'll laugh. You don't need to get the joke to learn that diffusion is your error eraser, your light stretcher, and your wash leveler. Your can put it in almost every fixture to good effect. Diffuse your top light. Diffuse your front light, especially if you have uneven light that you just can't seem to level out. Get the diffraction diffuser (Rosco 104) to throw light out like a hallway or staircase. Experiment, and make magic.

If you didn't get the joke, listen to oldies radio for a day or two.

<u>COLOR TEMPERATURE?</u>

You had to ask. Color temperature is light theory, useful when you know it, but a couple more steps into it than your basic trial-and-error methods common at our level. Here we go. Perhaps you have noticed, when driving at night, that some car headlights are not only brighter than others but are a different color completely. Some fog lamps have an amber tint, but I'm not talking about that. Some lights just look bluer than the others, which you would have sworn were putting out white light, but next to the blue lights, the white ones look yellow. Florescent lights work the same; in my garage, some are bluish (those are the "cool whites"), some look white, and a couple have a pink cast. And some streetlights are a powerful yellow—people hate them, but they are efficient and incredibly bright, and governments can't resist them, especially in high crime areas.

These are examples of lamps putting out light of a different *color temperature.* In some cases (streetlights), the color temperature is a best guess/closest fit kind of thing, but common theater lights put out a pretty good spectrum of light, which means the color temperature of the lamp can tell you what quality of light you'll be getting, usually compared to daylight. This comes in handy when you're forced to mix units with different power ratings, and when you mix different lamps in the same fixtures. In short, the long-lasting efficient lamps you should buy put out a slightly different-color light than the other lamp that fits your fixtures. Even without a gel. So you can get a real subtle gradient, just enough to bother you, and you might not be able to figure out what's wrong.

Color temperature is affected by the age of the lamp, the wiring (like a long extension cord), the lamp itself, the real temperature (to an almost insignificant degree), and by dimming the lamp down. So when fading a nice wash, it not only gets dimmer, it changes color slightly. Sometimes not so slightly, so your red-headed actress suddenly looks like a brunette.

You can safely ignore learning about color temperature for several years if you can afford to stock your lighting fixtures with all the same power and type of lamp (rule one again), and if you choose gels and lighting levels wisely. But if you try to make a movie, watch out—film is incredibly sensitive to the color temperature of the lamps you use. Remember all those yellowish color pictures in your photo album at home? That's outdoor film used with indoor lamps. The sun and the lamps have different color temperatures. It matters in video, too—one reason it's hard to videotape a stage performance.

My advice . . . ignore color temp until your scenic painting and lighting designs are so good you have to deal with it. Even then, neglect it. Rely on gels, paints, makeup, and your eye. There are too many other variables that affect things more. And you can fix still pictures in Photoshop. If the day comes when you put the same gel in your spotlight and your wash, and you notice that the color is different, and it bugs you, you can fix it with gels designed to correct for color temperature differences. Let me know how it turns out. Home videos of shows—live with it. Movies and broadcast TV—break out the color temp charts and do it right.

By the way, the reason those powerful yellow streetlights make things look so funny is that they don't put out any blue light at all; a spectrum analyzer would show a blank spot in the blue area. This messes up the color temperature reading, so there's even more ratings and adjustments and calculations to make to compensate. Don't worry, I'm not going to tell you any more about them, except to say that if you see a car running down the street with one bluish headlight, and one yellowish headlight, that's me. It says on the package to replace these lamps in pairs, but I didn't.

GOBOS

Gobos are fun, but sometimes annoying, tin cutouts that cast shadows (and light) in patterns. They look a little like those automatic cookie cutter dies that go in that cookie-making gun that looks like a caulk gun. Generally they are placed in a specially designed *gobo slot* on an ellipsoidal; some are set to a sharp focus so you can tell what they are, some are set out of focus on purpose (a soft focus) to help set a mood. I was never a big fan of the soft-focus, mood-setting gobo. Unless done very well, it gives more hot spots, and more shadows, and makes your lighting look *worse*—some effect!

Speaking of cookie cutters, a really *big* gobo in front of a really big light is called a *cookie.* You can make those out of Masonite, and you can make your own gobos, but you'll probably be happiest when you buy 'em. Hundreds are available, and custom-made gobos won't break the bank either. Stick 'em in the ellipsoidal upside down in their little holder, aim, and focus, and you too will agree that they are annoying sometimes. Since the ellipsoidal is usually hung a little askew, the image projected will look a little funny. It's called *keystoning,* this stretching out of the image. And, unless everything is perfect, you can't get every edge to focus right. Persevere.

SHOOTING A GOBO

My little trick for shooting a gobo is to carry the ellipsoidal around, like a bazooka with an extension cord, and aim it from several locations (you may have to climb a ladder). Decide on the best shot (like a photographer), then figure out how to hang the light there. Many times the ellipsoidal will have to *show,* meaning the audience will see it. This is no big deal (hide it if you can); the real trick is not to overdo it with the gobos. You can project images of clouds, no problem, but if it's *lightning* and you blink that lightning gobo more than three times, people will tire of the effect. I saw Joan Armatrading once (well, twice), and she used her trademark gobo throughout her entire show. I was sick of looking at it after the second song. And she could have afforded a *gobo rotator* (don't ask).

Anyhoo, hang and focus as best as you can. If part of the gobo is out of focus, just live with it; it's a teeny bit bent due to the heat. And if the gobo is in wrong, give it time to cool before you try to adjust it; they get red hot in there. (By the way, they are not tin, they are stainless steel.) It's best, but almost impossible, to put the gobo in right the first time. Try this—stand behind the ellipsoidal and install the gobo in its little holder so you can read the writing when you hold the gobo holder upright in your hand. Then turn it upside down and stick it in the gobo slot. Turn on the unit and see if you must rotate the gobo clockwise or counterclockwise. If the writing is backwards, you weren't following the directions. One more hint. If you are shining a gobo at the stage floor, and the audience can't see the stage floor, you are pretty much wasting your time. If the idea is to have someone wandering through the forest (dappled moonlight, so to speak), fine, just get some front light on 'em before they talk.

I bought a custom-made gobo with our school mascot on it. That's one gobo that got plenty of use. And the expensive color ones look intriguing. A great spot for these effects is a short scene when you don't have a set piece. Just make sure you have something to shoot the gobo at—a wall or curtain. I was once asked to shoot a red gobo at a black curtain, guess how that came out.

DONUT, ANYONE?

You can buy or make a device called a *donut* that serves to help sharpen a gobo image. It acts as an iris to help focus things. It fits in the gel frame holder and has a two-inch diameter hole in it. If you make one yourself, make it out of metal.

GOBO ROTATOR

You can rent or buy a sort of a toy that spins one or two gobos around— I just don't know why you'd want to. Maybe for clouds or dream scenes. I've seldom seen this effect pay off, but you are welcome to try it if you'd like. Just make sure the gobo rotator fits inside your brand of ellipsoidal light, or rent a unit made special for the purpose.

INSTEAD OF GOBOS

I'm sure you've seen someone giving a PowerPoint presentation using one of those newfangled media projectors. They can project a computer or television image pretty big, and pretty bright. These media projectors, while expensive, could be great in the theater, especially the ones that fix the keystoning of the image. I'm going to try to incorporate two into my next show. If you are going to try the media projector, remember they are not *really* very bright; you'll have to pretty much dim everything else out totally. This might be a cute trick for the beginning of Tevye's Dream in

Fiddler on the Roof. Hiding the thing is a problem. We've put them in the orchestra pit and hung them from the ceiling; you'll have to experiment a bit for the best effect.

BOTTOM OF THE CYC

You bought this book to learn a few tricks; well, here are a couple that can improve your light plot immensely with very little effort. I like these kinds of hints, so easy. You can set strip lights, extra scoops, or even Fresnels on the upstage floor, pointing up at the cyc (the back curtain), to set up complementary or contrasting light for background effect. Two or three colors. They point up, the cyc lights point down, the cyc looks cool. Red up and blue down is particularly striking. Now your background palette is almost infinite. You may or may not have to *mask,* or hide, these lights; luckily, they are so far away from the audience you can just stick a black board downstage of them so the audience can't see 'em. But you don't really have to do even that.

Play with tilting the very bottom edge of the cyc towards the audience and then away. You'll need somebody at both ends, and maybe the middle, as you sit in the house and watch. Have some of the crew slowly rock the cyc back and forth a few inches as the rest of you watch. Sometimes the cyc needs to be set a teensy bit off of the vertical to catch the best light. If that's true for you, you can lock the cyc in the correct position with a couple of sandbags.

AISLE LIGHTS

In an economizing move, the builders did not install a switch for the aisle lights in our new auditorium. Plus, they locked the electric box and chose not to give the stage director (me) the key. So our aisle lights stayed on all of the time. That is, until they burned out. I had the crew kids replace them all once, over fifty little lamps, one hundred screws—and of course I had purchased the bulbs that were just a little bit too big, even though they were rated correctly. The county electricians were supposed to handle this, of course, and now they do, but at the time we needed aisle lights. . . .

I did manage to convince the electrician (a great guy) to leave the electric panel open for me. Now when I throw the breaker, all of the aisle lights go out. Except six. Sigh.

Stock up on the correct lamps if you have to do this kind of thing.

GHOST LIGHTS

All theaters are supposed to have ghosts. I named ours "ATULAK." It took the kids about a year to figure out that that was "KALUTA" spelled backwards. Make up a great story about the ghost, tell it at the Friday dinners, and warp your crew's minds. You will also need a ghost light. This is a little dim light that stays on all the time so the theater never goes dark. Never goes *dark,* isn't that romantic? I heard that when the first construction workers went into the Ed Sullivan theater to rebuild it for David Letterman, there was a light on to greet them after all those years. Actually, I just made that up. But it is nice to have a teensy bit of light on for the first guy in the auditorium, especially as it's usually you.

Personally, I think the ghost light should be incorporated into the dim running lights that should be permanently installed in every theater to help the cast and crew see backstage during a show. What the architects are thinking to leave these out escapes me. If you ever get the chance, demand that "aisle lights" be placed backstage as well as in the house, slip a red gel in them, and there you go. Until that day, strategically place dim lights in useful locations backstage, with 15-Watt red lamps. Lots of folks use dim blue lights backstage; I like red. IKEA is a good place to pick up cheap lighting fixtures that will do the job. Don't use Christmas lights unless you have no other choice (see above).

Just today the school electrician (yes, the same guy) asked me where the light switch was for the aisle lights. "Ha!" I said. "There is none. The aisle lights run off of three different circuits, two of which nobody knows where they are hooked up!" I talk like that sometimes. It turns out that one circuit is controlled in the main office, one backstage and one . . . well, nobody knows. Be ready for these kinds of frustrations as you sort out the electrical systems in the theater. Find the bad outlets, put in the work orders, try to find replacement parts, never give up. But, for the run of each show, only use the circuits and components that you know work reliably. Don't count on something that may fail. Especially the intercom.

CUE 5.9 THE INTERCOM

To send messages back and forth you'll need some sort of intercom, and, knowing how things are, the one you have now is probably unreliable. It really must work if you are to have any chance of putting on a great show, so find some time and pay some attention to it, fix it, or replace it. Take a good hard look at what's there; it will probably be obvious if it's shot. Generally, however, the wiring in a hardwired system is fine except at the connectors. That is, you can probably fix up the house wiring and replace the plug-in headsets. If your expertise lies elsewhere, start pricing wireless units. As might be expected, Radio Shack usually has something to fit the bill. Find something with headsets or earpieces. You'll need at least six working units, unless you are in a financial crisis, where you can get by with four, or even three. In order of importance, here is who gets a headset:

➤ The stage manager (usually backstage)
➤ The light board operator
➤ The spotlight operator(s)
➤ The sound board operator
➤ The fly gallery (pulling scenery up and down)
➤ The assistant stage manager

During rehearsals the stage manager should be in the house with the director; during the show she is usually on the side of the stage that has the curtain pull. The light board operator should be at the light board, hopefully somewhere

where he can see the stage he is lighting. The sound board operator must be where she can hear, and she usually isn't; see if you can work on that.

Using the intercom is pretty self-explanatory. In theory, the stage manager gives warnings and cues, and everyone else speaks only when necessary. In real life, a strange and dangerous thing happens to those allowed to use the headsets. They talk among themselves during rehearsals, and during the show too. Inevitably a little clique forms, and they begin to insult the performers and the performance. Usually this is harmless, but if you ignore it, it can become a big problem. For instance, the lighting guy will say, "Look at that idiot, get in the light, oh, get in the light, you idiot, I can't believe he's so stupid, can't you see your mark, you idiot," and so on. What should happen, in rehearsal, is someone should fix the cue, or the mark, or the light (or the actor), but what *can* happen is the kids on headset consciously or unconsciously torpedo the show. The students, and adults, too, get an inflated sense of ego and power just because they have the headsets, and they can gossip throughout the entire run. About the actors, and about the staff. So you'd better listen in once in a while, enough to let them know you won't allow any hanky-panky. Plus you get to say, "Alright, let's cut the chatter," just like those guys in all those war movies.

EMERGENCY INTERCOM

Once upon a time, you could pick up surplus telephone operator headsets and build a serviceable emergency intercom that worked off of a battery. No longer. When our fancy-schmancy intercom broke down the other day, we just whipped out a few cell phones and finished the show flawlessly. Hey, it works. Set the ringers to vibrate.

Cue 6 Go.

Fix the Sound

The good news about theater sound is that it *can* be done. And it can be done without breaking the bank. The bad news is it can be the hardest, most frustrating, most difficult thing to do well. What I mean is, I always wanted to just do it myself and get it over with, because the kids were experimenting and I already knew how to do it right; I teach *electronics* for heavens sake.

But you must remember, the sponsor can't do every single stage job. *Your* job is to see to it that things get done and to teach the crew the skills to do things for themselves. And, for a few years, sound wasn't my job at all, it was the job of a coworker of mine.

Until I moved into my new school, I had never, *never,* seen a theater with a good sound system. Even in some pro locations. For instance, what they got away with at the Improv in New York was a crime. At least, back when I spent my summers in New York . . . They had a Shure Vocalmaster and a couple of beat-up old speakers. Most schools make do with even less. And, truth be told, the new system at my (new) school is so overbuilt it's scary—24-channel mixer, four (4!) EQs, a digital effects unit, eight channels of 300-Watt sound; it's just nuts. You can't hear in the football stadium, or in the gym during basketball games, but in the theater there's enough power to run a third-world nation. I'm reminded of a college pal's comment, from when he sold stereos for a living. Usually he'd try to sell the top models, but he was great at recognizing when a potential sale was fizzling and would steer the customer towards a less-complicated, less-expensive system. "Less to go wrong," he'd say, with a toothy smile that inevitably closed the deal.

Well, someone at Blair popped for the whole shooting match. There's even an infrared headset system for the hard-of-hearing. All too complicated for everyday use. And, after all that, there's just one set of speakers, hung dead center, facing the *beams,* not the audience. And the control booth hangs from the ceiling, in a glassed-in booth, where the operator can't hear. Awful. I exaggerate but a little. We ended up dropping a snake from the booth to the back of the house and running everything from there. The CD changer couldn't be removed from its case, so I'd bring in mine from home. And the architect would proudly bring in new customers to see his great theater. Sometimes I just don't believe those guys.

I guess I shouldn't complain. I remember being thrilled at the idea of this great new system. I figured the days of lugging in my band equipment and my home stereo components were over. Didn't happen. In the end, I gave up and bought two of everything. Was I getting wistful for the old setup? No.

At my old school we had a mismatched, patched-together system that nevertheless could do miracles if the right sound guy was at the board. One of our best sound guys was a sound girl (named Pia), so no sex-stereotype whining, OK? Usually, though, I felt it wasn't being utilized correctly, and said so. Many times. I was right, of course, but I didn't always get my way. It took a few years to convince my coworkers to have the kids move the sound board to the back of the house, where the sound operator could actually hear. Once it was there, it became *their* idea, a little thing kids do that still chafes when I think about it.

DJ SOUND VS. LIVE SOUND

One of the most difficult points to get across to the kids is that live sound for the theater is nothing like setting up for a dance, where you are just playing records. Or CDs, pardon me. And it's different from setting up for bands. For most bands, the mics just stand there, in plain sight, and the performer is always behind the speakers. In theater we hide the mics, either in the scenery, in the curtains, or on the floor. Or we tape a radio-controlled mic onto a performer's head. And the performers move around a lot. Area mics are notoriously bad at picking sound from a distance. You can use them for recording, but try to turn up the volume and then the troubles start. Well, here we go . . .

SETTING UP A SYSTEM

Let's pretend for a minute that you've got *nothing,* no sound system at all. This actually happened to me when we moved into our new building. Our supercalifragilistic sound system had not yet been installed. I brought in parts from my band setup and my home stereo and selected items from the media center. We had a few mics we brought with us from the old school, and we rented a couple of things. And we had pretty good sound for *Les Misérables.* It was the play version, not the musical; musicals are tougher. Some folks don't mic straight plays at all. I suggest you do for two reasons: one, it helps people hear, and two, it's good practice for the musicals. Musicals *are* tougher.

In a normal public address setup, you've got a mic, an amplifier, and a speaker or two, all hooked up with the proper wiring. For the theater, you are going to add more mics and sound effects (on cassette or CD, or even on computer). You'll need a *mixer,* a device to adjust each and every source of sound. Before you begin, find out where the nearest Radio Shack is. OK? Good. Let's take these things one at a time.

SPEAKERS (EASIEST)

Get the best you can. What more can I say? You may have some nice speakers installed in the theater, yet unused. Check it out. We borrowed the speakers from the old gym on more than one occasion. A teacher or a friend might be in a rock-and-roll band; try the music department. Nicest would be two powerful units you'll put to the right and left of the audience, so you can have primitive stereo effects. These must be hooked up to a good amplifier with some pretty heavy-duty speaker wire. You can use 18-gauge zip cord in a pinch, but keep your eyes open for that big sale. If the speakers need special connectors, pick them up at Radio Shack.

Speakers have a polarity and must be hooked up correctly. Pay attention to the "+" and "–" markings on the speakers and on the amplifiers. If this is your first show, don't try to get fancy by hooking up extra speakers. For one thing, different manufacturers have different ideas about what positive (+) means; more importantly, adding speakers changes the total load on the amplifier and you can overdo it, so don't. Just use the two best-matched speakers you can get ahold of. Wire them correctly to the left and right channels of a reasonably powerful amplifier. Yes, you can use your home stereo.

THE AMPLIFIER

Pro amplifiers do work better for this kind of thing, but if your system doesn't work, bring in the home stereo. Provided it has a little kick. Set it up in the back of the house; you can take up a couple of the back rows if you have to. Lay in an uninterruptible power supply; that is, tape the extension cord down real well with gaff tape. Run the speaker wires in such a fashion as to be safe, all the way to the speakers, which you have strategically placed at each side of the proscenium, in plain sight. Leave a bunch of extra wire at the speaker end, since you're going to move the speakers around to find the best sound. Hook up a tape deck and make sure everything works so far.

Move around the theater to hear your favorite tape from every location in the place. Sit in a few seats, close your eyes. Are the speakers too far apart? There may not be much you can do about that, but you can twist them or tilt them if that helps. Move around the theater a bit and listen carefully from many different seats. Whatever you do, keep the speakers between the actors and the audience, cheating closer to the audience. If the speakers are too far "upstage," you'll have unending problems when you add mics.

THE MIXER

You can't run the whole show with a home stereo. It would be fun to watch someone try, though. They'd have to click the selector back and forth from CD to tape, and whenever they played a tape, the mics would cut out, and there's no place to hook up mics anyway. You need a mixer. *Do not* buy the coolest one you can find, even if you are dripping in money. Modern mixers have extra gadgets on them (like inserts and submasters) that we don't really need. Look for a 12- or 16-channel stereo board; rent one if you can't buy or borrow one for the show. And you probably shouldn't be buying one until you get a little better at this stuff, OK? Even a modest 8-channel board will have far too many knobs—like my toothy salesman buddy said, "Too many things to go wrong." You're going to have to learn what each knob is for, so keep it simple.

LINE OUT

Find the "line out," "rec out," or "out" connections on the back of the mixer. These are going to go into your stereo's "aux in" input, probably with two RCA jacks, which are regular old stereo connectors, like on a tape deck. If the connectors are wrong, then it's off to Radio Shack. Be sure to save your receipts. Set your stereo to "aux in," and put the volume a little less than half.

If your mixer is really heavy and you find an output that's labeled "spkr out," you have a *mixer amp* (a powered mixer) and you can take your home stereo back home. In this case, hook up the speakers directly to the mixer amp and you're on the air.

TURN EVERYTHING DOWN

Well, it's time to check out the mixer. Plug in the CD player (get the kind that plays one CD at a time), the tape player (you'll need CDs and tapes), and one mic. Plug them into the *mixer.* CDs and tapes are stereo and may take up two channels on some mixers. That's OK. Plug the mic into channel one. Keep the mic near you as you test out the system. Having a crew member read from a book is much better than sitting there saying, "Check, 1, 2, 3"; find a script or something. Plug a different kind of mic into channel two (for later). You don't need any mics on stage yet. Before you turn *anything* on, turn *everything on the mixer* down. All volume knobs, sliders, gain controls to zero. Careful: Sometimes zero is in the middle. Good. If you are using your home stereo, you don't want to turn that down. Everything else. This is to protect ears and electronic components. OK, turn the power on. Play a tape and a CD. You shouldn't hear anything, since you turned everything down. Good.

Try the mic. A mixer has two or three or more knobs that can shut a mic off. And there might be a switch on the mic! To the right of most mixers are the master controls. Find the mains—there are probably two, left and right. (If your mixer lacks these controls, you've got a DJ's mixer. You should probably replace it.) Your job is to correctly adjust all of these knobs and sliders to get good sound from the mic, and then from all of the different sound sources. Turn up the mains to half. You still shouldn't hear anything. Look carefully at every knob and button along channel one. Now play with the mic settings on channel one—nudge up the gain and the slider. The gain control is usually at the top of the mixer board controls. The slider is usually at the bottom. Move the controls slowly; you are trying to avoid getting too loud too quick. Look carefully at each knob and button on channel one. If you have turned all of the tone controls all the way down, you might not be able to hear anything. I never said do that. Well, I said it, but I didn't mean it. Sometimes there's a "mix" button. This will take a mic out completely; make sure it's on. If you have a whole lot of buttons that say things like "sub 1" and "aux. send," you're going to have to get the book out. But if luck is with you, you should be able to hear mic one. Time to learn how to *listen*.

GAIN

This is the one that's going to kill you. It seems that every last audio device you buy has a gain control. Adjust just one of them incorrectly and you'll never be able to get a good sound. In effect, gain is *volume,* and it's important to know *when* and *where* to turn the volume up. We're going to experiment with the gain, then set it right. Turn the mains way down, then turn the gain on channel one all of the way up. Have your helper read from the book into the mic, as you can't talk and listen at the same time. Adjust the slider. Turn down the mains if it's too loud. Keep the talking going. What you hear probably doesn't sound very good. We've turned the gain up too high, overloading the preamps in the mixer. This is bad. It is also the one thing that happens again and again and again in the theater. I'll help you set everything right.

Turn everything on the mixer to zero again. Not the tone controls. If you are using a home stereo turn it up to about 80 percent. I know this is scary and you'd never do it at home, but we're setting up the amplifiers to amplify without distortion. You shouldn't hear anything since everything else is turned down. Put the mains up about 80 percent, too. If the numbers say 1–10, put it on 8. If the numbers have a dB readout, put the sliders at 0 dB. Now bring the "mic one" slider to about 80 percent. You shouldn't hear anything. Why? Because the gain is off. The gain is the first volume control the signal meets in the mixer. We made sure the system worked, and we've set all of the volume knobs to their normal settings. All that remains is to slowly bring up the gain until the volume is right. Slowly. Your helper is reading aloud, perhaps from this very book. Bring up the gain slowly. Slowly. Good. You should have good volume and good tone, and there is wiggle room on each adjustment knob. You can adjust the tone now with the tone controls, and you can control the volume with nothing but the channel one slider. Too loud? Slowly slide down. Too quiet? Boost the slider, leave all of the other controls alone. If it's way too loud, lower the amplifier volume on your stereo a little bit.

This trick works. You are going to have to practice, and tweak, but use this technique for every sound source and you'll get good sound.

TO REVIEW

We hooked up a mixer to an amp and hooked up two speakers. We turned up the mains and the volume of our home stereo, if we're using one. We turned up the slider on mic one to its normal position, about eight-tenths of the way up. We slowly brought up the gain until we had good sound. Done. It does seem a little backwards (the kids have trouble with this technique), but you have to remember, it's not a home stereo. With a home stereo you seldom control the *inputs,* you just control the *output.*

Adults have a hard time with this technique, too. That's because when everything's set up (we're not really done yet), the kids'll play the music too loud, then somebody'll come around and say, "Turn it down," and they'll inevitably turn down the volume on the power amplifier. In our example, that would be the home stereo volume knob. Big mistake. When you turn down the power amplifier, the only place to get gain is the gain control, and we've already seen what happens when you turn that up too high.

TRY MICROPHONE 2

Make mic two a different kind of microphone. A real cheap one. Set everything up the same, and you'll notice the gain settings are different for the different mics. The tonal qualities are probably different, too. Starting with all tone controls centered, adjust mic one and mic two for their best sound. Adjust for approximately equal volume. When everything sounds as good as it can get, stop. Compare the gain settings. The sliders should be set equally, in their normal (80 percent) location; the gain settings should be different to compensate for the difference in the mics. Congratulations. Now you know what a gain control does. The tone controls may or may not be different, no big deal. Take a few minutes to check all of your available mic cords now, by swapping them out. Toss all of the bad ones into a box or something for later.

BY THE WAY

If you turn down all of the tone controls on a Fender Twin amp (a guitar amp), you'll get no sound. So graphic equalizers and tone controls can screw you up, just not now because you know about it. The one and only rule for sound: Set your levels correctly.

THAT REMINDS ME OF A FUNNY STORY

Sometime before I was hired to run sound, a strange situation arose at my old school. By the time I came along, it was gospel; kids who would do just about anything would never break this rule. Ed would climb on the battens without any regard to his safety, George would bring a slingshot to school and break all of the mirrors, but *no one* would turn the power amp volume above 4. Why? Because my predecessor had attached a piece of gaff tape to the console with the words, "Do *not* turn above 4."

I was crying about the awful sound. I actually brought my portable sound system in, set it up, and tried to show the adults and the kids how it was supposed to be done. I won over the music director (immediately), but not the other crew sponsor. He was very reluctant to change anything, including the volume on the power amp. I loved the guy—still do—but when he retired, the sound for the shows finally got better. Well, complaints about poor sound went down. And compliments went up. You be the judge.

I was telling this story to the kids who run our school's closed-circuit radio station when they asked me to help them get better sound. We poked around the brand-new system (bought because the original system sounded bad) and I told them about someone presetting the power amp too low at the old school. The words were just out of my mouth when I spied the telltale piece of tape, "Do not turn above 3." Déjà vu all over again. I changed the 3 to an 8, went back to the studio, and reset the gain on the preamp. Now the radio station sounds good, except for the music they play.

Go ahead, laugh. But I bet there's a piece of tape on your power amp in your theater that says the very same thing.

MIXOLOGY

To return to the board: Using our newly learned technique, turn the slider for the CD player to about 80 percent, then *slooowly* bring up the gain. CD players pump out the sound, so the gain setting will probably look a little low. That's OK—bring it up until you have good sound, then do the same for the cassette deck. The tapes were already playing, so you should hear both, plus the kids yelling in the mic. Take control, turn the mains down. Not the power amp, the mains. The mains shut everything off. Bring 'em back up. Play just the CD for a while. Find the pan control. Move it, and get left and right action. Fun, fun, fun. If the left and right are backwards, swap the "line out" or "speaker out" connectors.

CD

CASS

STEREO OR POWER AMP

Simple Mixer/Amp Setup

TEST THE MICS

We will cover microphones from the simple to the complex:

➤ Mic in a stand
➤ The same mic handheld
➤ Floor mics
➤ Gooseneck mics
➤ Radio handheld
➤ Radio clip-on

MIC STANDS

If you are going to use a mic on a stand, for an emcee or for announcements or somesuch, make sure the stand is fully assembled and properly adjusted. If it has a heavy weight on the bottom, be certain that it is screwed on tight. And check the hand lever adjustment—too tight and someone won't be able to move it, too loose and the mic will slowly slide downwards in the most embarrassing fashion. This happened to my bass player during a "Battle of the Bands." The emcee left the mic stand knob a little loose and the mic slipped down just as he began to sing. We came in fifth.

HANDHELD

When an announcer or singer takes the mic off the stand, you have got to have someone awake at the sound board. If the talent covers the mic with his hand it'll squeal (feedback); if he moves into the house or too near one of the speakers—same problem. The sound operator needs to be ready to fade down that mic—it's the only way to stop the feedback. The worst part is when the mic starts to feedback, a beginner will instinctively cover it up with one hand, making things worse. Have every announcer practice with the mics. At school we had a "mic practice day" for student government candidates and talent-show announcers. Practice, practice, practice.

FLOOR MICS

Some folks call floor mics PZMs. I call them PIAs and suggest you throw them out. Or go put them on a desktop somewhere for videoconferencing; that's what they are made for. See, picking up sound for recording or tele-conferencing is very, very different from picking up sound for "sound rein-forcement." These floor mics are super sensitive and don't reject footsteps as well as they should. If you use them you run the risk of increasing the noise, but not the voices. We did attach a few to sheets of Plexi and hung them from the valence, to pretty good effect. Better to use gooseneck mics.

GOOSENECK MICS

I have found a pretty good gooseneck mic, the Peavey ALM 16S Podium mic. We used several in a show recently, and the gooseneck picks up better than any floor mic I've ever used. Plus you can hide 'em in the scenery and you can hang them from the electrics. When you place or hang mics you have to twist them *just so*—so they point upstage at least a little bit. Gooseneck mics are perfect for this; you may need to string up a little fishing line to keep them from twisting around. The ALM 16S isn't avail-able anymore, so you'll have to shop around for a similar model.

RADIO MICS

Radio mics are great—well, when they are working. Most come with a handheld mic (transmitter), a clip-on *lavaliere* mic (which is another transmitter), and one receiver. Don't turn on both transmitters at the same time, OK? When you are using the handheld, it'll act just like a handheld wired mic, except when the battery is loose or dying. Lay in a huge stock of batteries—always, always, always put in a fresh battery for a show. You'd be surprised at how many times the crew will put a battery in backwards—nerves, I guess. If a radio mic isn't working, that's the first thing to check.

RADIO CLIP-ON (LAVALIERE) MICS

Clip-on radio mics are a necessity for musicals, but if they are not used correctly, they will ruin your show. And they are very touchy, and they are easy to break. You're going to have to use them, so let's start practicing. First, you probably aren't going to clip on the clip-on mics. On television, you'll see newscasters and talk-show guests with the mic clipped to their dress or jacket. This is fine when the talent is sitting still, but no good for us. Our talent is moving around, dancing even, and a clipped-on mic will pick up every movement of the fabric. Plus, the sound levels will vary whenever an actor moves his head.

You have to attach the lavaliere mic somewhere where it will stay still relative to the actor's mouth. Lots of times this means hiding the mic in someone's hair, with bobby pins or tape. Over the ear sometimes works; hide the cord behind and tape everything down really well. You could try latex and spirit gum if you want; I think that's probably overkill. There are some very fancy mics available that sit on the ear and end on the cheek; you'll see them on Broadway, but they are *muy* expensive. Do the best you can.

More than attaching the mics, you have to practice *using* the mics. This is battery and time intensive, but your sound operators need to develop a gentle touch on the faders when using these mics. As two miked performers approach each other, the sound levels change, and when someone starts to sing, there's almost always an adjustment needed. Time spent here in rehearsals and practice will pay off big time; it's probably the single most important and overlooked aspect of technical theater.

One little detail. When you are watching a TV talk show look for the little clip-on mics. Sometimes you'll see people wearing *two*! That's how unreliable they are.

MORE ON MIC CLIPS

Full-sized mic clips are easy to find. That's a good thing, as they are also easy to break. The mic clips for the radio mics are tiny and get lost or broken very easily. These are hard to replace. You'll probably end up using hairpins as temporary mic clips here. Try a local cosmetics counter—you may find a little-bitty clip that can help you out. Also, these mics can be surreptitiously taped right at the hairline. Done well, the little mic is very hard to see. Done well. Usually the mics are placed in a hurry and stick out like a sore. Take your time. Try to get the radio mics out of sight in a performer's hair or something.

WHAT MIC TO BUY

I love EV mics for their great gain and anti-feedback properties. The only trouble is we've broken two, and that is unsatisfactory. If I were you, I'd borrow mics until I find a brand I like, then stick exclusively with that brand. There is no sense in collecting a hodgepodge of different brands and styles of mics—it just makes it harder to set the gain and tone controls. As you might suspect, expensive mics sound better than cheap mics. Listen and check out the setup in other theaters, but don't fall into the trap of buying a mic (or a sound system) just because you heard it work well somewhere else. Whatever you do, don't trust the salesman, especially if he has a toothy grin and an amiable attitude. Get a loaner, or rent some mics until you find something you like.

STEREO

There is a big debate as to whether or not to use stereo in live theater. As your audience is pretty well spread out, some people may not benefit from any stereo effects. My predecessor advocated center-hung monophonic speakers, and that's what we ended up with. My take is: Use what you've got. If you have to set it up yourself, set it up in stereo and use the pan controls when you want some kind of directionality from the speakers. At all other times, just center the "pan" or "balance" controls, and place the speakers by ear for optimum results.

PAN

On fancy mixers, you won't find a *balance* control; instead they call it a *pan* control, but it does the same thing. If you want a sound effect to come from stage right, set the pan control appropriately. You may find the pan works backwards because the sound operator is facing the opposite way from the talent. Not to worry; with a little practice everything will sound fine. If it really bugs you, you can swap the "line out" connections.

THE WORLD'S BEST AUDIO TRICK FOR DANCERS

A computer-savvy technician can put pre-recorded dance steps onto a computer and then slow down the tempo without changing the pitch of the music. This is a tremendous help to the choreographer as folks learn their dance steps. We slowed down all the fast numbers in *West Side Story* to 95, 90, 85, and 80 percent. When everyone was up to speed, they started dancing with the orchestra. This saves a lot of time, and it couldn't be done before the advent of computers.

Let's shift gears and do a little soldering.

SOLDERING

First, soldering is not welding. I'm leaving welding out. You need welding, call somebody. I think I welded three things in nine years at Blair, so it's not a skill that you need to cultivate, unless you like that kind of thing. Another guy came in to weld the broken metal doors back onto our light cage. Welding is fun (acetylene welding is the most fun) and pretty easy to learn; you just probably won't need to weld to built stage sets.

Soldering is different. It's a brazing technique that bonds metals together, but does not actually melt the original pieces like welding does. Soldering can be undone, unlike a weld. And soldering is usually done on a much smaller scale. You are going to need to know how to solder electric circuits and wires, and maybe plumbing, too.

OK, NOT PLUMBING

Plumbing involves soldering with a torch, special plumbing solder, and copper pipes. You are unlikely to need to do this kind of soldering in the theater, since you'll be able to use hoses and plastic pipe for the fake pumps and fountains you may build. If you have this sort of equipment laying around in the theater, lock it up, to be used only by trained personnel. And get a little training if you actually need to use the thing. Soldering plumbing, like welding, is beyond the scope of this book.

SOLDERING AUDIO CABLES AND MAKING CIRCUIT REPAIRS

I just spent a few hours fixing audio cables, trying to save the school a few bucks. These cables are expensive, so treat them nice and fix 'em when they break. For a while I thought myself wealthy enough to throw a broken cable away instead of fixing it. My rationale was that the repair would be undependable. The truth was I was just being lazy. My parents taught me well, though, and I never actually threw the cables out—I just put them in a big (really big) box of broken cables. Sure enough, in leaner times, I'd set up my soldering station, dip into the box, and fix a needed cable, or four or five . . .

Well, sometimes, when a crew member made a repair, it *was* undependable. So if you are not a *'lectronik genius,* or if the kids aren't, you may find a repair itself having to be repaired. Time for a bitter smile, a shrug or two, and a second repair. Perhaps this is a job you shouldn't relegate to beginners. Let's set up a little soldering station and try to get these cords fixed.

Audio cables are tricky little beasts. They have to be strong enough to withstand the rigors of stage use and they have to be flexible. They have to carry a low-level electrical signal in the audio frequencies with little loss, and they must shield the precious signal from interference. They must be able to be disconnected easily. And they must be cheap, except they aren't. The cable you'll use (and repair) the most is the one for a *low impedance* microphone. Low impedance just means the system is built and wired in such a way as to reduce signal loss. And it means there are three connections. Cross 'em, or disconnect one at either end of the cable, and you've got problems. Usually they break right at the end, through being tugged on too much.

THE SOLDERING STATION

Collect up some baby screwdrivers, nice wire cutters, needle-nose pliers, a really bright light, a magnifying glass if you think you'll need it, a soldering iron, and some solder. I use Weller irons. And I have this really cool battery-operated one from Chicago Electric, but I don't think it's available anymore. Get some black tape—electrician's tape. And you'll probably need a knife or a (real) razor blade. A wet sponge and a small file or emery board are nice for keeping the tip of the soldering iron clean. And, believe it or not, you should use safety goggles. Solder is melted tin and lead (almost four hundred degrees), and it can go flying, so goggle up. And don't wear shorts while soldering.

Before beginning, make sure the very tip of the soldering iron is first *tight*, and second, *clean*. Arrange a way to keep the iron safe when you are not actually holding it, as it can give a painful burn. They sell soldering iron holders; buy one. I usually set everything up on the dining room table, or the coffee table if I want to watch TV, but I'm single. If you do this, at least put something down to protect the table. Collect up all of your bad cables (in the box) and set up a way to test them, either right now as you fix them, or soon, before you need them. Open up a cable end (our example will be the ubiquitous mic cable described above) with the little screwdriver. Surprise! Some of the screws may go in instead of out. This was done thoughtfully by an unknown engineer so you don't lose the screw. As you disassemble, make a mental note of where everything goes. And do only one cable at a time, OK?

There should be a part of the (disassembled) connector that is on the big black wire itself. Leave it there! It's no fun to reassemble everything only to find the cover is not on the cord. Look carefully at the three "wires" connected to the three little posts inside the mic connector. If the wires touch each other, that's bad. If one or more wires are disconnected, that's bad. If one or more wires are *almost* disconnected, that too is bad. Unless you are really talented, or lucky, the easiest thing to do is take the whole thing apart and redo all three connections. If you just tug on the loose wire and resolder it, it will be a teeny bit shorter than the others and will break again in spite of the strain relief. Take note of what wire goes where, pry open (or unscrew) the strain relief, cut all three wires off, shorten the cord six inches (a knife comes in handy here), and trim the black plastic cover and a bit of insulation off of the two real wires.

You'll notice that the third "wire" has no insulation, unless you count the black plastic cover itself. This is not a mistake. This spiral or braided cable completely surrounds the two signal wires and is the "shield" that protects the signals inside the other wires. It is just as important as they are; it just does a different job. Plus it makes the cable stronger. Just twist the shield up tight (right-thinking people twist everything *clockwise*), tight, tight, tight, until it looks like a little wire. And be super-diligent that none of these little bitty wires unwrap to touch the others.

By the way, this "shield" is connected to the "ground" (yes, it's the real ground) and dumps unwanted signals. And the wires are multi-stranded to be flexible. So there you go.

Time to *un*solder. Pick up the broken mic connector and inspect it carefully. You are going to have to remove all of that old solder in order to do a good job with the new solder. I once actually had to stop a student from trying to reuse solder. There's a reason why it can't be done. Get your hot soldering iron right up on one of the little posts. The old solder will melt, but it's not going to fall out by itself, so quick now, smack it on the tabletop. Hope it didn't land on your leg (I told you not to wear shorts). This seemingly primitive technique works fine. They make de-soldering tools, and de-soldering "wick," but the heat and purge works; just wear those goggles! The little connector may get hot, so hold it with the needle-nose if you have to. Get as much solder out of the three little holes as you can. Good. Put the soldering iron *in its holder*.

Trim up the shortened cord so each wire properly fits in each connector. Time spent here will pay off in a moment, when you actually have to solder the parts together. If one wire is a little long, fix it; if there's too much insulation removed from a wire, redo everything. And don't despair about shortening the cord. Cut off six inches or so, just in case there is a weak spot near the end. Remember, the cord has been misused—probably stretched—so cut away the bad part. Test fit everything.

Before you reassemble you should *tin* each of the three wires. Tinning a wire puts a little bit of solder on it, sort of like a primer. This will speed up the real soldering. One way is to simply hold each bare tip of wire onto the soldering iron while the soldering iron is resting on the table. Add a dollop of solder, the soldering iron melts the solder, and the wire soaks it up due to capillary action. Cool. Overheat, and the insulation will melt. Not so cool. Underheat, and the solder won't flow. Definitely uncool. If it doesn't seem to want to work, it could be a dirty soldering iron tip (the tip should look shiny and new, with fresh solder on it), a dirty wire (it happens), lack of heat, or bad solder.

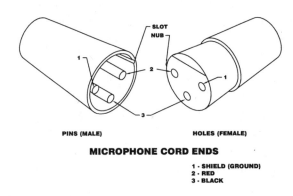

MICROPHONE CORD ENDS

1 - SHIELD (GROUND)
2 - RED
3 - BLACK

The Mic Connector

If the copper wires themselves are dingy, you're going to have trouble—the wires just won't want to accept the solder. You can try cutting back a little more, scraping them with your knife, or "washing" them with fresh solder, but it may be a no-go. Some audio cables sort of rot like that. Try again, then just pitch it. You're not that poor. But save the connector; you're not that rich, either.

If you are having real trouble, you just may have some bad solder. There are two ways to get bad solder. When I taught electronics, bad solder used to come in some of the electronic kits. Maybe it was just too old—whatever, it just didn't work. It took me a while to catch on; now I just throw it away and use Kester. The second way is more insidious. If you get a hold of plumber's solder, it will seem to work fine, but it's acidic and will later ruin your cords. Bad show. So pay attention, and don't try to economize too much. A lifetime supply of electronic solder costs about eleven bucks. Kester. Or Multicore. Whatever you get make sure it's *rosin core solder.* And get the thin stuff.

Time to reassemble. You did write down which wire goes where, didn't you? Generally speaking, the shield goes on pin 1, which you have to squint to find, but it's there. Place the tinned shield into the connector (not just beside it), and solder it. Hmm. Everything moved, didn't it? Soldering is a difficult job that takes three or four hands. As most of us only have two, you are probably going to have to clamp or tape the parts down while you manipulate the soldering iron in one hand and the solder in the other. I have soldered things together holding the solder in my teeth, but I don't recommend it. Try to arrange things so that nothing moves around too much (movement of molten solder is a no-no), and hold the shiny, clean, hot, freshly soldered soldering iron tip right on the connection. Don't wiggle it around. The connector should get real hot real quick. Daub in a little solder; it should actually soak in and wick up along the wire and the connector. Take away the heat (and the solder) and let the thing cool before you move it.

SOME DETAILS

Solder comes with this rosin stuff built inside it. Rosin is a flux; it works to clean the connections and to allow the molten tin (37 percent) and lead (63 percent) to flow. It's the stuff that smokes when you are actually soldering. Without it the solder becomes crumbly and won't adhere to anything. Bad, bad, bad. That's why you can't solder by just reheating an old solder joint. All of the flux is gone. So just daub in some fresh solder and off you go.

BY THE WAY

When I taught a high-reliability soldering course for a cable manufacturing company in Rockville, Maryland, I tried to find out if the smoke from the flux is bad for you. Even using the power of the Internet, I couldn't find any source that unequivocally stated that it does you harm. Lately, however, solder manufacturers have added a warning about the fumes and the lead in solder, so open a window.

TWO MORE WIRES

These next two wires are supposed to be red and black, but they probably aren't, so we must pretend they are red and black. Some unscrupulous manufacturers save a penny by not color-coding the wires, another petty aggravation that we will bear silently, along with never having the right kind of screwdriver handy. If you have to you can use an ohmmeter to figure out which wire is which. Solder the red wire to pin 2 and the black to pin 3. If you properly peeled away the plastic insulation there should be a very, very small amount of exposed wiring on pins 2 and 3. If you have the least concern that the bare wires may touch each other, you should weave a little strip of electrical tape in there to prevent it. It's the mark of an amateur, but it *will* prevent short circuits. Scrunch up the wires a little bit before you tighten the strain relief, usually by crimping with pliers, sometimes using screws. The strain relief is supposed to take the strain off of the delicate little connectors you just soldered; if the strain relief pulls at them, you've done something wrong. By the way, many times a cord is weakened right behind the strain relief. That's why we shortened the cord six inches.

REASSEMBLE, DONE

Hope you haven't lost any parts. Test the cord as soon as possible, just so you know.

SOLDERING OTHER THINGS

As you learn more and more about electronics, you will be able to repair more than just cords. Sometimes circuit boards crack and must be resoldered. Eventually you'll have to fix the radio mics, an almost constant source of aggravation. At least they now make detachable mics, especially nice for the clumsy among us. In time you'll find out that guitar cords are shielded too (the shield is the *ring* and the only signal wire the *tip*—this jargon from the telephone company). You'll learn that speaker wires are different from guitar cords (they sort of look the same). So much to learn.

THE KIDS CAN DO THIS

When I wasn't actually teaching electronics classes I never had a stage crew student skilled enough to solder anything—what had happened was, I had stopped training them. It was just easier to replace the cords, or do it myself. I got shown up by Roger, an actor who came in one afternoon and rewired all of the radio transmitters (the mic wires break from being stretched). He quietly, patiently, and quickly finished the work that had been piling up for months. So the kids can do it, if they know or are taught how.

ANYBODY NEED ANYTHING EPOXIED?

Just like *epoxying*—the act of using epoxy—you should do all of your soldering in one marathon session. There's a "touch" to it, and you should complete the work while the iron is hot. Sorry. Bad pun.

CUE 7 *Go.*

Publicity

In a perfect world, the stage crew sponsor wouldn't have to worry about show publicity. In the real world the sad fact is, if you don't make sure it gets done it won't happen, and the show will suffer. First look around and try to find a coworker to take the sponsorship. You might get lucky and find some grown-up, qualified help. This is easier in community theater where the jobs are more compartmentalized. If this doesn't work, start recruiting some kids into the publicity crew. Look for volunteers.

It's usually pretty easy to find a volunteer who *says* she wants to work on publicity; once you find her, it's pretty hard to get her to actually *do* publicity. Even with the best of intentions, a beginner usually doesn't possess the wherewithal to handle publicity alone. Combine the natural lack of experience with the reluctance of most media outlets to push a high school or a community theater show, and you have a recipe for disaster. Well, not disaster, but no publicity can stop a show in its tracks.

There are two kinds of publicity for a high-school show: in-house and in the community. *In-house* means in the school—announcements, posters, gimmicks; any trick to get the word out to the students and staff about the show. In the community, publicity can be more difficult. Many shop owners will happily put up a poster or two (though some won't); many newspapers will publish information about the show. You just have to make it easy for them. This means writing good press releases and sending them out in a timely fashion. Most students will need a hand with this, and even the best press release will be ignored from time to time. Chalk it up to profit and loss, but never stop trying to push the show.

One of the most difficult steps is to "know" the show soon enough to meet everyone's deadlines. Just reading the script may not be enough; you have to add a couple of details about the show to make your press release stand out from the flood of PR material coming into any newsdesk. And you have to start early. Some papers only come out monthly. The deadline may be two weeks before that, so you need to send things out more than six weeks early. I've been involved with a few productions where we didn't even know the *name* of the show six weeks early, so you see how this can be a problem.

FIRST PRESS RELEASE

Getting publicity for your show, especially outside of the school, is a tremendous challenge. It's a rare student who will want to spend the time to do this right. I set up a little system using a database and two press releases. This got us into most of the local papers; even the *Washington Post* would list our shows. Begin by assembling a complete collection of all the addresses and contact information for local papers and radio and TV stations. This is a lot of work, so you should prepare a computer database because you have to do it for every show. When the database is set up correctly, you can print out mailing labels, and, if you are really good at this, you can have the computer print out custom letters for each person on the list. This is called a *mail merge*. A good database will include the following:

- ➤ Contact Person
- ➤ Title
- ➤ Name of Publication
- ➤ Address
- ➤ City, State, Zip
- ➤ Fax Number
- ➤ Email Address
- ➤ Contact Number
- ➤ Deadline Date

Your publicity chief should be able to handle all of this, but many times she won't know her way around a database. I didn't either, until I took a class. Anyway, proofread the list very carefully. At the beginning of the production, print up a general press release with all of the necessary information:

- ➤ The Theater
- ➤ The Show
- ➤ The Dates
- ➤ The Times
- ➤ The Prices
- ➤ The Address

Add a little about the show (*A peasant milkman and his mouthy wife . . .*) and *your* contact phone number for interviews. Get this out early, in case someone decides to do a feature on your show. Have the crew fold, stamp, etc., so they get the hang of things. Mail the mail, and fax the thing to every fax number you have. Shoot out the e-mails. Then set your folks to work on two things: updating the database and *sending out a second press release.* They should call each contact number, check addresses and names (you'd be surprised at the turnover here), and check fax numbers (they change); *then* update the computer database. If you wait, not sending out the first press release, you run the risk of missing early deadlines.

The second press release should read like a news item. That way, a harried editor can crib off of it, or use it whole, and you'll actually get the publicity you desire. Include a little blurb mentioning that the kids put this together and ask if it was helpful (include your phone number). Some editors will call with helpful advice and may decide to run a little story on your hard-working stage crew.

We did two big shows a year, so we did this twice a year. Every time there were corrections to the database and some mail came back. Imagine that.

PRESS PASS

Print up some special press pass–type tickets and slip them into the second press release. Send to radio and TV stations as well as all the news-papers. Eventually, someone will actually use the press passes, and you'll make a new friend who's in a position to give you lots of free publicity. Good thinking.

UPDATE THE DATABASE

Anyone can make database corrections, but you must check them for accuracy.

SECOND PRESS RELEASE

Send out the second press release about three weeks before the show opening. Again, if you wait, you'll miss deadlines.

POSTER ART

The chances are pretty good that you are going to print your show posters on some kind of copier. Look around to find a copier that prints 11 × 17 inches. This sheet is twice the size of regular old paper and stands out—especially when you buy color stock to print the posters on. The posters need all of the show information. I suggest you print out all of the *type*—the writing part of the poster—on a computer. You can cut and paste the printing the old-fashioned way or do it all on a computer. Heck, you can print *color* posters from your computer nowadays if you have the money or the machine. . . .

For school shows, the art should be student art. This is great practice and exposure for the budding artist. In community theater, you may have artists available, and you may not. If you do, count yourself lucky. When you print up posters on a copier, there's just one little thing to remember. Be careful not to allow too much black space, or you'll jam up the copier. Even the newest, best copiers can't seem to fill a solid black space without jamming. Give the artist the right-sized paper, have her pencil in the art; then, upon approval, ink it in, trot on down to the Kinko's, and post the posters. Poster art that is not good enough for the posters is probably perfect for the program, or for a tee shirt. More detail on this whole process is included in the T-shirt section below.

ROUGH PROGRAM

As I am a big advocate of having the students do the work, you have to find a student typist for the program. You'll also have to go in after him and correct all of the mistakes. Also give him a little lesson on setting margins. A community theater program will probably have more advertising than a high-school show and will probably be sent out to be printed. If you do it yourself using a copier, check three times to make sure the pages are coming out right. Use any real program or playbill as a guide for your layout. And pay for fancy paper for the cover sheet. It's a small expense, but the program is the first part of a show the patron sees upon entering the theater, and it makes an impression.

Once in a while we go a little crazy with the program. If extra staff is available, you can go shill for ads, and include bios for everyone involved. I was very cruel in this regard and wouldn't allow the kids to print any of that "R U 4 me eggplant?" kid stuff in their bios. Perhaps they'll thank me later. Print up enough to last you, keep them safe, and you are home free. Well, you're home.

PUBLICITY PHOTOS

Cheesy publicity photos are an embarrassment and are better left undone. I have seen some nice displays of "snapshots," some taken with a disposable camera, so it's not the method or the equipment that's at fault. It's the composition. With all of the props, costumes, and theater lighting available, any journeyman photographer should be able to knock out some great publicity photos for any show. With the advent of digital photography, you can just shoot and shoot at no added expense. Costume-fitting day seems a natural for this kind of work. Take a little extra time (ha!) and snap away. If the photos come out lousy, find another photographer.

After you take the photos, you have to *use* them; we have boxes and boxes of unused photos laying around backstage.

THE OUTDOOR SIGN

All of us have driven by a school and seen a hand-painted sign promoting some event or another. In all honesty, they are usually hard to read and seldom bring in any customers. If you think about the sign as a vital part of the set and take a few extra moments to design lettering that can be read from a moving car, you may find your sign brings in more than a few customers, which makes it all worthwhile.

Keep the text as brief as possible. You can omit information like "The John W. Kaluta School of Performing Arts presents . . . " It will take up too much of your valuable billboard space. Give the reader the title, days, and dates. Include the show times. The price isn't needed, but if it fits in. . . .

You will usually make a 4 × 8' plywood sign. Use ½" or thicker plywood and be sure to secure it well. And put it where people can actually see it. Stand where the cars are (be careful) and make sure you've got a great line of sight. Near a stoplight is good. On school grounds, so no one hassles you about illegal signs. You can make the sign with the interior latex paint you use for the set; it doesn't have to last a particularly long time. Be sure to remove the sign when the show is over.

Use a computer to get a better layout. If you don't, you'll end up with one of those signs where everything does not quite fit, something like this. Draw a $4 \times 8"$ box on the computer screen (the paper will be in *landscape* view). Add text in text boxes. Poster fonts are good; vary the size and font until it looks great on paper. Don't fall for an *ALL CAPS* style if it can't be read. Show the design to a few people—can it be easily read? Hold the paper far away. Can it still be easily read? Wear your glasses; we're not checking your vision here, just the lettering layout. When everything is perfect, burn a transparency, project it onto a sheet of plywood, chalk it out, and paint it in.

If you don't go the transparency route (and you should), you can lay out a bunch of parallel chalklines and chalk in the text before you paint. Take great care not to compress the words on the right side of the sign. Or the left, if you are writing in Arabic. Or on the bottom if you are writing in Japanese. Be sure to calculate for the space between each line. This used to be called the *slug space,* on computers it's *line spacing.*

If you are faced with an unusual spot for the sign, make an unusual sign. You can attach a long, skinny (14" or so) vertical sign to a nearby telephone pole—just don't go near the wires. You can make several signs to place along a long driveway or shoulder, à la the Burma Shave signs from the thirties (do a Web search if you've never seen these). Photograph each sign and place it in your scrapbook. Before long, you'll have a set that can be perused for ideas, and the poor signs will stick out like a sore thumb, helping you prove to your kids that it's worth it to take the time to do it right.

Anchor the sign securely and safely. Real post holes, maybe two feet deep, and 2×4s for support. The vertical supports should be 7' apart, and 10' long. Remember, two feet of that goes in the ground. You usually can't leave the supports up year round, but, by all means, use the same holes every year. By the way, if your signs are good, people will want to borrow them—that is, paint over your sign and advertise their event. Actually, they'll ask you to do it, or to have your kids do it . . . it's up to you to decide how cooperative you want to be here. You can always cover a sign with another (¼") sheet of plywood—less total work, gets the job done.

Be sure to put something extra on the sign for added interest. A cut-out, painted Annie, for instance, for *Annie,* a Siamese skyline silhouette for *The King & I.* We had three-dimensional rotating dice for *Guys & Dolls.* Every evening I'd go out and rotate the dice by hand. A little attached sign saying "*Next week!*" or "*This week!*" or "*Closing tonight!*" is a nice touch. And get the sign up *before* opening night. That's why you made a calendar, remember?

T-SHIRTS

If the production is big enough, custom T-shirts can be ordered and worn by all cast and crew. Any local silkscreen shop will be willing to run a modest-sized order for about a $50 set-up fee and maybe $9 a shirt. So charge $10 and plan to break even. Students will resent it if you try to make money off of T-shirt sales. At Blair we usually trolled for student art; even when it is not the best, the authenticity makes a difference. With the best will in the world, you might not get student art in time. Once a parent pitched in with a great design, and once the T-shirt had only text, white ink on black cotton—very popular. You can save about a buck a shirt buying the 50/50 cotton/poly blend; if you have time, you can take orders for sizes. Otherwise, just order all XL. By the way, if you are quoted prices twice as high, you'd better shop around some more. Some shops just gouge, some serve the customer.

I must caution you that buying too many T-shirts for any event is extremely risky; the chances of selling them to patrons is usually quite slim. Our method was to show off the artwork, take cash orders from students in the production, check the teacher grapevine (good for a few orders), then call in the total. Most good shops can fill a simple T-shirt order in about three days, so try to back-time the order for arrival during the tech rehearsal. The shirts generate a lot of excitement when they arrive, which is useful after a grueling technical rehearsal. Of course, a few folks who did not order will want to buy a shirt when the rest arrive; you can add a few shirts to your order or order a second run or stiff 'em. If you make a second run you can charge the kids a little more. That'll teach 'em.

There are a couple of problems you must deal with when ordering custom T-shirts. The biggest is handling the money. School rules with regard to collecting money get real complicated. There are receipts to give out, deposits to make—it seems like way too much trouble, and it is. Just when the paperwork was finished and the check was complete and countersigned by five or even six people, along would come some kid with some cash to change the order, which would change the receipt, which changed everything. Cut a new check? Forget it. The school just couldn't move fast enough to make a T-shirt order in these conditions. So I usually kept the T-shirt orders off the books and handled the whole thing in cash. Don't ask anyone if you can do this, just do it. Adam, one of the orchestra kids, said it best: "Your T-shirt is your receipt."

Pick a shop close to work—getting the original artwork to the shop and picking up the finished shirts can be a hassle. I went at lunchtime. A friend with a car (and some time on his hands) is a big help here. But you can only rely on your friends for so much.

Silkscreen shops, especially the smaller ones, have certain things they can and cannot do. Try to keep the image, preferably student-drawn original art, to 12" × 12". Many shops can print bigger and fancier, but all shops can print 12" × 12". Stick to one color, especially the first few times. White on black is always striking, and very theatrical. The artwork cannot have any thin lines; the ink will stick in the screen. You must tell your artists to be bold and blocky. Use computer-generated text unless the quality of the handmade text is high. Poster Bodini and Cooper Black are good typefaces for silkscreen printing. Green ink on a gray shirt makes a great combination (especially for *Into the Woods*). We were less than thrilled with our white shirts, even when we had a multicolor run on white. Black on red is great if the design and the show (*The King & I* perhaps) warrant it.

WEARING THE SHIRTS

The T-shirts are the best advertisement for your show, because they walk around and talk. Encourage (can you require?) your troupe to wear the shirt every single day until the show closes. Try to get them to wash it every single night. This is particularly cool in a high school. Something happens in a school when fifty or more people are walking around wearing the same uniform, just like the football team should do every Friday. Teachers and students take note and excitement builds. People can tell who to ask about the show, and they will ask. Watching the buzz build is a great part of the fun. The students don't know any of this, so you must use your influence to get them to wear the shirts and advertise the show. It's funny—after the show they'll never stop wearing the shirts, but you'll have to order them to wear 'em before the show. Kids.

CUE 8 *Go.*

RehEArsALs, ANd LifE

Before you know it the cast will be on stage, rehearsing. This creates a couple of problems for you, and for them, as you probably have no other place to work. You have to reach some kind of agreement with the director and the other staff members as to when you can be noisy when you are sharing the space. I always felt it was good for the actors to have to practice while we were still hammering and sawing away; if they can concentrate through that, they'll have no problems later. As you might suspect, my directors usually felt differently about this.

Still, you both have to get your work done, and somewhere along the line you'll have to share the stage. Up until the technical rehearsal, I allowed the crew kids to work on the set while rehearsal was going on; the director would call on us to make a scene change when needed. After the tech rehearsal, it becomes more difficult to "work," as the crew kids are needed to practice the scene changes and set the cues. If they could break away during these rehearsals to finish painting or make repairs, fine; but the noisier work had to wait until rehearsal was over. This means your crew has to stay much, much longer than the cast—but of course you knew that already.

WORKING WITH THE KIDS

Drama kids are just like any other kids, only more so. I was fortunate to have worked with a pretty good bunch of kids for nine straight years. Even so, there were a few, um, situations, and a few colorful and memorable kids that I had to deal with. I had a fair amount of problems, some from pushing too hard, some from simple misunderstandings, and some arising from dishonesty on the part of the student. Dishonesty is the toughest one because you feel that, after all you have done for them, here's some kid lying to you or stealing from you. Lying and stealing got you kicked off of crew for a year, whether I liked you or not.

Drama kids are sensitive, just like all kids. A few were convinced I didn't like them. Generally they were wrong about that. I liked them fine. Most of them. Over the years, though, I did have a few kids on crew that I wasn't particularly fond of. It happens, sometimes from something they did, sometimes for no easily explained reason. I might be kidding myself, but I think that the kids I didn't "like" never even knew it, because I tried my best to treat them the same as all of the other kids. Don't get me wrong, if they *did something* I didn't like, they heard about it; I just tried not to play favorites.

Once in a while I wondered if the crew kids liked me, and, to tell you the truth, I really don't know. I pushed them pretty hard, and a couple of times I made a kid cry. Not on purpose—I just didn't see it coming and pushed a little too hard. I know there was some resentment because, like all kids, sometimes the crew just wanted to hang out and not work. I wasn't having that because they ended up wasting *my* time, and the show suffered. My emphasis was on producing better shows. The goal was to hear "Ahhh" when the curtain opened and to have the audience leave surprised and impressed at the quality of the production. Some kids didn't see it that way and joined crew for laughs. Most of them came around, and I still get comments (and thank-yous) when the kids see shows at other schools. So, I know they learned a lot about themselves, and what they were capable of, and left school better prepared for their future, and that's what it's all about.

DRAMA CLIQUES

Do what you can to break down cliques between the drama kids and the crew, the musicians, and the rest of the school. Kids like to be among friends, and they need to feel accepted, but generally they carry it too far. We fought this by making the actors sweep. And mop. Actually, we just encouraged them to help out, and encouraged the crew kids to try out for the cast. And we developed a very nice tradition of placing Hershey's Kisses backstage in the dressing rooms on opening night. Kisses from the stage crew. It's difficult to exclude someone who is giving you candy. Recently my director forced a change on this, as chocolate makes a nasty stain on costumes. Now it's "Hard candy from the hard-working stage crew." A nice sentiment, but I think we have to work a bit on the catchy phrase.

RIVALRIES

Sometimes cliquishness extends beyond excluding kids socially into an out-and-out rivalry, complete with poisoning friendships and choosing sides . . . it's ugly. We had this plenty of times in the cast, and a few times on crew, too. Kids will go so far as to quit rather than work with a rival. The best strategy here is the preemptive strike. Usually you can see these things coming a mile away. Try to intervene while there is still a chance of patching things up. If it's really bad, threaten to kick both kids off crew. That usually causes a little introspection and sometimes prevents trouble.

OFFENDING THE KIDS

One thing is for certain: It's easy to upset a kid, and sometimes very hard to calm him down later. Most of the time this is due to stress. The kids want to put on a great show as much as you do and may not agree with the way you are doing things. And, of course, they might just be right. It's a tough lesson for them when they have to bite the bullet and do it your way. It hurts, but they can handle it. Just try to keep the emphasis on what to *do,* not *who did what wrong.* If you can develop a way for someone to quietly approach you with ideas, you can prevent a lot of animosity later. You'll still sometimes have to shoot 'em down, due to time, money, or other pressing issues, but a lot of the time the kid just wants to be heard.

COMMUNITY THEATER KIDS

Community theater kids are probably pretty much grown-up, so you won't have to deal with adolescent-type issues as much as the rest of us. You'll still get the gamut, from enthusiastic beginner to well-qualified technician, clueless to talented, helpful to surly. Luckily for you, if someone is unhappy, they'll just leave. So no petty fights. Well, fewer petty fights. Usually it's a bit easier to train volunteers in the community theater setting, since they actually listen to what you say.

WORKING WITH MUSICIANS

Generally, the musicians are not your concern. They may ask for extension cords or help with the music stand lights, or have you look at a broken guitar amp. One thing to be careful of: Since they have been rehearsing elsewhere, they may feel like outsiders. Ask the cast and crew to make them especially welcome the first few days. One great undercurrent to this job at the high-school level is to break down the artificial barriers the kids are constantly putting up. Drama kids have always been thought of as cliquey; you'll have to manufacture ways to break up the little groups. One great way is by forcing the musicians to mop. That way, you don't have to do it. Or you can have each group help set up for the other group—musicians, crew, cast . . . And the kids make new friends.

Since I am a bit of a musician myself, I did try to have a dialog with the musicians, even bringing in my electric guitar on occasion. That opened their eyes and was usually good for a few laughs, which breaks the tension, which allows people to relax and gather their strength, which makes a better show. Feel free to do something silly once in a while; just don't overdo it.

A LITTLE TACT

I still speak up a little too soon at some staff meetings, or maybe I just talk a little too quickly. But backstage I have developed a little tact. When you are explaining things to students, put the reasons first, and take the time to explain things thoroughly. If they are paying attention, they'll reach the same conclusion you do most of the time, preventing disagreements. Establish a time to give direction, and a time to listen to student suggestions. During "notes" is not the time for suggestions from students and not the time for debates. The kids need to learn a little tact too.

WORKING WITH THE STAFF

It could be just you, or just two of you, but in big shows and musicals, a surprisingly large number of adults can be involved. In community theater, the number of administrative positions can be huge. Usually this division of labor is a good thing, leaving you with a smaller share of the responsibilities, and a lot of adult help and advice. Let's see . . . there's the director (hopefully *not* you), there's you, perhaps someone to run the costume committee (you should be so lucky), sometimes an adult assistant director, folks to help with auditions (three's a good number here), a publicity manager (probably you), a house manager (probably you), a set designer, art director, head electrician (you, you, you), a choir director, orchestra conductor, and choreographer for musicals, and a bevy of folks you have to answer to on the board of trustees or in the office at school. Lots of grownups, or maybe none. One of Blair's directors had *eighteen* adult assistants. Eighteen. I dunno, Kelly Newman, Blair's current theater director, and I are kind of used to it being just us for plays, adding a choral director and orchestra conductor for the musicals. In really big shows, like *West Side Story* with a cast of eighty, we got several more adults to help out. Parents are sometimes willing, but this is a wonderful misery, if you know what I mean. Ask around, get some help—but if you know what's good for you, you'll try to keep the number of cooks down to a reasonable minimum. Director, crew sponsor, costume manager for plays; conductor, choir director, and choreographer for musicals. It seems like the hardest person to find is the choreographer.

A CHOREOGRAPHER FOR THE SHOW

Musicals have dancing, and chances are you're not qualified to both choreograph the show and run the crew. Besides, you're busy. And the director may not want to bother, fobbing the job off onto the choir teacher, who may or may not want to be a part of it either. Directors I have worked with sometimes chose students to work up the dance steps; we have had both good and bad luck with this method. A student choreographer needs to be a superb dancer and a sort of born teacher, but finding these two qualities in the same package is difficult. Look to the dance teacher or a qualified parent. If there is no adult for the job, the director should choose a qualified student. Your part in this is to support the director and maybe call the kid aside if you see she is being too bossy or unfair to the others.

I got to add a little bit to the barroom dance in *Fiddler*. Due to a shortage of dancers, the crew kids were on for this scene. I found a couple of real barrels and had them doing some very athletic stunts, like a Ukrainian dance group I had seen. Since the crew kids weren't really gifted dancers, there was a lot of spinning the barrel, leaping over the barrel, and jumping onto and off of the barrel. The bar scene turned out terrific. Funny, the kid cast as the bartender actually turned down the part, giving a hardworking underclassman his first role. He did a great job and eventually got a lead in *Les Misérables*. L'chaim!

If you find a good choreographer, try to keep him happy—or send him my way if you don't need him.

TOO MANY COOKS

There were many years when I had a coworker to share some of the jobs I'm describing in this book. When we agreed on things, this was great. Sometimes, of course, we'd feel differently about something, and occasionally this would pose a problem. Help from others is a classic double-edged sword, since you have to give up some of the decision-making power in order to get the help. In community theater you'll very likely have a set designer and a lighting designer who are not the same person. If these two grownups don't get along, things can get pretty childish. That's the saving grace of having the *director* be the big boss. Professional disagreements can be worked out; if not, the director decides. Personal disagreements are the same—the director decides. Make it a precept to support the director, even if she's wrong. Support the director when someone else comes meddling, and support the director when the cast gets uppity. (In high schools, many of the crew and managerial positions are taken up by students under your tutelage. Either you or the director will have to jump in and make a decision from time to time to stop the bickering.)

Theater is collaborative, so have little sit-downs and collaborate. Work out the disagreements before someone gets angry. Take advice, give advice. If you're lucky, your coworkers will smooth the way for you, and give useful suggestions, and everything will turn out peachy. Unless they're idiots.

WORKING WITH IDIOTS

I'm on thin ice here, as I'm not talking about the kids. I'm talking about other adults, so forgive me if I couch this paragraph in euphemism. Y'know how sometimes, in a Little League game, some parent will get up and do something boneheadedly stupid? You are not going to totally escape that by working in the theater instead of in sports. The directors have it worse, of course, since lots of parents think their kid deserves a lead role, and many of them are willing to point that out to a director in great detail. Luckily, crew sponsors are spared that trial. You'll still bump into problems where you least expect them, because somebody in charge of something just doesn't understand. Well-meaning teachers can unwittingly put extra pressure on a kid, even when they are trying to be helpful. Someone in charge can make an offhand decision that causes you hours and hours more work. Someone not in charge can raise a stink because they think you are doing something wrong. The most frustrating part is when they don't even realize they're making it harder on you.

They are not really idiots. They are just uninvolved and don't really understand the mechanism of putting on a show. Or they are involved and just don't understand you. Try to forgive. Especially since someday, you'll be the idiot.

WHEN YOU ARE THE IDIOT

It's very easy to forget that an entire world is running while you are pre-occupied with your little show. We have a pretty big school, and even when we have 100 kids involved we only account for about 3 percent of the school. So sometimes you expect concessions that can't be granted. And, once in a while, you're the one making a bad decision, or being thoughtless or inconsiderate of others. I did it a couple of times, and of course it feels horrible when you finally realize that the problem this time is you. Since you have banked up an incredible font of internal goodwill by forgiving others, go ahead and forgive yourself when this happens. No one else will.

CUE 8.9 FOOD BACKSTAGE

When you are working long hours backstage, you are going to want to have a snack, or even a meal, and so is the crew. Stock up on trash cans and try to develop a plan to control the mess. We had certain rules about no food in the light booth, no food on the catwalks, and no food backstage, but these rules are almost completely ignored. All I can suggest is, try to develop a workable system that does allow kids to eat and provides a way to keep the place clean. Any rule forbidding food backstage creates more problems than it solves. We tried "Eat in the hall," and got complaints about kids eating in the hall; we tried "Keep food in the scene shop," but that was a flop too. Some directors have had success with a system of fines for being caught eating backstage. That may be the best compromise.

FRIDAY COMES

Let's assume for a moment that, while things are pretty well in hand and there hasn't been a crisis for at least an hour, you still have a nagging feeling that you just aren't going to get everything done in time for opening night. Know this . . . this is a completely normal sensation. You will get this feeling even when things are perfect. So don't trust the *feeling*. Instead, take a good hard look at everything, and determine, with some sense of priority, what "needs doing." Then schedule a Friday dinner meeting. I had these just about every Friday—one, because they are fun, and, two, you get an incredible amount of work done.

After school Friday there is a nice sense of relief; no one has a test tomorrow, and almost everyone can sleep in (unless you *really* need 'em). So there is a built-in good mood. There might be a football game, but not everyone goes to those. Anyhow, have kids bring in some bucks for carryout or delivery dinner. We had an acceptable Chinese restaurant nearby and several delivery pizza places. Keep the delivery phone numbers nearby. Work till six, place the order, then *keep working* until the delivery stuff actually arrives. The kids will want to knock off to wait for the delivery guy; this robs you of a lot of time. When the stuff arrives (you may have to pitch in some extra $$$) have everyone sit together, even the few who brought their dinner because they hate Chinese food. We had a rug we rolled out right on stage, a violation of the "no eating" rule that made things more fun. Any actor still hanging around was invited to join in; as a matter of fact, not socializing was forbidden. Buy a supply of plates, napkins, and plastic ware.

Eating with teens is an experience. I had to lay down a few ground rules. Miss Manners would have been proud:

1) Everybody must socialize.
2) If it's pizza, take one slice at a time.
3) Chew with your mouth closed.
4) If it's Chinese food, you must share your order. Which meant there were *eating* forks and *serving* forks.
5) No *eating* forks in the Chinese food boxes.
6) Sponsor gets the leftovers.

All good rules. When you place the order, make sure you get enough fortune cookies, unless you are ordering pizza. When cookie time comes around, read out the fortune, then say "backstage," as if it was part of the fortune. Something

like this: "You will find happiness this year (backstage)."
Here's another, "You will be successful in everything you do
(backstage)." This is a barrel of yuks. We stuck about a hundred fortune cookie fortunes on the door to the paint room.
And Alvin put up an "Inspected by #14" sticker he found in
his shirt pocket: "Inspected by number 14 (backstage)."

Then it's back to work. You'll have about ninety minutes more from the kids; then the parents show up to take
them home. Have the parents come inside; I hate it when
they wait outside, then yell at the kid because it's six minutes
after nine . . . Nine is a good quitting time, which gets you
out about 9:30. Not bad for a Friday night, especially in
Cleveland, where things don't really get going until about
10:30, if at all. Yes, I've been to Cleveland.

What you get when you do this, besides the leftovers, is
almost five hours of work from the kids, plus almost ninety
minutes more after dinner. And, while some kids can't stay,
others will be able to drop by after soccer practice, or cheerleading. So they can still participate in stage crew, even if it's
only part-time. Just make sure the kids stay on task as much
as possible. With this concentration of labor, and the benefit
of not having to clean up right when things are getting
started, you can get almost as much work done on one
Friday as you got during the all of the other days combined.

When you are out for Chinese food with your somewhat more grown-up friends, you can say "in the sack"
instead of "backstage."

Cue 9 Go.

Working Backstage

Rehearsal time is the time to train the crew on proper use of the stage equipment. The most important part of the stage equipment is probably the fly system, since there's so much danger of misuse. A *fly* is an area in the wings where crew members raise and lower scenery pieces for the show. There are a couple of different kinds of fly systems and several combination systems. First is pulleys and sandbags, very old-fashioned, tied to something called a *pin rail*. Better is a counterbalanced system with off-stage weights. Some theaters have a hand-cranked or motorized winch system, especially for the electrics. Of course, you might have nothing, in which case you build everything on wheels. . . .

FLYING TO THE GRID

If you have any kind of fly system, you've got pulleys attached somewhere near the ceiling. If you can get to them, you have a *grid* (a steel gridiron); lucky you, you can make changes and adjustments without a lot of trouble. If the equipment is installed directly to the roof trusses (an economy move on the part of the builders), you won't be able to change or adjust anything without setting up a huge scaffold. Too bad. With a grid you can change curtain positions, add mic lines, "dead hang" something when necessary—a lot of versatility comes with a grid. I relocated our act curtain at the old school. It was hanging up on the valence and I simply moved the pulleys a bit to fix it. If you have a grid, make sure you block access with lock and key; the temptation to climb up there, or even on the roof, was too much for most kids and a constant problem for us at the old school.

COUNTERBALANCED MEALS—I MEAN, COUNTERBALANCED SYSTEM

Most theaters with a fly system are going to have a counterbalanced system where you put weights on an *arbor* (a hanging rack) offstage to balance the weight of whatever you are putting on the pipe on stage. Generally these systems have a 2:1 weight ratio; the arbor gets loaded with twice as much weight as the piece being hung, and the pipe wires run through a compound pulley. This just saves space offstage, allowing the fly gallery to be up in the air a bit. When you attach something to a pipe (also called a *batten*), you throw enough weight on the arbor to balance the system. Then everything can be "flown" with a minimum of sweat and muscle. Two things to be careful about: one is affixing scenery to the pipe well, two is loading and unloading weights without killing anybody. This is harder than you might think.

ADDING SCENERY AND LOADING WEIGHTS

When a pipe is "flown in" and something attached to it, the corresponding weights are way up near the roof. There is a "loading gallery" up there so the crew can add weight while the pipe is down. This is extremely dangerous for several reasons. First, the controls for the pipe, the lock and latch, are down below. No one should be down there when someone is loading, since these weights weigh forty pounds each. Second, it takes a bit of a gymnast to get to the arbor from the loading gallery, and it's usually an awkward squeeze. Third, if the weight added is too much, the pipe will rise, and there's no way to stop it. There is a system for doing this safely.

First, design stuff for the pipes to be as light as possible. Canvas, scrim, paper, thin wood—you get the idea. Don't try to fly something that's extremely heavy. Second, attach the thing to the pipe really well. Aircraft cable is usually the way to go; double-up and double-check those saddlebolts, though. If the loaded pipe is light enough to raise without a lot of strain, go ahead; then you can load from the fly gallery for perfect balance. Clear everyone out from under and load up. If you have any *real* weight on the pipe you won't be able to do this, and you shouldn't try, since letting go would be catastrophic. Get up to the loading gallery, clear everyone out from below, and safely begin adding weight. This might mean using a safety line, to keep you from falling if you overbalance. After each weight is added, check the strain. You can get almost perfect balance with these systems, so much so that the pipe won't raise or lower itself without some tugging on the lines. That's what you are shooting for, of course. This is sweaty, nasty work, so be extra careful. You need a spotter on the ground to keep idiots away from danger. Once the system is balanced, you're pretty safe; notice that there isn't much strain on the rope part of the system when everything is balanced. That is good. Inspect these ropes after every show, or have someone come in; this is just too dangerous to leave to chance.

Once in a while, someone will thoughtlessly put a line out of balance. This is extremely dangerous, but you must have a procedure to cover the problem. What I always do, since I'm not about to trust anyone's setup but mine, is test the lines before unlatching the lock. Clear out everyone from below. Grab the two lines closest to you with one hand. Give them a little shake. If you see the pipe move, that's a good sign. Carefully unlatch the lock and open it, then quickly close it again. If something is way off, you'll be able to snatch the lock closed quickly since you are hanging onto both lift lines. If the pipe starts to run away, you can usually stop it with the lock. If not, get the heck out of there.

I once caught a kid climbing on the battens. That meant that the line was about 150 pounds out of balance. Which meant all of that strain was on the lift line, which is a piece of rope held in a little cam-type lock. If the rope slips, the pipe falls, and so does the kid. Once he's off of the pipe, it just may go back up. Then when it hits the ceiling, it may break loose and come back down, landing on the kid. Would've served him right.

ZIPPING THE FLY

When everything is balanced and safe, train the crew on flying things in and out. You'll have to attach spike marks to the lift lines so you can stop things in the right place. Stress that anyone moving a pipe is to call out (loudly) that they are moving a pipe and to check below for people and things that might be in the way. When crafting cues, make sure you time the movement of the pipes to not interfere with the movement of the other set pieces, actors, or crew. During a show, of course, the pipes are moved as silently as possible, with no calling out. It's best not to change fly assignments during a show (like when someone wants to help). They'll pull the wrong rope every time.

WINCHES

Some electrics are counterbalanced, which is a pain when adding and taking off lighting instruments, but most are on some kind of winch system. All you have to do is crank things in and out for service. You'll learn to plan ahead after you've cranked these things out a few times. Some of the winch systems are motorized. You should be so lucky.

BASKET LADDER

Hopefully you have a basket ladder to facilitate stage work on high. One of my predecessor's greatest achievements was raising enough money to get one for our school. A basket ladder cranks up and down and rolls around, making setting lights and hanging mics a million times easier. Basket ladders have brakes and outriggers and guards and safety manuals, so take the hint. We roll ours down the hall twice a year to reset the big clock for daylight saving time. Plus, they come in handy when setting up for the homecoming dance. We've also run it down to the football field and put a camera operator in it. They are great. Ours is a Genie.

PULLING THE CURTAIN

I don't know why, but when kids pull the curtain, they always seem to pull it too slowly, and they always stop before the curtain is fully open. It could be that the job gets fobbed off onto somebody at the last minute. It's supposed to be the stage manager's job anyway. Take a moment and practice with the curtain pull. You need to know which rope is which, and you need to begin the pull with authority, both opening and closing. You need to practice so you don't cross up the ropes halfway through the pull. And you need to pull until the curtain stops. That is all.

SCENERY

Moving scenery on and off is a skill and takes practice, too. During rehearsals, look for things coming on from the wrong side. Try to design a flow to the scene changes as rehearsals progress. Find convenient offstage locations for everything; you may have to have a *storage* position and a *ready to go on* position. Mark onstage and offstage positions with spike tape, or even paint. Have the crew move half-built scenery items on and off so the actors can get used to them. Think about what items should be moved by the crew and what items should be moved by the cast. In *Guys & Dolls* we had a couple of kids put on waiter vests and slowly clean up the Hot Box while the scene was winding down. They brought out a mop, placed chairs on tables, and struck the entire set while Nathan was pleading with Adelaide downstage. The waiters (crew) were in silhouette, and it looked great.

PROPS

We had a semiautonomous Props Committee that found as many pieces as they could and set up the props tables, etc. This is a task for any responsible person that wants to do it. As the years went by, the "Queen of Props" would pick a successor for next year without any interference from the director or me. If you keep an eye on the props list and help find any unusual or costly item, the "Props Queen" can take care of the rest. One year it was "Props Mistress," one year "Lord of Props." Whatever. If problems develop you'll have to intervene, but usually it's clear sailing.

Most scripts have a props list in the back, which you will probably simplify, and a one- or two-person crew is usually enough to take care of even quite a large number of props. Help them out by reserving a large, safe space for them to lock everything up. Let the stage manager and the "Chancellor of Props" knock out a customized props list for your show, then look it over carefully. It's probably best to get the director involved here, just in case. The regular crew can help build props when they aren't working on painting the staircase. If you start early enough, you'll be well propped up before showtime.

That's not to say you won't have problems finding props. For *You Can't Take It With You*, you need a printing press. I had one in my garage, but you—you might have to look around a little bit. Look for the hard parts first. Wagon wheels for Tevye's cart, milk cans—not the easiest things to track down at the last minute. Eddie, our Tevye, tied the cart wheel into place during *Fiddler* rehearsals; I have it on video and tease him about it every chance I get. "We're leaving for New York . . . well, in a minute, when I get this rope untied."

One thing to watch out for is not getting an expected piece when you need it. This is true for props and set items alike. Days march by, and it finally becomes clear that the promised device isn't going to arrive at all. You can circumvent this with regular meetings with the "Prime Minister of Props." You say, "Say, where's that dress mannequin?" and watch his eyes *very* closely. Shifty eyes mean you have to go out and find the stinkin' dress mannequin yourself. I never messed with the student tradition of selecting a "Props Commander" on their own. It's good to have a tradition or two like that backstage. In a venue where you don't have the luxury of tradition, you will have to cast about and find a props leader as quickly as you can.

CUE 9.9 PREPARING THE TICKETS

Take a moment to think about your price structure. If you don't want to think about it, make the student price $4 and the adult price $8. Make senior citizens the same as students. If you do want to think about it, consider that the student price should be as low as possible, to encourage students to attend. Some parents will not give extra money for this kind of event, and most students won't dare ask, so keep the price low. Every year I spoke to my students about how to wheedle the money from their parents, and every year they looked at me like I was crazy. As far as I know, not one student went home and said, "Mom, can I have four bucks to see the school play?" The deal these days is that kids are forced to budget whatever money they get, and there is no room or money for special occasions. So, as far as the kids are concerned, asking for money is out. They are forced to part with their own money, from their allowance, or job, or whatever, and that money is precious to them. So, for us, four dollars worked out.

On the other hand, parents should be able to scratch up real money, and your show should rate the same as a movie these days. Around here that's eight bucks, so there you go. Having senior citizens pay the student price is a kindness to those on a tight budget, and the truth is, not many come anyway. Well, one year an entire retirement home came, and they loved the show, but none of them would have come if the price was higher, so, all things considered, four bucks is fair. Usually only a coupla dozen senior citizens make the show, so the discount doesn't hurt you too much.

You may bump prices up or down to compensate for local conditions, but if you go too high then no one will come. So don't do that. And *do* do discount student tickets on opening night.

MAKING TICKETS

At most venues, the tickets are supposed to be numbered, and usually you are put through a pretty thorough accounting process to make sure you aren't skimming the ticket money. This rule (the numbering, not the skimming) is broken pretty regularly, but I suggest you follow it. A school will usually provide numbered tickets ahead of time; they are, of course, the ugly municipal kind. And you can buy pre-numbered tickets at an office supply store, or on the Web. You can print up your own tickets on a Xerox machine if you want, but you'll have to number them by hand. We used a computer to print up numbered tickets in color, but I've got to warn you—it's kind of a pain, even if you know what you are doing.

As I'm typing this, I'm printing a set of tickets for our fall show on my Macintosh computer in the next room. I use ClarisWorks, which I think is unavailable in the stores anymore; you'll have to use FileMakerPro, which is just as good or better. If you know your way around a database, set one up, and decorate the ticket as nice as you like. Set up a serial number, which will probably be the only entry in the database, and go to town. Hold on a second, I have to reload the Mac printer. . . .

I print ten tickets per page, and I print the adult tickets beside the student tickets. Everything would be easier if you set one price for everyone, but you shouldn't do that, as I've discussed previously. I have used different colors for each day, and I can tell you that's a royal pain. So this time, it's yellow ink for the students (and senior citizens), and goldenrod for the adults. The colors are different enough to tell apart, but similar enough to represent the same date when that's necessary. If you choose to do this, you're going to have to print far more tickets than you think you'll need, more than a full house, because of the possibility of selling more adult tickets than student tickets, and vice versa. Don't forget to print up press passes and comp tickets for staff. You'll have to buy some *cover stock* to print on; make sure your printer can handle it. I'm running 67 lb. cover stock from Staples through my DeskWriter 660 printer. Buy extra ink cartridges. And keep an eye on the house and the ticket numbers as you sell tickets. You don't want to oversell. We went years before selling the house out; when we did, panic struck, because my girlfriend didn't have a seat!

AN INTERNAL DEBATE ABOUT ALL THIS TICKET STUFF

Truth is, I prefer the municipal school tickets, sold at the door, no presale, one color for adults, one color for students, same two rolls for the run of the show. Why? Do you really have to ask? It's easier. Printing up the tickets isn't a job you can just fob off on somebody; you have to design them, print them, cut them, sort them (numerical order), and it takes forever to print them; fifty seconds a sheet on my printer. I did it because the director wanted them, and she wanted to pre-sell (y'know, sell throughout the week), and you know how persuasive directors can be.

Also for the challenge—it is a great computer graphics training lesson.

IF YOU'RE GOING TO TRY IT

Drop by a sewing shop and pick up a couple of *tracing wheels*. You can run these over the printed ticket sheets before you cut them out, and it makes a nice little seam for tearing the tickets. Use a ruler to keep the tracing wheel running straight. Then cut out all of the tickets. Here, I had the tremendous advantage of a "guillotine"-type paper cutter. As a matter of fact, without one, the ticket cutting-out job is just about impossible. These industrial paper cutters can cut five hundred sheets at a time—you might see one in a print shop, or even at Kinko's. After cutting, have a crew member sort the tickets into numerical order, show them to the bookkeeper (a pro forma step) and start selling. Our attendance secretary was kind enough to do the ticket-selling job for the past few years. Having students try to sell tickets at lunchtime runs a distant second to having an adult on the job all day long.

BY THE WAY
There are companies that will handle all of this for you. Also, there are computer programs that will let you set up your own little Ticketron right in the school. Maybe the business department could handle the whole thing—check it out.

SO YOU WANNA MAKE YOUR OWN TICKETS WITH A TWO-TIERED PRICE STRUCTURE AND RESERVED SEATS, DO YA?
It can be done, but shouldn't. Especially reserved seats. In addition to slowing down the ticket line, you'll have to train the ushers to seat people. And, let's be honest, someone will *always* sit in the wrong seat, a problem we don't need at this critical moment. We did it once, and it *was* cool, the ushers did a great job; but it still left a bad aftertaste, complaints about the seats, arguments . . . yuck. Just don't do it. Besides, you'll have to print the seat number on every ticket—almost impossible unless you pay somebody or buy a commercial ticket printing program (about a thousand bucks that you don't need to spend).

Reserved seats are *expected* in community theater. Sorry, get the job done.

Cue 10 *Go.*

Patching the Lights

Hoo boy, prepare for confusion. Patching can get complicated, especially if you have an older lighting system. Here's an explanation of the concept. You probably have a light dimmer located somewhere in your house. Rotate it, and the lights can be adjusted from "out" to "full on." The dimmer is hardwired to the lights. The controller is the knob, which you are turning by hand. A volume control for the light, so to speak. You could, if you wanted, buy four or even six dimmers and wire them up to a whole bunch of store-bought lights. I did this very thing when I built a controller for my first portable light show, which I still have. Then you can click and twist the dimmers and play with the lights. Eventually, you'll want to control the red light with the dimmer on the right. For your own personal reasons. So, instead of keeping everything hardwired, you just add plugs and sockets, and then you can sort of control which dimmer runs which light. This is the makings of a patch system.

A true patch system has another refinement—several really—which is where things can get a little hinky. The knob you spin—actually some sort of slider—can be connected to any dimmer you want. In addition, one slider can control several dimmers. And nowadays you can automate the whole process, so once everything is figured out and programmed in, one simply presses the "go" button.

The primitive way—one light is hardwired to its own dimmer, and someone has to turn each and every knob to the right position (quickly) to change the lights. The elegant way—add several outlets to the same dimmer all over the place (for convenience) and control the dimmer remotely via a patch system. So slider 4 can be patched into dimmer 23, because the plugs connected to dimmer 23 are in a convenient place on the pipe to hang that one special light you need to light up Willie Wonka when he finally appears in the chocolate factory. And of course dimmer 23 breaks. No problem; with a patch system, you can assign which socket (outlet) goes to which dimmer. Meaning you can reassign socket 23 to dimmer 24 (whew!) and reassign slider 4 to dimmer 24—then the light will work. Don't forget to get that dimmer fixed.

Right about now, you're probably saying that a patch system was the product of a sick mind. That's just because you haven't joined into the spirit of the thing. As you develop skill with lighting, you're eventually going to want to backlight somebody (with a little haze or fog), then gradually bring up a purple high side light, then a slow warm front light as it becomes clear it's not the killer but the postman, then change the purple to something more normal. You could never hardwire a show like that. You are going to need that front light at other times, and the regular side light, too. You'll quickly run out of lights, dimmers, sliders, and extension cords if you don't plot out the system for versatility. When we got our new theater we got 98 (I think) new lights. Nirvana. But we still ran out; lights will always have to pull double duty. I was counting the lights at Wolf Trap Farm Park for the Performing Arts and stopped at 500; you're lucky if you have 60. So plot, patch, program, produce the best show you can with what you've got.

In order to keep from going nuts, you'd better figure out a way to test everything and make certain it all works. The simplest way is to patch everything up, one-to-one-to-one. Be thorough, and write everything down on some kind of cheat sheet. I worked one summer at a different school and went through this process. The next year (I was rehired), I had my notes, so I remembered that slider 3 was broken, as was dimmer 19. Dimmer 3 would only go full on and full off (no dimming), and I patched accordingly. The worst part of it was, their cross-fader was damaged, which made running the board "live" an absolute bear. Almost every lighting board has a cross-fader—it's just a knob that allows you to segue between two different preset lighting cues smoothly. I hope yours works.

Figure out your system and patch everything up one-to-one-to-one. That is, slider 1 to dimmer 1 to socket 1. The slider is on the lighting board, the dimmer is somewhere relatively close to the lights (in a room or on a pipe), and the socket is in the beams somewhere, or in the wall near the light pipe. If your system incorporates a patch panel, that's the place to connect dimmer one to socket one. Otherwise, most of the "patching" will be done at the control board. By the way, lots of lighting systems have a plurality of numbered sockets; they have the same number and will all turn on together. So don't panic if you find two locations labeled "socket 1."

You might also have some extra dimmers, but don't worry about that right now. Plug a (working, repaired) light into socket 1. When convenient, you can use a bright desk lamp on an extension cord or an adapter, which will help you move faster. Usually socket 1 is in the beams or some other remote or inaccessible location. So employ extension cords, helpers at the board, and runners, and use the intercom or a wireless mic so you don't have to yell. And if the light is bright, and it should be . . . sunglasses. You'll be looking at these lights for hours.

Say, "number 1 at full, please." It is a tradition, and a requirement, that you always add *please* to your instructions here. Always. The worker bee at the board is just sitting there while everyone else is having all of the fun, so say *please*, please. "Thank you" means it worked, since not everyone is in a position to see the light. You can see it though, (through your sunglasses), and you might even be able to read the number of the color of the gel in the gel frame. At this stage you don't need color, but it's good to know you can actually read the numbers when you need to. If slider 1 works dimmer 1, socket 1, and lamp 1 perfectly, great! If something is wrong, you must determine where the problem lies:

1. Check the lamp.

2. Check the circuit breaker on dimmer 1, probably at the patch panel.

3. Change the patch so slider 1 controls dimmer 2. Change the patch panel so dimmer 2 controls socket 1. If this works, *dimmer* 1 is bad.

4. Change the patch so slider 2 controls dimmer 1, and socket 1. If this works, *slider* 1 is bad.

If you have everything working, take a moment and test all of the socket 1s. There may be another place on the pipe that has an outlet hooked up parallel to the one you are testing. Find it, test it, and note its location on your lighting cheat sheet. This pre-lighting plot can be as simple or as complex as you like. During this process it'll probably become a scribbled mess, but persevere. You need to know what works and what doesn't. And take note of where all of the sockets are (what pipe) so you don't have to hunt around later.

You might not be able to find any other outlets numbered "1." This is typical; remember to keep checking, or plot it all out ahead of time. I *never* found socket 106 over at Whitman; go figure. At another school, someone had numbered a few dimmers incorrectly. Someone else had *renumbered* them, also incorrectly. I wonder what their shows looked like. I renumbered (using white gaff tape), figured out which dimmers were out (number 16—it's in my notebook), and patched around them.

If you find something wrong, write down the problem and mark the suspect device with white gaff tape: "Socket 23 dead," or "This is socket 10" (it was cross-wired and labeled 11). Keep your black Sharpie handy. Put the note on white gaff tape, which can be removed when the problem is fixed. When you come across a broken socket, label it and fix it as soon as possible. Make friends with the county electrician. *Floor pockets* (sockets in the floor) are particularly notorious here. They get filled with dirt and dust. Assign someone to vacuum them out (be sure they are off) and inspect them very carefully.

Here is a short list of things I have found in an electrical socket: dirt, dust (small dirt), broken pieces of plug, hot melt glue, balsa wood, hair, a popsicle stick (which is maple, I think), a paper clip, wire, a plug—connected to nothing—a screw, a gum wrapper, gum, a pencil lead, a pencil, water (yikes!), an outlet with no plastic (just the metal parts exposed and live), a screwdriver blade, a fan (I'll explain later), and paper. Hmm. By the way, lots of people say "plug" when they mean "socket." A plug is on the end of a lamp cord and isn't a lamp. A socket is in the wall. Got it?

DID YOU SAY "A FAN?"

I once found a fan plugged into the dimmer system. This was not a good thing, as fan motors are not built to be "dimmed." You *can* patch these loads directly, through something called a *non-dim*. These are switches that are either on or off, with no dimming. You are not supposed to dim fans, or fluorescent lights, or induction motors. So patch them into the non-dim circuits. You can assign some dimmers to work like non-dim circuits as well. The astute reader may comment, "Hey, maybe that's what was wrong with dimmer 3 a few pages ago!" Maybe. But I couldn't fix it.

THOSE PESKY FLOOR POCKETS

Once, at the old Blair, with the power off and the dimmer system shut down, the floor pocket itself gave me a pop that knocked me to the ground. Funny thing, electricity. It'll go *wherever you let it,* and I let it go through the floor pocket case, through my arms, and through me, and it hurt. That's why we cover everything with rubber and keep water away and invent ground fault interrupters; you see, electricity doesn't choose or think, it just goes. So be careful. Floor pockets are exposed and neglected and in a vulnerable location. Treat them nice, paint a safety stripe around them—don't mop them. After a crew member cleans them out, custom cut some kind of foam to keep the dust out of them. They do come in handy.

You may also have microphone sockets in the floor. If you do, the chances are better than 50/50 that they don't work. Repair them or have it done. You are going to need those sockets when it comes time to run mics.

RUNNING THE BOARD

Well, if you've gotten the hang of things, you have developed a list of problems with the patch system that need to be avoided in the short term and eventually repaired (fat chance). Plus, you've got a pretty good idea how to run the equipment. Find someone who really can run a board well, and you can do amazing things with just the lights. Amazing things. Our problem as a sponsor is that we mostly get beginners to work with, and we don't often get enough time to become expert at the board ourselves. In truth, it's not really necessary for you to be the expert. You just need to know what to ask for. The crew will be on the board for hours, and they have so much experience with computer games that they should be able to figure out the light board. They will need some lessons, though, from upperclassmen or someone from the supply house, or from you. And as the years go by, certain lessons don't get passed on and folks will not be aware of all of the capabilities of the system. And they'll think they know what they are doing. But they don't. I found out after our last show that none of the lighting crew knows how to save a light plot to disk—the knowledge graduated away without being passed on! So students (and many adults) rely on a shorthand version of things that sort of work, but really hobble the system—and everyone's creativity. So stay alert. Remember what happened with the audio controls because someone didn't know the proper way to adjust them. It had to do with an *audio* board, but the idea was the same. By the way, if you are the sort of person who can't program the clock on a VCR, you are going to have a really hard time with the newer lighting control panels. Take deep breaths; keep your first attempts simple.

EXTRA DIMMERS, EXTRA SOCKETS

Remember, as you test your system, you are trying to be thorough. Re-patch to check all dimmers, and re-patch again (at the patch panel) to check all sockets, including floor pockets and wall sockets. Mark any broken thing on your cheat sheet and on white gaff tape at the problem location itself.

BOX BOOMS

Sometimes you'll find some lighting pipes installed on the side walls of your theater space. Usually folks ignore them, since using them means a lot of ladder work. I suggest you get a couple or five ellipsoidals onto these *box booms* and learn to use the dramatic high side light they create. It's definitely worth the trouble.

OLDER SYSTEMS, NEWER SYSTEMS

I put my time in when there were still a very few mechanical lighting systems around, all the way through the introduction of computer-assisted patch panels—about as long as the run of *Cats*, which I never saw. You can search the Web and find cool stories about saltwater dimmers and all kinds of junk, but most theaters you're going to work in will have a mechanical patch panel and a computer-assisted control board. The computer is in the control board, so it won't look like a computer. It'll look like an audio mixer. If your stuff is older (like a two- or four-scene preset panel), you're going to have to modify some of your techniques. There are still systems around where electric motors control huge rheostats to dim the lights. As long as it works, be happy.

If you have a newer system (what joy), you'll be able to make more mistakes more easily than ever before. That is, you'll be able to do great work once you learn the board. The biggest improvement is that the mechanical patch panel, with the big bank of controllers that were hard to read, hard to move, and hard to place, has been eliminated. Except in a refit, where it probably hasn't. Oh, well. In the newest systems, the dimmers are purely electronic and built right on the pipe near the socket they control. And each socket has its own dimmer! Which means no patch panel, and you'll almost never run out of dimmers! And the dimmers have built-in overload protection that resets itself! And you can assign any dimmer directly to any slider. So cool. You will, of course, get more dimmers than you have sliders on your control board. This is normal, the same as older systems. Fine. Until you realize that they should have given you a slider for every dimmer. I mean, if they really wanted to make things easier, more sliders is the way to go. You might end up with one hundred dimmers, but only forty-eight sliders. You can use the other fifty-two dimmers, you'll just have to utilize the keypad or assign the dimmer to another slider. No one-to-one-to-one. Maybe it's just me, but if I have a hundred dimmers then I want a hundred sliders. Then I could set each and every light, press "record," and be done.

Of course, it's not really done that way, and it would be expensive to pay for a board that could do it that way. I happen to know it *can* be done. But maybe not at your school. You're going to light up the lights in groups anyhow; forty-eight sliders is plenty. Twenty-four is enough, provided they all work. A hundred sliders would be kind of cool, though; maybe if I hit the lottery. . . .

If you have less than twenty-four channels, or an older system, you just smile and do the best you can. If you're creative enough, you can still do magic.

TAKING ANOTHER LOOK AT PATCHING

Once you've sort of figured out your board, you should sit down and think for a while about the best way to use it. When I was working through the summers, I had the opportunity to work with several different systems. Each one was picky, and it was difficult to think the way the board needed me to think. That is, I was trying to do something at Landon the way I did it at Whitman or Blair. You probably won't have this exact problem, unless you change locations from show to show, but you still have to figure out the best way to use the board. I found it helpful to take the plugged-up lighting completely apart to hook up fresh for every show. As a matter of fact, the one time I didn't do this, my creativity was blocked by the fact that the lights were already aimed a different way, left over from the last show. You can, and should, have a general setup for assemblies and outside groups, but for a *show* you should decide what you want to do, then assign your channels accordingly. This is the job of *lighting design.* Let's fake up a whole project the way it might be done for a new guy in a new location. First, do everything from page 1 up to here. Then . . .

KNOW YOUR LIMITS, AND SURPASS THEM

For our example, I'll use a 24-channel controller, 32-dimmer, 105-socket setup. This is a typical high school installation from the sixties and seventies, so your theater may have something similar. Generally, the sockets are numbered ascending from the front light locations to the cyc light locations. This means it would be stupid to try to assign socket 1 to a scoop facing the back wall; the electrical socket itself is too far away, probably up in the beams. If you did a good job testing out your system, you have a little chart (the *cheat sheet*) that shows socket locations. It doesn't really matter exactly what the numbers are; each installation will be a little different, and modern systems can be numbered any way you please. Most folks still follow the conventional configuration. If you are the one numbering everything, start with the front light and work your way to the stage, then to the back wall, then to the floor and wall pockets. *Wall pockets* are floor pockets on the wall. Actually, they may look just like conventional outlets, except that they have a number beside them. If you are doing the numbering, use white gaff tape, as you are bound to screw something up. Really. I once misnumbered fourteen flats that had to be in order, and I went to college. Done? Good.

PATCH IN THE CYC LIGHTS

The easiest place to begin is with the cyc lights. We have twelve, which is enough. Less, and you are going to have to make sacrifices. With twelve you can set them up on the back pipe, lowered for the purpose, and arrange a pretty good spread along the cyclorama or back wall. Four sets of three, so you can shoot three colors. Standard colors: red, blue, green. One thousand–Watt lamps. This is going to suck up three of your sliders (channels); might as well use channels 1, 2, and 3 (lucky you, your slider 3 works). Let's put red in the middle. Remember, it's not red yet, since the gels aren't in, but these four lights are in the middle of each set of lights, four sets, and they will eventually be red. (The gel—the color—is pretty much the last thing you do.)

At this stage of the game, the twelve scoops are hung facing the right way, and all of their C-clamps are facing the right way (or at least the same way). As far as I'm concerned, the right way is with the "C" facing the audience (easier to get to when aiming), but people argue about this. The twelve plugs are all hanging down. Your mission, should you choose to accept it, is to plug the lights that are going to be red lights into convenient sockets nearby. If you have 2400-Watt dimmers (proof—a 20-amp circuit breaker on the patch panel), you may plug two scoops into the same numbered socket. Let's pretend it's socket 86. Lucky you, there is a socket 86 located near every one of the red lights. So you plug them all in. And you begin to think, "This patching stuff is easy. What was I so worried about?" Assign socket 86 to dimmer 2, to slider 2. And you say, "Bring number 2 up to full, please," because you are ready to see them light up, and voilà! The circuit breaker pops. You haven't been paying attention, have you?

You put a 4000-Watt load onto a 2400-Watt dimmer. Bad boy. (To the girls, *bad girl.*) Unplug two lights. Reset the breaker. And think. The other two lights must go to the same *slider* (channel 2), but cannot go into the same *dimmer.* So use dimmer 22. At the patch panel, assign socket 87 and 88—since they are near the lights in question—to dimmer 22. Plug 'em in. At the lighting control board, assign slider 2 to dimmer 2 *and* dimmer 22. Cross your fingers, and squint. Better yet, put on your sunglasses. Say, "Number 2 to full, please," since somewhere along the line you did turn it off. . . .

Success. Slider 2 now controls dimmer 2 and dimmer 22 and turns on all four lights, because they are patched into those dimmers. Say, "Thank you," to your light board operator, then, "Take 2 out . . . *please.* Thank you." Later you will aim these lights and add red gel. Start on the next batch. Before you get too far ahead, take a moment and update your (redrawn, neat) cheat sheet. There is a sample in the back of the book. You've used up channel 2, and dimmers 2 and 22, and sockets 86, 87, and 88. You have to cross them off of your cheat sheet, since they've been assigned. From now on, you don't look at the pipe to find an open socket, you look at the cheat sheet. Otherwise you'll plug something into a circuit that's already been assigned. If you want, you could put tape over the unused assigned sockets, but that's too much trouble and you'll probably miss some of 'em anyway. Time for the next batch, green.

Greens, on slider 1, again using two dimmers to safely carry the load. Looking at the cheat sheet, you see sockets 84 and 90 are located perfectly. Divide the load, assign, and patch . . . darn! The cord is eighteen inches too short! You could pick another socket or use an extension cord. Don't use a household cord made for a living-room light; the current demands would melt it in about five seconds. Then you'd have some explaining to do. Buy or make (or repair) a huge selection of tough, durable, medium-length extension cords (cables). You could rent 'em if you want, they're pretty cheap. Plug in and test, "Number 1 at full, please. . . . "

ISN'T THIS FUN?

The best reason for starting with the cyc lights is that they are easy, patching them is pretty straightforward, and you can use the time to better plan the rest of the lighting plot. OK, that's three reasons. The problems you are going to bump into are running out of sockets (you can double up or even triple up on fixtures as long as you don't overload the dimmer or the cords), running out of dimmers, running out of lighting fixtures, and running out of channels on the light board. Also shadows. Unexpected shadows can cause major disruption to a light plot. Spill is a problem. Spill is lighting up something that's supposed to be dark. Unwanted reflections can also be an issue. Anyhoo, with cyc lights, most of these problems are no big deal. So it's a great place to start. Raise the pipe, aim the units, and slap a jelly on 'em. That is, put in the gel. And pay the bucks for diffusion here, or buy gel with built-in diffusion. Diffusion will soften and smooth out the light. Note that some diffusion must be put in using a certain alignment. If you get it wrong, you'll know it; just rotate the diffusion if it is square, or go buy more if it's not square and cut wrong. Play with sliders 1, 2, and 3 to find an enormous number of great color combinations. You can get orange, lavender, pink, and more. Setting the cyc light is a great way to establish the mood of a scene. Changing the cyc light is a great way to show time passing, or a change of location when nothing actually moves on stage. Dimming the cyc light can move focus to a well-lit actor downstage. Raising the cyc lights while dimming the front light gives dramatic silhouettes. *Cool.* Update your cheat sheet. By the way, if you put diffusion and gel in the same gel frame, install the diffusion closer to the lamp. Two reasons. Reason one, you'll still be able to read the gel color number you wrote on the gel, and two, the gel will melt if you do it backwards. Perhaps that should be reason one.

MORE ABOUT THE CHEAT SHEET

We're going to skip the detailed drawing of a lighting plot. When you have the time, experience, and talent, you really should work one out, but for the moment we'll save time by not drawing a light plot perfectly to scale. Instead, develop a shorthand code for your lighting inventory: square boxes to represent the scoops, rectangles to represent ellipsoidals, small boxes to represent Fresnels, etc. Use arrows to indicate the direction of the light. You can draw this right on the lighting patch cheat sheet and connect the units to the socket locations with a little pencil line.

You are bound to make a lot of changes as you go, especially in your first few shows, so drawing a real nice scale lighting plot with the little templates and all of that would probably just be a time-waster for you. Promise yourself that as the years go by you'll learn how to do it; just don't bother right now.

FRONT LIGHT

Without question, front light is the most important light you can set, and it must be done well. The trouble is, while front light is the most *important,* it is not the most *dramatic.* Side light and top light are dramatic. So you can't scrimp, as I sort of implied earlier. You need top light and side light. But, the audience has to *see*—front light comes first. Don't argue with me; people have to be able to see. I had an enormous disagreement with the kids during a production of *A Midsummer Night's Dream.* I wasn't in charge of lighting and could only suggest. I suggested more light; specifically, "More front light, I can't see!" "But, Mr. Kaluta, it's supposed to be *night!*" Sheesh. Front light comes first. I know we put up the cyc lights first, but that was just to learn the routine. Plus, they're easy. Front light is most important. To work!

The front light for the downstage areas usually comes from above the audience. In high school (Washington-Lee, in Arlington, Virginia), my buddy Mark had to climb a rickety thirty-foot ladder to set each light. The foot of the ladder was nestled among the seats of the auditorium. What a pain. If you have this sort of setup, buy some new ladders.

Most of the time the lights are accessible from the balcony or encased in some kind of catwalk or crib, commonly called the beams. So someone has to climb up into the beams, where it is unusually hot and stuffy, to aim, focus, and gel all of the front light. The kids would sometimes take off their shirts because it was so hot. I had to tell Penelope she couldn't do that.

There are two major theories about front light. One is, aim the lights straight at the areas right in front of their positions on the pipe and rely on side light (from the wings or the apron) for depth. The other, commonly called the *McCandless System,* is to aim the lights at an angle to form interesting facial shadows and fill in the shadows with more front light from the other direction. The two "banks" are toned warm and cool with gel. It actually works pretty well. Some folks deride it these days; other people say it with respect. The McCandless System. As famous as his system is, it's unlikely they've even read his book (written in the 1920s!). Here's a similar technique that'll get you through a few shows; then you can go to a lighting seminar (costs big bucks) and become more of a pro.

Depending on the width of the stage, and the number of high-powered ellipsoidals you have, divide the stage into four or five sections across. Four sections, for this example. This'll take sixteen ellipsoidals and an undetermined number of dimmers. And a minimum of two sliders (lighting control channels), but probably lots more. If you don't have enough lights to do this well, then just do the first half, or just make three sections and leave the edges of the stage dark. And start planning fundraisers. You are going to arrange four of these lights on the right-hand side of the pipe (in the beams) and four on the left. You have to space them out a bit, and even overlap them. And you'll aim them so the light crosses like an "X." Actually, more like a bunch of upside-down *V*s. One set will be *warm* (gelled with Rosco 02, which is a color invented by accident called *bastard amber*), and the other four will be *cool* (Rosco 60 is fine). On the pipe, it looks something like this:

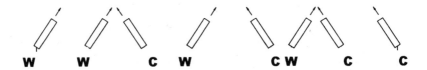

Aiming the Front Light

Aim each unit down to light the very front edge of the stage. You can take care of spill with the shutters later. You'll have to focus these lights one at a time, in a very dark auditorium. And you have to keep your cheat sheet up to date. And keep safety in mind. (During *Les Misérables*, our lighting designer accidentally got smacked with a gel frame from on high—*be careful.*) Reading from left to right, the first warm light (and the first cool light) go to area 1, and the system follows for all eight lights. I call this the *McCandless Rolling Over in His Grave System,* but it gives a pretty good light in a pretty short amount of time. I'm not mocking McCandless; he helped invent the ellipsoidal fixture, so his fame is deserved.

IN FOCUS

When focusing the ellipsoidals you can usually change the aim (the hot spot), the size (zoom in or out like a video camera), the focus (soft or hard), the shutters (which we'll get to), and the color, of course. 'Smatter of fact, that's pretty much the routine. You can patch before or after or as you go, which is probably best. If you have an old-fashioned patch panel, you can turn off all of the breakers, plug up each light into a convenient (unique) socket, and place them all in the test position. Then you can click them on one at a time, saving lots of time. I am ashamed to say I didn't think of this; it was one of the kids. Aaron, I think. Anyhow, you hang the light, plug it in, turn on the test button, open the shutters, set the approximate zoom, aim the hotspot, focus the edges, go back and forth a little if it's not perfect, tighten up the nuts, set the shutters, and place the gel. Of course, it's not always that simple. Some architects spec a piece of steel right in the way, so you need extension pipes and a lot of extra time. Some places were designed for a light called a *360,* and the newer lights you now have don't quite fit, so it's best to ignore all of the cussing you'll hear during a focus.

AN AMUSING STORY

When novices are focusing (ignore their cussing too), they take it very seriously. That doesn't mean they do it right, but boy do they take it seriously. The "please" and "thank you" rules must be strictly followed here, since time is probably running short and tempers are flaring. It is not the best time to mention all the days they wasted a couple of weeks ago, but just try not to say it. You see, your temper is flaring too, and a focus takes forever even when it's going well. OK, here's the amusing part. Your stage is forty feet across, four areas, and each ellipsoidal has to light a 10 × 10 box. That's actually asking a lot from the light, but I made the math easy for the sake of the example. The kids will measure these areas to the inch, and take forever to do it, and they'll shutter each area into a perfect little box on the floor. They'll focus the warm light to this box, and then the cool, then they'll check both for a perfect match. Then the next area, and so on. Eventually the first eight lights will be focused and patched and turned on together. The kids are always surprised that there are dark spots on stage. That's the amusing part—they are *always* surprised. Take an imaginary seat in the auditorium, and I will try to explain.

Each ellipsoidal sends out its own little cone of light. You can shutter this so it's not round, but it still expands as it gets farther away. There is no place farther away from the light source than the stage floor (think about it). So, where the actor is, where his *face* is (unless he's dead on the floor), the cone is a little smaller—it has to be. By focusing the light to the exact inch of the area you are trying to light, you guarantee that there will be a dim spot that begins about two feet off of the floor. By the time you get up to a (standing) actor's face, the dark area will be large enough to be noticeable. Plus, even the best ellipsoidals have a hot spot, and even diffusion won't entirely erase it. So, as Professor Harold Hill strolls across River City, he goes into a hot spot, into a dim spot, into a hot spot . . . it's maddening. My buddy Mark says, "Fifty thousand watts of electric light, and I can't see." I suppose I should have run a few strings from the light to the stage floor to illustrate this to the kids, but I never did.

THE FIX

Just demand that the areas overlap about two feet and save yourself the trouble of trying to explain.

FINISHING THE PATCH

These ellipsoidals probably have 750-Watt lamps (plan on replacing these, as they blow, with more efficient versions). Clearly, you'll have to do the math and be sure not to overload anything. And, restating our number-one lighting rule, these should all be similar units with similar lamps. Otherwise, you get real hot spots. If you still are working with mismatched equipment, match it up as best you can. For instance, the warm light can be the 750-Watt lamps, and the cool light can be the 1000s; that won't look too bad. Patch, patch, patch, and assign slider 11 to the warm and 12 to the cool. Play with your front light. Cross-fade from warm to cool and back. Get some stand-ins to walk around on stage so you can actually see the dark spots. Put them in a gray sweatshirt and watch the *shirt* as they walk side to side. Look for dark spots in warm light, cool light, both. What are you, up in the light booth? No, no, no, you have to be in the house to watch this—that's where the audience is (same thing with sound—listen from the house, not the booth). Again, across, cool, warm, both, looking at the shirt, fix the dim spots. The downstage front light is critical if you want your actors to be seen. Spend the most time and effort here, use your best and most powerful units, and you'll be a hero. You can roll out the costumer's mannequin here as a stand-in if you must. Put a sweatshirt on it and a volleyball for a head. Update your cheat sheet.

One day, when you are much, much more confident about your lighting skills, rig a photo light meter on a stick to point at the gray-sweatered mannequin. Push the mannequin around and take note of the readings. You'll probably learn something.

NO REST FOR THE WEARY

You've got eight more lights. They hang among the first set and are aimed at the midstage areas, which you'll number 5, 6, 7, and 8. Hardly anyone has sixteen sockets in the front of house, so you'll have to use what I call *creative extension cording* to get all of these working. Think, and be sure your are not overloading anything. Think, and patch correctly. By the way, you are probably going to change the patch later. Got good front light? Good—it's Miller time. For you, not for the kids. And keep it off campus.

SO ISN'T THIS LIGHTING SCHEME A LITTLE COMMON, AND NOT PARTICULARLY ORIGINAL?

Yep.

AREA LIGHT

You've used up a lot of dimmers, but so far we've only patched in two sliders. You have a patch (a partial patch) that I call *The Assembly Setup*. Good for assemblies and the like. That's about to change. We're going to skip ahead and repatch the front light for areas. See, I had to get you through the simple part without giving too many details, so now we're going to change things and get a more versatile plot. Suppose you've got Macbeth standing alone, right between areas 1 and 2. Actually, the director put him there; you've got to light him. If you bring up slider 11 to full and 12 to half, you get a sort of daylight thing going. Of course, it's all across the stage, and that's the problem. But before we move on, let's have a little fun. Make Macbeth stand there for a while. Change the front light to mostly cool (swap the sliders). Remember, you have to be in the house watching with the house lights out, y'know, like it will be at the show. Hook up the intercom and put the student lighting designer at the board. Or sit her two seats away from you (for the obvious reasons) and put the assistant lighting designer in the booth.

The obvious reason is that a student should not sit right next to a teacher in a dark auditorium late after school with no one else around; isn't that obvious?

Play with the front light. Bring in some cyc light, for instance, 11 and 2 at full (please), 12 at half. Gradually change the cyc light to blue (slider 3), and gradually change the front light to cool (slider 11 out slowly, please). Slowly take the cyc out—in effect, it brightens Macbeth. You should be getting some pretty cool comments from your student lighting designer. Make sure you try to fade slowly; generally the kids program the fades too quick. At this stage, someone is just pushing a slider, so it's easy to go slow. Cool. But the front light problem still remains. The whole stage is lit up, not *just* Macbeth. Time to repatch.

PROGRAM THE CHANNEL SLIDERS

You have to rethink your slider assignments so you can turn off the upstage lights and the stage left area as well. And you still have two colors to deal with. You can easily use up eight slider assignments here. And we haven't even begun top light, side light, or specials. Try this. Think about only the warms for now. Reassign so you can light just area 1 and 2 (slider 9). Put 3 and 4 on slider 10. Keep the midstage light on slider 11. Figure out the assignments for the cool lights on 12, 13, and 14. You've sacrificed six sliders (out of twenty-four, you have fifteen left) and you can heat up three different areas with varying amounts of warm and cool light. And the slider assignments actually make a bit of sense too. Good thinking, champ!

CONFUSED?

The work I just described is done at the *lighting control panel*, up in the lighting booth. Changing a socket assignment is done at the *patch panel*, usually backstage (if you have one at all). OK? Having trouble with the lighting control panel? There's got to be an instruction manual some-where. Try a Web search.

FINISH THE PATCH

"Finish" is probably the wrong word; we still have specials after this. But they're, well, special, and they get their own section. Right now we're adding top and side light. Side light is terrific, extremely dramatic. But you might be running out of fixtures, and that's the one place you can sort of spare them. So, for the moment, for your first few shows, we'll lump side light in with the specials, even though that's not really true. We're skipping a few other important concepts, too, but we can catch those later.

MORE ABOUT THE FIRST ELECTRIC

Instead we are going to load up our *first electric,* the pipe directly above the actors when they are standing on stage. This is probably going to be the place where you cram in the most units, so stock up on electric cables, two-fers, and Fresnels. You sort of copy the system you used in the beams, lighting up the mid- and upstage areas. A bit of overlap with the downstage lighting is essential; ask your crew to light up all areas as the focus progresses. Generally you are hanging Fresnels for front light here, as the electric is pretty close to the stage. Keep the same 45-degree tilt and the same "warm and cool" approach. Slap in some diffusion if you have a hard time getting even light. You are also going to put in top light; if you plan ahead you can load all of the units at once and patch them in later. When it comes time to focus these lights, check for spill onto the curtains. Re-aim, or block out the spill with *barndoors,* which work sort of like shutters, *tophats,* which look like black coffee cans, or with some *blackwrap,* a tough black tinfoil you can buy at the supply house.

TOP LIGHT

For the past few years, I've used high side light as top light. It just means I angle the units in so that the lighting is a little more dramatic. Try it—you'll probably like it. By the way, you don't have to gel top light. Its purpose is to put a sharp edge on your actors (a halo, if you will), mostly on their hair and shoulders. This pops them out from the background, giving the illusion of depth. It's probably best to set high side light from the warm side, so in our example that would be stage right. Collect up all of your Fresnels and hang 'em on the first and second electric. That's the first electric pipe behind the curtain, and the second. At least two of these lights will be in the wings off stage right, since you are tilting them. You can hang them, and even patch them, with the pipe down (flown in), but you have to aim them with the pipe in its normal spot, up out of sight from the front row. Update your cheat sheet and patch (assign sliders) frugally; you are going to run low soon. If you get in a pickle, you can put all of the top light on one slider, especially if you don't have a lot of set pieces (like in *Our Town*), but it's better if you can control each area, same as front light.

If you have a lot of Fresnels (par cans will work), put in a lot of top light. Every five feet would not be overdoing it. Aim them down about 45 degrees and exactly sideways (in the spot position), then move the adjustment knob and flood them out. Aiming them using the spot position is just easier. Top light should be diffuse, so set them to flood after they're aimed. Plop in some diffusion and you're done.

TOP LIGHT WAY DOWN FRONT

When an actor walks way downstage, close to the audience, it's extremely difficult to hit him with top light. The problem is, if top light hits the actor, it's also going to hit the audience. You can use some side light, but you'll get a lot of spill. Luckily, because he is close to the audience, the need for top light is lessened. You see, the main purpose of the top light is to punch the actor out from the background (by shining up his top edges); if the actor is way down front, the background is naturally farther away and less intrusive, and the actor is both bigger and louder, diminishing the need for lighting tricks. Just heat him up with front light and he'll be fine.

THE ALTERNATE PLAN

Some people like it better when top light comes in from (up and) behind instead of directly down or, my preference, from the high (warm) side. These people learned lighting from a photographer, and their system works fine. C'mon, just do one or the other. Stop playing around.

Let's see if you've done it right. It might be a little hard to hit Macbeth with top light from the first electric; he's probably too far in front of the curtain. For the moment, however, we must assume that you can. You've assigned a slider to bring up the top light for just that area. Bring up only top light (please). As Macbeth begins to speak, bring in the blue cyc (slider 3) and the cool light on his face (slider 13 if you are systematic in your channel assignments). Warm him up as you slowly change the cyc lights to show dawn. Pretty powerful, huh? Except the mood doesn't fit the speech. Go from warm front light to cool and change the cyc light to blood red. Have Macbeth turn into the cool light (to his left). Take the warm light out completely. Try all of this with and without the top light. Wow. You, my friend, are getting pretty good at this.

SPECIALS

Well, we skipped a few things, as you'll soon see, but right now our little show needs some specials. The way we've got it set up, we can set a mood and manipulate three areas and we have top light to give us some depth. We're going to add two specials. One, an ellipsoidal from the beams to turn Macbeth red, and one, purple, or orange—some crazy color that looks real cool. An ellipsoidal, a powerful one, with a rich gel. Hang it on the first electric and aim it right in the middle of areas 7 and 8. Tight spot, hard focus, gel it, patch it (slider 24, what the heck), update your cheat sheet. Put a little *spike mark* (an "X") on stage at this special purple hot spot, and place someone sitting, dying, on the floor, looking way up. Use glow tape, as they'll take their mark in the dark. They may need top light too, but that's getting ahead of ourselves.

So here's Macbeth downstage, with his knife, and you're going to turn him red after doing all of the other tricks we've tried. Figure out the patch yourself. Play with the lights, then right at the right moment you'll bring up the purple special, and the supplicant will reach up, as if for mercy. Macbeth twists the blade . . . the purple spot fades while the red spot comes up, the other lights slowly fade, not to black, but to top light, only on Macbeth. The red light glints off of the knife as he twists it. Then out. No one spoke, no one moved, it was all done with light. Whew.

Actually, I don't think there's a scene in Macbeth exactly like that, but you get the idea.

FOOTLIGHTS

I never used footlights. At two recent shows I saw them used, and now I know why I never used 'em. Awful shadows occur whenever you use footlights. Ugh. The only place I might countenance them is for comedic effect. Use side light instead.

BACKLIGHT

Many times people in theater (and in photography) say "backlight" when they mean "*top* light," sometimes called *highlight*. That would be light that shines on your head and shoulders. To me that's top light, and a high side light does the same thing. I usually put it sideways, and some people point it straight down onto the stage, but it works pretty much the same for both.

You probably don't want to *really* backlight an actor on stage. If you did, the light would be shining right into the eyes of your audience. Instead, light the scenery *behind* the actor *really* bright. This throws the actor into silhouette, which is probably what you wanted.

In photography, when something is *backlit,* it means the background is brighter than the subject. It does not necessarily follow that the source of the light is back there.

You *are* allowed to shine lights directly at the audience if there is a train coming, or if Jacey Squires is showing his stereopticon slides in *The Music Man.* One cute little trick is to "fly in" your second electric right at the end of your show, just enough so the top lights can be seen by the audience. They have to be turned a bit downstage for the best effect. Then blink 'em. Very cool, especially if you have three colors up there, like on strip lights. Don't overdo it. And don't do it for *The Crucible.* Wouldn't be prudent. *Grease* would be a better choice.

Another trick is to set up an ellipsoidal or Fresnel to shine on the cyc or back wall from offstage. When your talent comes on, a huge shadow will be cast on the back wall ("looming" and "menacing" are some adjectives that come to mind). You have to practice this a million times or so or it'll look stupid.

BLACKLIGHT

Something "new" in theater is to paint a drop with fluorescent paints that glow under blacklight. Done right, the entire look of the scene can change. I never tried this, as I didn't have the very expensive blacklight equipment, but if you can swing it, it might be fun. There are several companies that rent and sell this kind of stuff. It's not really new, but the technology has come a long way and is getting trendy again. Anybody doing *Hair*?

You can hide a small blacklight in a shadow box and make a fake neon sign out of old garden hose. Paint the garden hose with ultraviolet fluorescent paint and get a pretty convincing neon sign. Build the shadow box in such a way as to keep the audience from seeing the blacklight itself, and have a care that you don't put the fluorescent light on a dimmer—it's bad mojo. Use a non-dim.

SHADOWS ON THE CYC

When you use a lot of front light, especially when you try to light any upstage areas from the beams, the lights will "catch" on the valence curtain and cast a nasty shadow right across your cyclorama. You have to deal with this line. The easiest way is to shutter off the top edge of these lights (surprise! you use the bottom shutter) so no light from the beams ever hits the cyc. When you do this you will no doubt have to add front light from the electrics; try to aim this front light in such a way as to avoid the cyclorama. The most versatile light plot will have the front light lighting up only the talent, not spilling onto the set or backdrops. Correct the most egregious mistakes; you'll probably have to live with a less-than-perfect situation from time to time. Accept a little less than perfection only if the audience can actually *see.* If you are sitting in the house and it's clear to you no one can see the action, then keep a couple of kids late and fix it. This can be done during lunch if you are really pressed for time.

DIM SPOTS

Because you'll usually be using beat-up old fixtures and a cranky dimming system, even your best lighting layout will have dim spots. Any unwanted dim spot in center stage simply must be fixed. If you can track down a poorly functioning fixture, swap it out while you have the time. Otherwise, you just add a few more light cannons and aim 'em at the dim spots. You'll have to customize the patch, but you need the light, so quit whining and pile 'em on. One common place for dim spots is at either wing entrance. It's because you're not supposed to light the curtains, but you are supposed to light the entrance. High side light aimed from center stage out will usually cover the downstage entrances pretty well if the unit—probably an ellipsoidal—is hung slightly upstage of the entrance. When an actor walks on from the wings, she'll be facing this light; by the time she turns downstage, the regular front light should suffice.

HIT IT FROM THE BEAMS

An alternative to this plan is to add a couple of powerful ellipsoidal units in the beams, aimed straight ahead at entrance one and two, just up from the act curtain. Shutter carefully to heat up just the entrance. If you choose to do this, your light plot will have become even more like the original McCandless plan—not necessarily a bad thing.

THE TRUTH HURTS

Well, we've not patched a full show—far from it—but the essentials are there. We skipped a couple of things, and they're very important. First, you're going to have to light the upstage area, near the cyc or back wall (but not on it). And the midstage is probably a little dim too. As you go farther away from your light source, the brightness diminishes rapidly (it's exponential, actually). And you can't hit those areas from the beam position. So you're going to end up loading your first electric with more and more lights. Plus, you can project high side light from two directions if you want (I wouldn't try it for a few shows because it divides your resources and uses up a lot of dimmers). We sort of glossed over side light almost completely, even though it's the coolest. Tell you what. Let's set some side light, and then solve all our other problems.

MIGHTY SIDE LIGHT TECHNIQUE

There is a school of thought that says use a lot of side light. And it is incredible. But usually at the level of production we are talking about, if you rely too much upon side light, you are going to get some horrible shadows and a lot of spill. Plus, the lights are right in the way in the wings (true shin-busters). A great compromise is to put the lights on pipes in the wings, high enough so they won't brain you (this from a guy with four stitches in his eyebrow). From that height, the light won't spill onto the opposite side of the stage, and they will send out a pretty good beam. Ellipsoidals. You might need three per color per entrance, but you also might be able to get away with only lighting two entrances. Later you can experiment with low side light— very cool.

So let's put a whole bunch of ellipsoidals in the wings off stage left, on pipes. Aim, focus, patch (aiming side light is an art—spill and shadow are a big problem). Update your cheat sheet. If you have good front light, you can go a little gaudy with side light colors. A very powerful effect is to use side light only in the most exciting or dramatic moments, like the conclusion of a showstopper. Then, slowly return to normal lighting as the applause fades. It's a powerful, dramatic shift and can carry a lot of emotion, especially when you combine it with a change in the front light and cyc lights.

It's almost like a cue to the audience. Don't rely on this trick too much; like anything else, it gets old fast. One of the true lessons about theater . . . keep some of your stage tricks for Act II, meaning don't show every lighting effect or scenery piece in Act I, and don't overuse any of the tricks or else your show will get boring.

When you get good at side light you'll find yourself using it more and more. This allows you to bring down the front light a bit and still let people see. When you reach the stage where you are subtly manipulating the light levels to give a variation to each and every scene in a show you will have gotten your money's worth from this book. You're welcome.

Now that you've seen it you know you are going to want a different color side light on the other side. Face it, you're out of dimmers, and out of control sliders. You've reached a limit. What to do?

SURPASS YOUR LIMITS

The title of this entire section was "Know Your Limits, and Surpass Them." Things are going well. You've got great front light, particularly way down front where it's most important. The top light is working, and you've got specials aimed and patched and a little side light. But you want more. You've got a couple of spare dimmers, but no more slider channels are available. You've already loaded up your non-dim circuits with effects and equipment that don't need to be dimmed. You need another special, and you really want a third color for that moment just before the end of Act I. It's time to get creative. A second color gel can be flipped into place from the beams, while the lights are off, as long as you have some talent that can move around up there quietly. The gel is removed at intermission. Write it into the cues so you don't forget. Slider 24 can be repatched whenever it's not on, meaning it can be your purple light, then later it can run a gobo aimed at the back wall. Just make sure it's repatched *correctly*. And a circuit breaker or two can be tripped on purpose (by hand) so your area 1 and 2 lights become area 1 lights only. An ellipsoidal can be lugged around like a mini-spotlight and held in someone's hand, as long as it's not on too long. And it can be run from a plug in the wall. You can always rent extra equipment, including dimmers and controllers—good for shows where you have disco lights and chasers. If you are just dying for three more dimmers, you can replace all the 1000-Watt lamps in the cyc lights with 500s, repatch the socket assignments, and there you go. You did keep those 500-Watt lamps, didn't you? And you can have the director change the blocking so that a special can be used twice. You can turn on the work lights if it gives the effect you want. You can patch a socket into the test circuit and use it as a non-dim. Whew. Now you really are a lighting designer.

On some systems, there is even a way to hook up an intentional over-load on a dimmer, then patch and program it so it only goes to half, so it won't really overload the circuit. You *can* do it, but it's not wise and not appropriate for this book. If a lighting professional teaches you how, I'll let you do it. By the way, most "lighting professionals" aren't. They're just people like you and me who have been around a while and figured all of these tricks out on their own. Heck, once I got introduced to some folks as a "lighting expert." Made my day.

Whatever you do, don't overload the circuits.

IF THIS IS ALL TOO MUCH FOR YOU

If you don't have the equipment, time, or enough help to set up a light plot as described above, you can still get by, especially in simpler shows, with my buddy Mark's favorite shortcut. Use this when the deadline is too close or when you arrive too late in the game to do better. The secret: medium amber gel (Rosco 20). Load the entire front of house with medium amber (forget about mixing colors, forget about side light), place the most primitive no-gel top light, and escape, maybe even get a few com-pliments. Since you have simplified the light plot to its absolute minimum, you may just be able to produce a nice even wash, which is fine for a lot of plays, especially where lighting tricks could detract from the mood.

The great advantage of this system is its simplicity. Almost everyone looks good in medium amber (but not everyone), so you're pretty safe there. Be careful to avoid hot spots, which can really spoil the wash. And slap diffusion on every last unit. When you use this trick, you have to promise yourself it's just for this *one* time. Once only, in your whole life. That's what we did for *Frankenstein,* and, um, *Charley's Aunt,* and, um, *I Hate Hamlet*!

DMX

Modern lighting control systems are run with a technique called *DMX.* I don't know what DMX means, but I do know how it works. A DMX light controller sends out a code for every single one of the lighting circuits several times a second. About forty-four times a second, actually, which is faster than the blink of an eye. Each circuit can count, and decodes the information for itself and no other circuit. All of the circuits are strung up in a row. Each dimmer reacts to the control code. Pretty cool. The whole system just stands by in a ready state waiting for a change in the code, which would correspond to some change in the lights. The cool thing is that this can control the position of moving lights as well as the brightness, so we can have all sorts of fun. The technology is already racing forward beyond the abilities of the code; but that really isn't a problem for us—just folks like Paul McCartney and Britney Spears. If you get to the point where you are manipulating DMX codes for moving lights and effects, pat yourself on the back. Just don't repeat the effects too many times, or people will notice.

I think "DMX" means "digital multiplexing."

IDEAS I SHOULD PATENT

1) Theater lights that have their own built-in dimmer, controllable by radio or on the power line (which is actually possible).

2) A mini-radio mic that bonds to a tooth, transmitting to a hidden repeater with no wires (which is probably possible).

3) A theater light that can correct for keystoning (coming in 2005).

4) A lighting control panel that works like a Theremin, with just a wave of the hand.

CUE 10.8 SMOKE, FOG, AND HAZE

Somewhere in some show you are going to want to add some kind of fog effect, either to accentuate the lights or to set some kind of mood for a scene. There are a great variety of fog machines for the theater. Rent 'em. That way you don't have to maintain them. The disco-type fogger (with "fog juice") works for most shows, but the fog usually floats away, which could be a good or a bad thing, depending. Also, it's bound to make someone cough. As a kid I worked on the world premiere of *K-2,* the mountain-climbing play, and therefore got to see it free when the revival came around. I think they used a chemical fogger; everybody was coughing, which kind of ruined the effect. Experiment with powerful exhaust fans. Dry ice foggers make a fog that stays low. A *hazer* makes a fine mist—great when you want to see the light beams themselves. One thing you can say about fog: It never works the same way twice. Works perfectly in rehearsal; with an auditorium full of people it behaves differently. Works differently during the daytime and the nighttime, probably due to the temperature of the auditorium. And if the elephant doors are open, watch out. (The *elephant doors* are those big garage-like doors that roll up so you can get your elephant, and all of your other set pieces, from the stage to the scene shop.) Fog effects are best used sparingly, kind of like side light—great except when used too much.

CUE 10.9 BLINKY LIGHT SHOW

When you're not running your own shows, the theater space is going to be used by other groups. Heck, *during* your show the space will be used by other groups. Get used to it. They are going to want lights, and sound, and everything else. They are going to want your stage crew. And they are going to want you. You have to decide how much help you are going to give them. I tried to make myself available to the school groups, but couldn't say yes to them all. We opened the paint closet for most school groups, but not for outside groups that were renting the space. Seemed appropriate.

School variety shows are the shows where you can allow your student lighting designers more freedom to try something wacky. Why? Because it's not *your* show, and the person running it needs someone with ideas to help them out. A perfect opportunity to let students help direct, design, and show their independence. At Blair we have *Indian Night, Ethiopian Night,* the *Black History Show,* and the *International Show; Magnet Arts Night,* the *CAP Cabaret,* and the *New Faces* show. Our Thespian Club puts on shows of its own, including a student-directed one-act festival. We used to hold a coffeehouse. Tori Amos played there. And of course we have our plays and musicals. So you see why I couldn't work on them all.

Be aware, however, that the novice sponsors of these shows don't know exactly what to ask for. That is, they haven't read this book. Feel free to buy them a copy. So the sponsor, particularly in a variety or talent show, not knowing what *can* be done, will ask for a blackout after every little act. Because it's the easiest way to get acts on and off. This is the dreaded *Blinky Light Syndrome* and will turn even a good talent show into a bore. Lights up, lights off. Lights up, lights off . . . *please.* You could let them do this, but your conscience will gnaw at your vitals, and you'll die young. Show them how to do simple cross-fades, cyc light color changes, spotlight the emcees—anything to prevent the stage from going black after every act. . . . If they have an emcee, cross-fade to an ellipsoidal spot set up on the apron—anything—just don't let the stage go dark except when it needs to go dark for effect. And don't let them use the curtain like a jack-in-the-box, either.

In a blinky light show, or an assembly, you can usually get away with running the light board *live;* that is, with a minimum of preset cues. Due to the unpredictable nature of these shows, it's probably best to do so. If you have the ability to set submasters (any modern light board can do this), do it; otherwise, play the channel sliders like a piano and have a finger on the blackout button. Keep the fancy stuff to a minimum, and remember the most important part of theater lighting: Let the audience see everything they are supposed to see. If you're stuck with more archaic equipment, simplify the light cues as much as possible and preset as many things as you can.

We're not done with lights (you've got to set the cues, for goodness sakes), but you've been ignoring the sound guys.

CUE 11 Go.

MORE ON SOUND

A big part of running sound is playing sound effects. You can record these yourself, buy a compilation of sound effects on CD or tape (try CD), or copy sound effects off of old records or videotape. In short, anything goes—*almost*. We pinched a "horse trotting" sound effect off of some movie for a show. I suppose it would be a copyright infringement if we were a commercial house; I just chalked it up to "fair use." Understand, however, that sound effects and music are two different things.

You are supposed to pay a royalty when you perform or play someone's copyrighted works. Pinching the alarm clock sound off of Pink Floyd's *Dark Side of the Moon* album seems like a venial sin; having the orchestra perform the entire album without paying a performance royalty is a crime. Especially if you charge admission (although a school project is a different story). And if you're doing this as a commercial venture, you are bound to get a call from a lawyer eventually. But for a school show you are allowed a little latitude. A little. Use your judgment. Buy a complete sound effects library on CD and your worries are over.

Collect up all of your sound effects and put 'em together in order.

TAPE/CD/MINIDISC

I have seen people try to play sound effects from several different CDs and tapes. They end up trying to change tapes in the middle of a show in the dark, then put the CDs in upside down. Please. Let's gather all the effects and put them in order on a tape or something so we can play them back properly every time.

I am a big advocate of doing this on cassette tape. My predecessors just as strongly pushed using an old-fashioned reel-to-reel machine. Fogeys. I'm the fogey now, as the best way to do this is on a custom-made CD or MiniDisc. Since you may not have CD-burning equipment, we'll make a cassette tape.

GAIN

Remember gain? That's the magnitude, for lack of a better term, of a signal before it reaches the tape or the main amplifier. Remember also that whenever you *play* music you are just adjusting *output* controls. When you *record* music (or run a mixer) you are playing with *input* controls, and the gain settings are critical. If we're going to make a tape, we have to pay attention to the meters on our cassette deck. Listening as we record is not good enough; if the meters (the gain controls) are set wrong, the tape will sound lousy on playback. Back to school.

SIGNALS AND NOISE

Tapes make noise when you play them, even if they are blank. It's a little hiss, and that Dolby guy has worked very hard to reduce hiss, so try to find the best cassette deck you can for recording and use the Dolby controls. Some hi-fi addicts don't like Dolby too much. Fine, you guys do it your way—we want it to sound good. Reduce the hiss, reduce the noise, use the Dolby controls. And pay extra for a chrome tape. They aren't naturally that much quieter—they just allow you to put a louder recording onto the tape. So the noise comes out quieter compared to the music. Nice loud music (a good signal), not much hiss (no noise). This is the magic *signal-to-noise* ratio that stereo magazines used to crow about. Let's pretend we are cribbing the jackhammer from the Lovin' Spoonful's *Summer in the City* off of your record collection at home.

As you play the song the first time, have the cassette deck all prepped, set on "record." Be sure you have rewound the tape and reset the counter to "000." Record a little silence to get away from the beginning of the tape, press pause, and watch the little meters on the cassette deck. Not the counter that now probably says "003," but the *VU meters*— the left and right level meters that show the signal level during recording and playback. One other thing: The real volume in the room is not an issue right now, just the meters, so set the room volume at any comfortable level.

With a chrome tape, you're allowed to record up to something called +3 dB. If you see it on the meter, fine; otherwise, it's the yellow lights, with maybe the briefest of red lights blinking. Modern tape decks don't have the yellow lights, just look carefully for the proper markings. On a cassette deck with real meters (peak meters with needles), it's just into the red. You might see the magic Dolby mark on the meters. Adjust the gain (the input level) until the needles or meters are perfectly aligned with the marks just described. Too low and you won't be able to hear the sound effect later. Too high and the tape won't be able to properly record the signal and it'll sound funny later. Fancy cassette decks have two input controls (left and right are separate); most have one. Be sure you have set the levels in stereo by watching *both* meters.

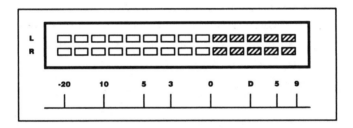

Cassette Meters

Chrome tapes are pretty forgiving, so you might be able to record the signal a little hot. Just watch the meters for egregious misalignment, high or low.

Replay the original music, push pause at just the right moment (this act unpauses the cassette deck), and then, at just the right instant, push the pause button again. Great. But you aren't done. Stop the music and record silence for ten more seconds. This separates your sound effects. Now you are done. Rewind and listen. If it's right, you may move on to sound effect two; if not, do it again. You have got to record extra silence every time and listen to each sound effect as you make it if you want to avoid pips and pops and unwanted noise on the recording.

Our next sound cue is the previously mentioned alarm clock from *Dark Side of the Moon*. Set everything up afresh and *check the levels*. No one ever said Pink Floyd and the Lovin' Spoonful had to play their music at the same level. You are going to want this effect after the jackhammer, so listen to the tape and watch the counter. After the jackhammer you have about ten seconds of recorded silence. Listen and watch the little counter on the cassette deck. Push pause at the appropriate moment (then stop), set up to record (*please* check the levels), then record as above. This admittedly painstaking process assures you of a tape that plays at a constant volume (since you set the levels every time), with no start and stop noises, and with plenty of time between sound effects.

If you are watching the VU meters more carefully now and saying to yourself, "So that's why my homemade cassettes didn't used to sound so good," then I think you've probably got it right. Let's move on.

Our third sound effect is the jackhammer again. "Fine," you say, "I'll just rewind and play it again when the time comes . . . "No, *no*, NO! Sorry to yell like that. Your job here is to record *all* of the sound effects in order so that it is easy, *easy* to play them back in order. No rewinding. No flipping tapes over. Take your time and do it right. Put all the sound effects and prerecorded music cues in order, properly recorded onto one tape. Write down the counter numbers so you can pause the tape during playback. Make a spare tape (a duplicate—just in case), and when you are done remove the *record lockout* (that little plastic tongue on the back edge of the cassette). Good job.

FOGEYISM

I have a CD burner, and I have recorded sound effects and music cues onto a CD and played it during a show. When it works, it's the greatest. Your kids will look at you funny when you insist on using cassettes; they are used to making CDs and mini-discs and consider cassettes to be Stone Age–remnant technology. They don't even steal the blank cassettes from me anymore. But I have a little problem making CDs that I don't have making cassettes, and that's why I still use cassettes. When I input a sound effect into my computer, I find it very difficult to set the level. It could be a software issue, an incorrect setting, or operator error, but it's enough of a problem that I don't use the computer except when I must (for instance, when I want to use some kind of sound-editing program). The truth is, if you can do sound effects on a CD, do it. That way you can make changes on a daily basis and just burn a new CD. (They cost less than fifty cents.) Changing a cassette is a pain. Whatever you do, don't run the sound effects directly off of the computer. The off-chance of a computer crash is far greater than the very slim chance of a CD or cassette failure, plus there's reboot time . . . just don't do it.

PLAYBACK

Let's have a practice run-through of our sound effects. You may have recorded the sound effects at home, or elsewhere, but for real playback you have to use the real system in the theater. Everything set up for playback? Good. You have to watch the counter on the cassette deck and the setting on the mixer (for volume). Play the cassette from the beginning and pause it a moment before the counter tells you the sound is coming. In our example, that was at reading 003. I hope you have all this stuff written down. Set your volume (and gain) on the mixer, about 80 percent, remember? When the cue comes, push the "pause" button (unpausing the tape), play the sound effect, and bring the volume down on the mixer. Run the tape up to the next sound effect, note the counter reading, pause, volume . . . you'll get the hang of it. Keep the volume down while setting things up, especially when the director says, "Do it again . . . "

Changing cassette decks usually means changing the counter readings, so avoid doing that. Use the best deck you have, even it you have to carry it back and forth from home. Keep meticulous notes of counter readings, volume settings, fades (you do them live), and changes.

<u>NEVER</u>

I have never, *never,* had a problem with playing good sound effects I'd made on good equipment. The counter works in forward and reverse, the tapes lasted throughout the run of the show . . . never a problem.

Except . . . when other people brought me tapes. This sometimes meant big trouble, as they usually aren't as careful as they need to be when they record the thing. And sometimes they bring in a really cheap tape that plays in their machine but jams in yours. And most school cassette players, forget it. Make sure you use a decent cassette deck and a high-quality tape, and record at the proper levels. Then it's clear sailing. Until the lawyers from Pink Floyd come after you. . . .

TESTING THE MICS

The other job for the sound technicians is practicing with the board. During rehearsals, the sound operators need to be at the board running sound as if were for real. This includes floor mics, if you have them, wired and wireless mics, and sound effects. Beginners need an unusual amount of practice time to develop skill in running the board live, especially when there are a bunch of sound effects and a lot of mics. This is a task that is usually ignored, as right about now there are a million things going wrong, but if you want good sound you must get the crew to practice. I think the biggest complaint at this level of theater is, "I couldn't hear the voices." If you are to excel you must, must, *must* practice sound. Set up everything. Test everything before rehearsal. I remember getting quite upset when the real problem was a broken wire somewhere; test everything. Put the radio mics on the talent, even for rehearsals. This is a huge job—assign labor to help.

THE SNAKE

You may need to line up some custom audio equipment in order to properly run mics. One thing is called a *snake,* and it gets the wired mics on stage connected to the mixer somewhere in the back of the house. I have used two snakes in one show. If your theater has some installed mic wiring, use that first, but if it isn't enough, or if it doesn't seem to work, go ahead and hook up everything to a 100-foot-long snake. Try to "snake" the device safely through the house to a convenient location near the wired mics. Take note of the mic numbers, and there you are.

THE TRUTH HURTS

Here we are, in pre-publication of this book, and I just sat through two shows with poor sound. Awful sound. Not my shows, thank goodness. It was bad enough that I could recommend hiring this job out to a professional. It'll cost you, but poor sound ruins a show, so it might be money well spent. Just be sure the company you hire really is professional and can do what you want. Generally I am all for the students doing as much as possible, but if it's *not* possible, well, admit it and hire it out. A coworker of mine *always* hired out the sound for her rock revues, and it was probably a wise move. Use your rapidly developing Solomon-like wisdom to do the right thing here.

CUE 12 *Go.*

SETTING CUES

Like everything else in this book, I've tried to simplify the cue writing so you can get the job done. Purists will cringe, like they did when we read dimensions off of an architect's scale (usually a no-no) and like they did when we bench focused the ellipsoidals by eye. Phooey on them. If you were teaching a higher-level technical theater course, or working in a pro location, you'd put a lot more time and effort into every step of the productions. Plus, you'd be working with people who already knew what they were doing. Here we must simplify so we don't get bogged down in minutiae. Still, in a couple of pages you're going to find some stuff that's hard to read. Well, it's not meant to be *read,* it's meant to be *studied.* Poke through cue by cue until the system makes sense. (Some mistakes are included as examples.)

Stage cues are written by the stage manager with a lot of input from the lighting designer. Or perhaps by the lighting designer while the lighting is being worked out, then turned over to the stage manager. The cue list includes every little thing, such as: turning off the work lights before the show, sound effects, curtain pulls, on- and offstage scenery movement (like putting things in place offstage during intermission for Act II), and every lighting cue. I have always let the kids write all of the cues, telling them what I want beforehand and what I don't like after the technical rehearsal. Then I lean on them to practice and improve the cues. So cues must be roughed out long before the technical rehearsal. Or, when real life intervenes, the night before the tech rehearsal.

During the tech, most of the flaws will become apparent and, hopefully, fixed. Then improvements are made through the dress rehearsals, then you're on, and improvements are still made all the way to closing night. In a perfect world, you can sit with the crew after the show closes, watching an archival videotape of closing night, and still rewrite cues: "See how this didn't work—what should we have done?" This doesn't help the show that just closed, but believe me, it helps the next show, already a twinkle in the director's eye.

The crew will need a short list of blackout cues so they can assign jobs for the stage left and stage right personnel. Usually they can do this themselves. The "prop pope" (prop master) will need to have some kind of list, too, for no other reason than to see that everything is ready. The stage manager will need a complete list of all cues.

When writing real cues (for the moment we'll concentrate on lighting cues), the lighting designer is supposed to consider time of day, the action, the mood, the direction of the main or motivating light, the "flow," the shape of the visual frame, the focus of the audience attention, the focus of the actor's attention, pattern, balance, what's happening offstage, the effect of mixed colors, movement . . . uh oh, we have a problem here. We are going to have to attack this a different way. We need to simplify. You can write cues in strict chronological order, or you can begin with the most important scenes, or you can start in Act II, then go to the end and start over at the beginning, but you have to set the light and the cues for the *whole show*. And you are probably in a hurry. So we'll deal with the above items only on an as-needed basis. Meaning we're going to set lights by eye. Try a blue cyc. If you don't like it, switch to red. This may seem short-sighted or time-consuming, but I have found that the best-laid plans (and the most thoughtful light plots) don't always work out and will have to be scrapped anyway. Your lighting designer may not have a single show's worth of experience, the director is going to want to make changes, some things simply won't look right; just let it go and set it by eye. Plus, it allows for happy accidents. And, lastly, we don't need to spend a lot of time discussing the *mood* of Juliet's death scene; we'll be able to tell if the lights look too cheerful.

Of course, you've already thought the thing through enough to have specials when you need 'em, and you've experimented a little bit with color; we're just skipping the part where you try to imagine if your paper lighting plot is balanced, and we're balancing it on the spot. We're doing this because none of us have enough experience to "see" the plot until we actually *see* the plot. For real. So, taking a sort of holistic approach until we develop our talents is in order. Besides, at the last minute, the director may change an entrance or an exit or cut an unnecessary scene, throwing the entire lighting scheme into disarray. On the other hand, if a precocious LD wants to try to preplan the whole show, let 'em.

Take a moment to establish complete freedom to a young lighting designer, subject to your approval and the director's. That means the LD is submitting cues to *you* for *your* approval. The LD has freedom, but the cues *must* satisfy you and the director. This gentle reminder will soothe the LD's feelings ahead of time. It's an important position, and sometimes it's difficult for a young LD to take direction. He thinks, "I thought *I* was the LD," and resists your suggestions. Point out that your suggestions are *not* suggestions, they are *directions.* So what the LD says goes, unless you change it; you say, "Please," he says, "Thank you." And of course the director trumps you. If the director wants blue, it's blue.

GETTING STARTED

A few days before the technical rehearsal, the stage manager should have a pretty good idea about the stage action, since he's been working closely with the director and has written down exactly what she wants. The lighting designer should have enough of a plot figured out to know what can and cannot be done. It's time for them to sit together and peruse the script and begin to figure out cues. This is called a *paper tech,* and if they do a good job it makes everything that follows much easier. You can prime the pump by mentioning little things that you want a few days before they have to get started. Once they have everything on paper, it's time to set it up for real, again before the tech rehearsal actually begins. Some folks call this pre-tech rehearsal work a *dry tech,* and it's a good term. I might actually start using it. Budget a lot of time for this stressful setting-up period.

For our first attempt, we'll take a show in chronological order. This method has some flaws to be aware of: The beginning of the show might be poorly lit, since your crew hasn't reached a "groove" yet, and the end of the show may be poorly lit since the lighting designer's eyes are bleeding and everyone else is exhausted. But you have to start somewhere. If luck is with you, you are beginning a few days before the real technical rehearsal. (Anything to get a jump on the tech rehearsal, that's what I always say.) Let's take a few scenes from *Fiddler.*

We gloss over the opening cues:

Cue 1—Places! (And all presets)
Cue 2—House lights dim
Cue 3—House lights out
Cue 4—Spot the conductor
Cue 5—Curtain warmers out
Cue 6—Spots out
Cue 7—Curtain

The show opens with a fiddler—hopefully on a roof—and Tevye talking. Decision time. What do you want the audience to look at? Do you want some of the stage lights on before the curtain, or do you want the lights to come up as the curtain opens? Do you want to light the fiddler with a special? Do you have your fiddler walk on (playing) just before the curtain opens? Most of these decisions have already been made, of course. Circumstances may have forced your fiddler off of the roof because it was just too weak. The director can make an inspired (or an insipid) change. We'll try this bit a couple of different ways just to get the hang of things. This should be fun because *Fiddler* is my favorite show.

HERE WE GO

Cue 7—Curtain
       Cyc lights (red) silhouette the fiddler as he plays
       House and barn dim
Cue 8—Tevye enters as curtain is still moving—Spot on Tevye
Cue 9—Tevye says "Tradition," ensemble enters, front, top, and
       side light up
       Tevye wanders (still in spot) to each family group

or

Cue 9—Brighten up DS, take down the ensemble US
       Groups move to CS for their moment
       You'll probably take out the spot . . .

or

Cᴜᴇ **9**—Each group has a mark; bring up area light for each
vignette

This could end up being 20 cues, and too many changes

OR TRY THIS . . .

Cᴜᴇ **7**—Fiddler enters DS of closed curtains—in spotlight

Cᴜᴇ **8**—Tevye meets fiddler CS

Cᴜᴇ **9**—Tevye says, "Tradition"—Curtain opens to pre-lit set

This allows the fiddler to dance around, since he's not really on the roof. Then the fiddler can draw attention to each group in turn.

ONE MORE . . .

Cᴜᴇ **7**—Cast enters silently in no light, freezes in place

Cᴜᴇ **8**—Fiddler enters in a spotlight and plays and walks to Tevye

Cᴜᴇ **9**—Lights up on Tevye as he turns towards the audience

Cᴜᴇ **10**—"Tradition"—Lights up for song as cast comes to life

ONE MOMENT PLEASE

You can see that this is going to be a long, tedious process. Unexpected problems will crop up, further shredding your well-thought-out original plans. Plus the levels of every light must be adjusted for every scene, to move focus and avoid hot spots. Let's set a couple of guidelines and try to streamline the process. First, set all of the lighting cues. They will have to be numbered according to whatever system your light board uses, and usually the light cues far outnumber all of the other cues combined. Usually you just number the cues 1, 2, 3, 4, 5; then if you have to squeeze a new cue in, you can add a cue 4.5. Most computerized boards work the same way.

That was so easy to write: "First, set all of the lighting cues." The truth is, this is going to take hours, especially since you, the director, and the LD are all going to have strong opinions about light levels. Aren't you glad you followed my advice and firmly established a hierarchy of command? Remember to give the LD plenty of time to set everything. Of course, you'll probably have to coax him into moving along forthrightly; the show is long and he'll never get done if you don't push him a little.

What's supposed to happen is the LD will sit in the darkened theater with an assistant in the booth, the scenery in place, the cast on stage, and a couple of helpers to re-aim lights when needed. They poke through scene by scene and set the intensity of every single light in every single scene. To return to our example, *Fiddler,* the LD may choose to brighten or darken the spot on Tevye, and might remove the top light completely. He writes everything down (be sure he is writing everything down) and sends the messages upstairs via the intercom, and the crew resets the lights until the LD is satisfied. Then the director butts in and changes everything, which will elicit, "She's ruining my plot!" from the LD . . . sorry, I was having a bad dream. Again, start this procedure *before* the real tech rehearsal, get a sort of rough plot, and save a lot of heartache.

Next, let's get the spotlight operation down. An actor is not supposed to wait for a spotlight, and the spot operator is not supposed to wait for an actor. I have had long philosophical discussions with some directors about this when they say, "Enter when the spot comes on," or worse, "Wait for your light." This, of course, causes the tiniest delay. And the spot operators, in spite of everything, are reluctant to open the shutter until they have something to aim at. So they end up waiting for the actor, which they shouldn't do, and the actor is waiting for the spotlight. This is a problem.

When the cue is called (Tevye's entrance, for instance) the actor should enter and the spot should pick him up. At the *same time.* Imagine you are the stage manager, with one hand on Tevye's shoulder. You say, "Cue 8—Go!" and slap Tevye on the shoulder. He enters and the light picks him up. The spot operator didn't wait for *Tevye,* and Tevye didn't wait for the spot. Hesitation is little less than a crime here. So the actor goes when the cue is called and never waits for the spot. The spot operator should know where Tevye is entering and pops on the spot at the word "Go!" Then he "picks up" Tevye if his aim is a little off. Practice this or pay the consequences. Done well, the entrance is seamless.

AND ANOTHER THING

Since we're beginners (never admit this, of course), it's probably best to set the grossest of light cues and then refine. Then, at the tech rehearsal, set everything as perfectly as possible. That way you get the whole show set before you run out of time. Consider *Fiddler;* we could spend an entire day on this opening at the expense of later scenes. And the point where we ran out of time will be obvious to the most casual observer. So set rough cues and refine.

CALLING CUES

A note to the stage manager: If you wait until a cue is needed, you'll surprise the crew when you call it. The clever stage manager anticipates the cues by back-timing from the cue itself and giving warnings via the intercom or by a system of lights and switches. The intercom is far superior to any kind of cue light system, but we used cue lights on the fly and in other locations far from the stage manager. We'll take our original nine cues and add warnings (the words in parentheses are not said aloud):

    Cue—Places! (And all presets)
        (Cyc lights red silhouette the fiddler)
        (House and barn dim, no front light)
    Ready Cue 2
    Cue 2—Go. (House lights dim)
    Ready Cues 3 and 4
    Cue 3—Go. (House lights out)
    Cue 4—Go. (Spot the conductor)
    Ready Cues 5, 6, 7, and 8
    Cue 5—Go. (Curtain warmers fade out)
    Cue 6—Go. (Spots out)
    Cue 7—Go. (Curtain)
        (Fiddler plays, lights have been on since Cue 1)
    Cue 8—Go. (Slap) (Tevye enters as curtain is still moving. Spot on
        Tevye)
    Ready Cue 9
    Cue 9—(Tevye says "Tradition")—Go. (Ensemble enters, front, top,
        and side light up. Tevye wanders, still in spot, to each family
        group)

Anybody who has really set cues is giggling right now as they see the weaknesses of this system. For one thing, the spotlight operators are certainly not following the script, so they may not remember what "Cue 8—Go" means. So cues for the spot operators usually add more detail. To be honest, spotlight cues don't even need to be numbered. Here is an alternative:

    Ready Cue 3. Ready spots on conductor
    Cue 3—Go. (House lights out)
    Spots on the conductor . . . Go.

Ready spots out. Spots out . . . Go! Ready spots on right entrance one.

You get the picture. Some folks like to differentiate the tasks, and the cues.

Liᶃ**ht Cu**ᴇ **5—Go.** (Curtain warmers fade out)
Ready spots out . . . Spots out—Go. (Spots out)
Rᴇᴀ**dy Cu**ʀᴛᴀɪɴ **Cu**ᴇ **1.** Curtain—Go. (Curtain)

The stage manager is the only crew person concerned with all of the cues. So numbering them separately is not too much of a problem. If the stage manager clearly calls "*Lighting* Cue 1," we probably won't hear *Sound* Cue 1. That is, if everyone is awake, alert, and on task. Besides, it's much easier to set the light cues independently of all other cues, since they have to be programmed into the lighting control board. (In an old-fashioned system they'll have to be written down on paper, then pre-set as the show proceeds, then reset, and reset, and reset . . . aren't you glad you have a computer-controlled board?)

CONFIRMATION

A nice refinement when using an intercom for calling cues is to have the crew member involved with the cue confirm that they heard the stage manager's warning. So "Ready Lighting Cue 6" would be followed by the reply, "Lights," a simple response that confirms that the light operator is indeed ready. If the stage manager doesn't get this confirmation, she knows to give the warning again or find out what's wrong.

PRACTICING CUES

The crew should rehearse all of the cues, concentrating on the most important ones and any that are causing trouble. It gets a little dull, but the only way to perfect the show is to practice the cue, refine it if necessary, and practice it again. The same goes for set changes.

PRACTICING SET CHANGES

Set changes are a huge problem, as they usually take too long. Get the crew all dressed in black, hand out some of those cute little flashlights that look like cigarette lighters (ushers get these too), and practice those set changes. Practice, streamline, reset pieces, do whatever it takes to make them run flawlessly. Unfortunately, you are usually just about out of time when you're ready to practice these changes; but remember, they are just as important as the other parts of the show. There is no question that a smooth-running show is going to be a better show, so practice the set changes until they are perfect. Ninety percent will do in a pinch. If the crew is having a difficult time in the dark, the LD can add a very low-level light cue in between scenes. Helps a lot when placing set pieces.

If the cues and scene changes need polishing (and they will), you can try to run a Q2Q. That is, a cue-to-cue rehearsal. I hate these, but they do have a place in the scheme of things. Let's suppose you've just run a dress rehearsal and things look pretty good but it's obvious that the crew hasn't solidified the scene changes, and some of the other cues aren't sharp enough either. Before letting anyone go home, you run the whole show again, and the stage manager deletes everything that isn't just before or just after a cue. Sort of like running a show in fast forward. I don't like the zany intensity of a Q2Q, but it does allow everyone to practice the cues in order without having to add an entire rehearsal. Use it if you need it.

CUE 12.9 VIDEO CAMERA HANDY?

Most performance contracts forbid the use of video cameras; fortunately for us, an archival copy for rehearsals and teaching is a fair use that nobody'll sue you over. What the theatrical companies are trying to prevent is you selling copies of their copyrighted work, so don't do that. Many parents will come in and want to tape a show—or every show. You'll have to treat them diplomatically by printing a notice in the program forbidding the process. Then maybe it's best if you look the other way and don't raise a fuss when parents set up a video camera they bought brand-new today, just for tonight's show, because they want to send a copy to Grandma. . . .

For you, video is a teaching tool. Videotape dance rehearsals; with modern equipment you can play the tape back in slow motion. Use video to help show flaws in the lighting; your eye can compensate for less-than-perfect lighting, but you can't fool the camera lens. It's particularly good at showing hot spots that you might otherwise ignore. You can usually find an interested student or volunteer to shoot a video record of the entire production. If you want to videotape the show and sell copies, you have to ask the production company for permission first.

Cue 13 Go.

The Week Before the Show

As you get closer and closer to opening night, your notebook is going to fill to bursting with little notes about the show. Somewhere along the line you must realize that it's not all going to get done—just the most important 90 percent. You have to develop a very flexible sense of what can be fixed, and what you have to settle for. Sit down and watch rehearsals, which at this stage of the game are going on side-by-side with the painting and the last-minute set repairs. Take notes just as if you were the director. You need to know the show, and you need to watch to see where the technical aspects of the production need improvement. If you spend all of your time backstage, you'll get a rude awakening when you finally sit down and see everything together. So, somewhere around "T minus 2 weeks," move bodily out into the auditorium. Take notes.

Share these notes with the director somewhere where you can't be overheard. There's bound to be a couple of places where you disagree with the director; defer to the director even when you know it's a mistake. Then present your changes/improvements to the troupe as "notes." You cannot give acting notes unless you have run them by the director. You may give technical notes about staying in the light, entrances and exits, safety, and scenery issues. The director can, of course, give technical notes, and should, as a courtesy, run them by you, mostly so you can both show a united front to the cast. The idea that both of you have conferred and agree on notes gives a powerful message to any cast, undercutting their "she doesn't know what she's talking about" mentality. Lots of people have a difficult time taking direction; they don't see the benefit of doing a certain thing a certain way and will stall or oppose both you and the director.

This was proven in a recent show, as every single staff member associated with the show gave clear and simple instructions not to move one particular scenery piece ever, at all. (It was a painted door.) Yet any kid anywhere near the piece moved it, not out of spite, but because it seemed to them they should. It was never meant to move, it wasn't built to move, and every last kid tried to open the non-working door.

When this happens to you, you'll have to call out all of your reserves of patience and explanation to convince the kids to do it the way they are instructed. Try to stay calm. If it's important enough, yelling "Don't touch the stinking door!" may work, but if you yell too much you'll torpedo your own show.

PROPS ASSIGNMENTS

Props are laid out on offstage tables; the tables are first covered with white paper and labeled as to what prop goes where on the table. Touching someone else's prop is forbidden, even if the prop is way cool, and actors that forget to replace their props are shot, unless you are short on actors. Never allow a student to bring in a prop if it is important to them, and don't bring in something from home if it's important to you. I still have Sally's broken candlestick (I promised I'd repair it, and I've tried, but I can't). Props that go offstage on the wrong side are given to the props crew on that side and are secretly run across as needed. I have seen two kids on "props" run something across stage without being too secretive about it; that is, they ran the prop across the stage. With the play going on. Oops. They are supposed to run around back.

KEEPING COSTUMES CLEAN

My director had a hard-and-fast rule that concerned food and costumes. The rule was that there was no such thing as food *and* costumes. Even at dress rehearsals she'd make the kids change for dinner. I convinced her that if the kids wore robes (from home) they'd protect the costumes and save a lot of time. Just have all kids bring in nice big robes from home, put their names in them, and keep 'em in the green room. This will comfort the director and get dinner done with a little bit less waste of time. Parents would occasionally provide a pizza lunch for the kids during tech rehearsal; imagine having fifty kids standing in the hall in bathrobes eating pizza. Kind of makes you giggle, but it works. If I was feeling cruel I'd make the crew kids work through the cast dinner—at least the lighting kids. If things were going better I'd let everyone take a break at the same time. Don't forget to reserve a couple of slices of pizza for yourself. Getting a couple of slices of pizza to the custodian wouldn't be a bad idea either.

CUE 13.9 TEASERS

A teaser is a school assembly where you present a little bit of the play to the entire school to try to drum up business. It's a little like a pep rally for the play. Our school is so large we have to set up four separate teasers of about forty minutes each so that everyone can see a bit of the show. Of course, you put these on just before opening night. Pick the best parts of the show, or the parts where kids kiss, and you'll be sure to get a reaction from the audience. Plus, it's good for the actors to hear laughter and applause from the audience before opening night. Remember, they've been playing to an empty house. Legally you might be obligated to pay extra royalty for a teaser assembly, but I've never heard of anybody being sued over something so trivial. And, of course, the teasers attract a bigger audience, which results in more royalties in the long run anyway. Remember, a teaser is just a tease, so only show good stuff and don't give away any too many surprises.

In community theater you may choose to give previews at a discount, or even for free. If you do this, you are still supposed to pay a performance royalty; perhaps you can negotiate a discounted rate.

COSTUME PARADE

Sometime just before opening night collect up all your kids, put 'em in costume, and parade 'em through the school. This can be done at lunchtime or as the kids arrive or leave. Lunchtime is best. The chance that a costume will be damaged is heavily outweighed by the buzz created by all the kids in costume in the hall. This can be done the same day as the teaser assemblies to great effect. One last trick: After the teasers, and after your kids have had their lunch, convince them to return to their last class, not in costume, but with their makeup still on. Warn them that they'll get a little teasing, especially the boys, but when a kid walks into a class *just a little late* still wearing his stage makeup, the other kids in the room will talk about nothing else, and more and more of them will decide to come and see the show. This minor interruption to the school day is well worth it, as it makes the show more of a success and raises school spirit.

WEAR BUTTONS/STICKERS

Buttons and stickers help publicize a show; not quite as effectively as T-shirts, but better than nothing. Easiest might be those horrible little convention badges, with a computer-printed announcement inside. Kids just can't seem to resist stopping to read a sticker or badge another kid is wearing.

Cue 14 *Go.*

Curtain Up

When the curtain was about to go up, I would vacate the backstage area. For the duration of each act, the show was in the hands of the cast. I sort of liken this to the job of a football coach. The coach may be intensely involved in the game, but he's on the sidelines, not on the field *doing* anything. The only adult who actually had to work between the curtains was our orchestra conductor. The rest of us took a place in the house, and sat, and pretended everything was under control. Plus, I sort of ran the house. You can delegate this, but it's kind of a do-nothing job unless there's a crisis; then you'll have to take charge anyway. All a house manager does is see that the ushers are well dressed and ready, stock up on programs, check the restrooms, assist in the set-up for any vendors (flowers, candy), open the house, deal with questions from the patrons, set up a lost-and-found, run for change if the ticket sellers run out (or send someone), and send word that the house is ready to the stage manager. I liked doing this, as it left the show part of the show to the kids but still gave me something to do. Sitting still and doing nothing was not my style. So I'd also be hovering near the sound board and fiddling with the video setup for the archival videotape.

One of the most important parts of this job is making certain the house is prepared for the audience. We'd check the aisles for trash and hide all of the bookbags and coats. I'd give a quick lesson on ushering, and open the doors.

USHERS

Drama kids that either didn't audition or weren't selected are usually up for ushering. Adult theater lovers volunteer to "ush" as well and get to see the shows for free. Extra stagehands can ush too; remind them to dress nice and to bring work clothes in case of a backstage emergency. The quick lesson on ushering is: Dress nice, stand up straight, always smile, say something to each customer (they can repeat themselves every fifth or sixth customer), hand out the programs right-side up, and have an answer for simple questions regarding the bathroom, the phones, and the length of the show. At halftime (intermission), ushers can sell refreshments, block backstage access (very important), and watch the sound board so the technicians can get a little break. After the show, ushers can help tidy the house, keep people from entering the dressing rooms, and fold programs for the next show. They can also give you a break, allowing you to go backstage if necessary. You'll have to go back for green room if nothing else.

GREEN ROOM

All staff, cast, and crew should assemble in the green room prior to the curtain for last-second instructions and a pep talk from the director. The green room itself is wherever the actors cool their heels between scenes; *green room* is the pep-talk/warm-up ceremony that occurs before every show. Absolute last-minute changes are noted, and frayed nerves are attempted to be smoothed over. You should be there, so leave the house under the responsibility of the head usher or the house manager and get backstage. Be sure the musicians and the crew find their way to the green room as well. On closing night you'll probably receive a little gift, so prepare a short thank-you speech. Your job during green room is to say something exciting and perfectly appropriate for the moment. I always like to breeze in after green room starts and mention that we're holding the curtain because there are so many people in line. Another good one is to sort of interrupt and demand that the musicians take their places. This never fails to elicit a cheer from the troupe. Two particular reminders that may get overlooked (mention them if the director forgets): safety, and not changing things. Don't change routines, don't change blocking or entrances, don't jump too high just because you are excited, then fall flat on your face because you overdid it (it happens).

Call the crew to their duty at the appropriate moment; the director or the stage manager will call "places." Then scoot back to the house and watch the musicians enter.

THE CASH BOX

Whenever admission is charged, someone ends up in control of the cash box. The box can be the classic cigar box—now getting hard to find—but is usually a little tin box with a tinkeytoy lock, and no key. Presuming the tickets have been made and cut, all that remains is to sell them all at the right price, make the right amount of change, give out the correct ticket (adult/student/senior citizen), keep the extra tickets in order (because they are numbered), and keep the money safe. Worst of all, the ticket sales almost always must be audited, which entails a tremendous amount of paperwork. Like you couldn't cheat 'em if you wanted.

It's surprising how many sponsors entrust ticket sales to a student. We weren't allowed to do that; our adult chaperones took care of selling tickets. They were scheduled to arrive about thirty minutes early and sell until about fifteen minutes after the curtain. Chaperones in a high school are usually teachers. Nevertheless, the prudent sponsor keeps an eye on ticket sales; at least once a year we'd end up with a teacher who would count change *verrrry* slowly. In addition to making the school look bad, this lets the ticket line get objectionably long. It's worse when the seats are reserved; again, I caution you to think long and hard about the negative aspects of reserving seats.

There is no way to hurry up a slow ticket agent. The only thing to do is to grab a handful of student tickets and walk down the line selling student tickets for exact change. It's important to start with student tickets. Parents don't seem to mind if a student gets to cut in front of them in this situation; it's clear that someone who knows what he is doing is getting the customers inside, and they'll stay quiet. It's also important to sell exact change only. That way you can cram the cash into one pocket and move along pretty quickly. Make sure your pocket does not have any of your own money in it. This is also a great way to resupply the cashbox with ones; it's almost a given that you won't have enough. Some schools supply a change fund. At our school, the phrase "blood from a turnip" comes to mind, and we usually had to live without. Again, the sponsor (you) will have to provide some cash. Ones. Planning ahead is useful here. Twenties you can get from a money machine, but that won't help you make change. Ones are available from the bank, but only when it's open. In a pinch, you can send an usher or a crew member to the closest store that does a lot of business with the crew. I'm not above using T-shirt money if you've managed to collect it. Don't forget to pay it back.

KEEP AN EYE ON TICKET SALES

It is critical that the amount of money you've put in the change fund is documented, because the ticket sellers almost never come out even. If they're short, it'll be your money going in there to cover, and it's nice to know how much. Take it off your taxes as a donation, or chalk it up to experience, but be sure the deposit is balanced. You could turn it in unbalanced, but think about the looks you'll get and the scrutiny every future financial transaction will incur. And then someone will ask about all that T-shirt money. It's not worth it. Remember, you are the person who runs things right; you can't come out uneven. During *Fiddler* I made up a $56 shortfall out of my own pocket. It never seemed worth it until I overheard the principal tell the new financial secretary, "He's always right to the penny." It means they trust you, and when you have that trust you'll have the freedom to do a lot more—with the money and with the rest of the production.

So, we're selling tickets to students with exact change, and then to parents with exact change. Feel free to joke about scalping tickets, it's inevitable. Usually a few minutes of this is enough to get the ticket line down to a respectable size, although occasionally you'll have to stay there and sell tickets until the curtain. If that's the case then *hold the curtain.* First, you want the customers inside, and happy. They won't be happy if the show starts while they're waiting for their change. Besides, people in line love hearing that you'll hold the curtain for them, and the word magically filters back to the cast, "They're holding the curtain because there's so many people in line."

You are the one that makes sure the word magically filters back to the cast. The effect is, well, magical. They don't have to know that there's a slow ticket agent, just that there's a long line. If green room is over, your sound operator can be instrumental in getting the word backstage, since she is, or should be, in the house close by. When you are holding the curtain—anytime, actually—be sure, through the headset system, to make it clear that the show never starts until you say so. Only the director can trump you on this. Technically, it is the student stage manager's job to start the show; just make it clear that it is your job to tell her when she may begin. It wouldn't be prudent to say you are holding the curtain, only to stroll into the theater to see the second scene. Hold the curtain as long as you need to to seat your audience. Then get to the sound board and use the headset to turn the show over to the stage manager.

After the curtain rises, you'll have to put the cash somewhere safe. We had a real safe that my predecessor had purchased, used. It was a monster, and the movers almost balked when it came to moving it to the new theater. It's still there, the strongbox for the Montgomery Blair Players. I still remember the combination. There is no question it is worth the time and trouble to track down and buy a nice-sized safe—actually, a big safe. It'll help you keep things . . . um, safe. In addition to the cash, there's the prop pistols, microphones, expensive theater lamps . . . you'd be surprised what a comfort it is to know these things are out of the way, mischief-wise. Never give a student the combination to the safe.

Lock up the cash until everything's over. If you are required to turn in the money immediately, keep the ones. Always keep the ones. I'd keep the ones even if my ticket prices were $5 and $10, but that's just me. After the show, or after the weekend, count up the proceeds, reconcile the account (a real pain), and make your deposit. Be absolutely certain the deposit is correct.

By the way, if the money ever comes out over, you can't keep it. Turn it in. Or use it to buy Hershey's Kisses for the kids, or hot dogs, or something else for the show, off the books. This is one of those situations where no one must know when you pitch money in, and you must not skim any gravy that comes along. Inevitably, someone will ask, "Hey, where'd that extra six bucks go?" You must be able to answer, "I used it to pay for the carpet spot cleaner." And there it is, no spot on the carpet, testimony to your complete honesty. Good karma.

OPEN THE HOUSE

Let people choose their seats as they arrive, but don't let them into the theater too soon. I tried to open the house at 7:12 or later for a 7:30 show. You don't want people sitting in their seats for a half-hour before your show—it makes them restless. Better to have them restless out in the hall and getting a little excited; then when the doors open, there's a surge of enthusiasm that penetrates the crowd. I call this *critical mass.* When I was playing in a band you could tell when the crowd was ready to rock, even with your back turned. There's just a little buzz that you can feel if you are sensitized to it. You can prime the pump, so to speak, by making the audience wait outside, just a little bit. My coworkers think this is crazy, but I swear it works.

ARCHIVAL VIDEOTAPE

Sometime before the curtain opens you'll have to set up your video camera to make an archival videotape for educational purposes. As a courtesy to the playgoers, you should put this up in the back of the house, out of the way. If you're lucky you can pinch the audio off of the sound board, but you had better practice this beforehand. The best compromise might be to run one open-air mic and take one channel of sound off of the board. This takes a little doing, so most people rely on the camera mic to record sound. Unfortunately, especially from the back of the house, the camera mic just isn't going to give great sound. If you have the time you can experiment, dedicate a wireless mic to the task of "videotape audio," or even hire it out. It's not as important as it may seem, since you aren't selling videotapes. Definitely use a tripod and find a talented camera operator, or do it yourself. Since you've turned the show over to the stage manager, *officially* you have nothing to do, so this might work out. Besides, you can just pan out to a wide shot if you are called away. Make sure you have enough tape to get through the show, and don't rely on batteries; hook up an extension cord and run the camera plugged in. I have even rolled a full-sized TV down and connected it to use as a monitor; you'll get awfully tired of peeking through that little viewfinder on the camera. The archival videotape can be a great teaching tool, if you can ever find time to watch it.

CURTAIN UP!

If you blinked or were busy, you probably missed the orchestra's entrance. We tried this a few different ways; you probably don't want them sitting idle throughout the seating of the audience. We'd have them enter and pretune, then slip out as we opened the house. That way they get to make an entrance and get some applause. The conductor, of course, enters after the fire announcement and gets a spotlight of her own, doused out just before the curtain. After intermission the procedure is the same, except no fancy entrances, just spot the conductor at her seat. And awaaaaaaaay we go!

SWEATING IT OUT

Once that curtain rises there is pretty much nothing you can do until intermission. You might as well sit down in the house, relax, and watch the show. You could take notes, but if you are the restless type (like me), you'll be pacing the back aisle, trying to force the show towards perfection with every tensed-up muscle in your body. There's no proof that this *doesn't* help, so go ahead if you want to. If a crisis occurs, you must very quickly decide if you should intervene or let the cast and crew solve the problem. Don't be a busybody; minor quirks are part of what makes live theater so real. You could run the videotape recorder if you like that kind of thing. Somewhere along the line you should force yourself to sit still and just enjoy the show—closing night, perhaps. I liken this to putting your camera down while on vacation and actually vacationing. You worked as hard as anybody on this show—sit down and enjoy it.

INTERMISSION

Your one important duty at intermission is to see that everyone remembers that the show isn't over yet. Post ushers to keep well-wishers away from backstage and to keep the cast out of sight. Deal with any crisis, then announce that the curtain is going up for Act II. "Curtain going up!" you say, and ring a little bell, just like Broadway.

LEG BROKEN, DO IT ALL AGAIN TOMORROW

After the curtain calls are over comes one of the most exciting and rewarding moments in theater. Make sure all of the equipment is safe, then post ushers near the dressing rooms to keep the hoi polloi at bay. Near, so the cast and crew can feel the excitement. Far enough away to allow the cast a bit of privacy. The ushers can act as guards; don't let them overdo it. Of course, little kids somehow magically get through the phalanx of ushers and get a backstage tour from their older brother or sister. Parents and other well-wishers have to wait outside the stage door. This is a particularly important moment for everyone in the show; there will be flowers, hugs, and lots of laughter. It was my favorite place to be after a show, but someone has to watch the sound equipment and any other vulnerable thing. I did have a video camera stolen once; it was "Happy Blair Day," and everyone was happy except me.

THE NEXT DAY

The second day of a show is the first opportunity to neglect something you thought was taken care of. Things need to be reset, props need to go back where they belong, and no one will be in a mood to concentrate. This is the *sophomore syndrome,* where young actors and crew can get the feeling "This isn't so hard" and lose concentration. You might fall prey to the syndrome, too, and figure your work is just about done. This is deadly, as it means you've forgotten the purpose of all of the work that has gone into the show. The goal of *everything* you have done is to *put on a good show*. Now is not the time to lighten up, now is not the time to lose concentration. Don't let the excitement trump your good sense. In *The Sting* there is a scene where the grifters come into an office dressed as painters in order to commandeer the office. We had the actors actually begin repainting the set. At the conclusion of the first night, everyone was ready to run off and party (or sleep). I had to remind them to repaint the set its original color. (By the end of the run, the paint was nine coats thick.) Anyhow, you must be careful not to let your guard down. Plus, you will no doubt have some improvements to make, which you give as notes.

NOTES

Giving notes during the run is a bit of a problem. Try to see the stage manager concerning any egregious errors and get them corrected, or at least noted, before everyone goes home. Add some time before the next show to fix everything else. For instance, if you find you need to practice a scene change a few times (and you will), budget an extra hour or ninety minutes especially for that task. If everything is going smoothly, congratulations—make the "call" for an hour before the curtain. Lock up the money and go get some sleep. Tomorrow you may actually get to see a bit of sunshine for the first time in weeks.

Cue 15

Go Home, the Show's Over

When a show closes, there is always a tremendous urge to get out of the theater and go have a party or something. This euphoria will last until everyone falls asleep, then wakes up, and that sometimes takes an entire day. Upon awaking, everyone finds the euphoria gone and *no one* will be willing to come in to do *any* kind of work, not even you. So you'd better plan to get everything you can dismantled the moment the show closes. Invite all cast and crew to help dismantle the set, carefully; don't break anything up. You will want to save all of the useful parts for next time. You'll get about ninety minutes of labor before everyone sneaks away, and if you plan well you can get just about everything dismantled in that time. If you are in a situation where you simply must vacate completely, make plans to work all night. Have a strike party.

STRIKE PARTY

The purpose of a *strike party* is to get all of your dismantling done while enjoying the reverie of the moment. In a community theater there may be alcohol involved, but that's probably not wise. In a school environment the regular rules apply, and you have to be extra-vigilant for safety violations. You'll be surprised how quickly things get dismantled; if you don't take care, some things will get destroyed. Arrange for snacks—if you are putting on *Guys & Dolls* don't forget the cheesecake. Have the tools ready and instruct the crew to help the cast. Be sure everyone is involved in the action. It's not healthy for the cast to run off while the crew stays behind to work, so make sure everyone gets into the spirit of the thing. Get all of the trash into bins or boxes, then clear out—it's over.

Off-campus cast parties are not your official concern, but it would be wise when working with youngsters to make certain that a responsible adult is actually on-site and in charge. I usually didn't go to the kids' cast parties, but I did check to make sure somebody's mom was there.

TAKE DOWN POSTERS/SIGNS

Get the crew to take down all of the posters they can find on the last day of the run. That way they'll be gone when the show is over. They can hang the posters in the green room for autographs and keep them as souvenirs. You'll probably have to print up a few extras especially for this purpose. Don't forget to dismantle the outdoor sign.

CUE 15.9 BETWEEN SHOWS

Stage crew work never really ends. There will always be a show to clean up after and another show to plan. In between gigs you may find a bit of time for housekeeping and stage improvement, and perhaps a moment to reflect upon the job you did. Here are some things to think about between shows.

BUILD A STAGE MODEL

When we moved into our new theater, we were so excited we built a ½"-scale model of the stage. This was a big mistake, since we make layouts in ¼" scale. If you have the time and desire, go ahead and build your own three-dimensional stage model in ¼" scale. Use foam core, Elmer's glue, and pins. Then the crew can make set models with Play-Doh. One little note. When you are standing in the lighting booth staring at your almost-finished stage set and it begins to look like a teeny-tiny stage model, it means you are doing good. It also means you need some sleep, so go take a nap.

BUILD A SCRAPBOOK

I'm sure you had the presence of mind to take photographs of all of the work everybody did during your little show. I'm the keeper of our scrapbooks, and I bring them in every year to allow the new crew to page through them for inspiration. Make up your own, keep them safe, show them off whenever you get the chance—just don't lose 'em. And write down all those names and details you think you'll remember—'cause you won't.

BUILD A WEB PAGE

A scrapbook on the Web, featuring photos of all of your work, punctuated with little stories from the cast and crew, is a great leisure-time activity, and somehow helps in the design of the next show. Actually, looking at other Web sites is a great inspiration, and helps your designs, too. Poke around enough on Google and you'll be able to find my stage crew Web sites. If you have no experience making Web pages, just use Netscape's Page Composer. It's free and will help you put together a nifty little Web page in no time. You'll hafta scan photographs and find a Web host, but these problems are very small; just ask around until you find someone willing to help.

ORDER REPLACEMENT PARTS

This is never going to really happen. What will happen is you'll be driving by a catalog store, or Black & Decker repair shop, or some such place, and you'll decide it's time to finally fix or replace some idiotic little thing that's been cramping your style. You'll pull in, whip out Mister Credit Card, and scratch one thing off of the list in your little book. The idea that you'll actually have the luxury of sitting down, maybe with a cup of coffee, and methodically filling out replacement parts orders—well, it sort of makes me laugh. I'm sure I did it sometime, but I don't remember when.

HOLD A COSTUME SALE

As the years go by, you'll probably end up with far too many costumes, some of dubious quality. Hang 'em on a pipe on October 18 and have a Halloween costume sale. You'll clear the closet and refresh the petty cash account at the same time.

THINK ABOUT THINGS YOU DID WRONG

I don't really want to admit to doing *anything* wrong, but I did. I lost my temper sometimes, and I pushed a little too hard sometimes, and I refused to listen sometimes, and I stuck with bad decisions sometimes . . . hmm, that's about it. To my credit I did notice these things, and I have seldom made the same mistake more than five or six times. You'll know, when the same problem crops up again and again and again, that you are doing something wrong. Try to figure out a new approach. And don't be too hard on yourself—these things happen to everyone. If theater were easy, there wouldn't be much of a challenge—and no reward, either.

THE SHORT LIST

After writing a whole book on how to put a show together, people still ask me for a short list of tasks that must be done. Here you go:

Clean up
Fix everything
Design a great set
Build and paint the set
Hang lights and set up the sound
Practice, practice, practice
Send out publicity, make T-shirts, all that jazz
Practice, practice, practice
Perform
Close the show

I knew you could do it.

ACKNOWLEDGMENTS

It's my book, and I think acknowledgements should be in the back. Kind of like the credits in a movie. Nobody likes it when the credits for a movie run before the movie—c'mon, just start the movie. Nobody ever reads the acknowledgements in a book until after they have read the book, so, *acknowledgements in the back*. I'd like to thank my latest director, Ms. Kelly Newman, for spending a lot of time with me during the writing of this book, discussing all the little details and tidbits included herein. I'd like to mention my first director at Blair, Mr. Thomas Mather: Thanks for giving me absolute, complete freedom in stage design and production at the old Blair. The staff at The Bethesda Academy of Performing Arts deserves recognition for allowing me the opportunity to really stretch my lighting skills. I'd also like to thank all of the folks that read preproduction copies of this book and gave praise and encouragement when I needed it the most, especially Heather.

I'd like to acknowledge all of my coworkers, most particularly Matt Shibla, and everyone else I shamelessly stole ideas from. I'd like to thank my brother Mike for the artwork and for the great advice. By the way, if you ever meet him, call him Michael—only his family gets to call him Mike. A special acknowledgement goes to my family, particularly Mom. Hi, Mom. My publisher, and of course my editor, Nicole Potter, deserve many thanks for their efforts.

Over the years I have worked many, many shows with my childhood friend Mark Wray. He got me involved in stage crew while we were both in high school. He stayed in the business professionally while I worked in the schools. His advice and help through the years has been enormous. Plus, he gets me work outside of school. Thanks, Mark.

Finally, I'd like to thank the crew kids from Wakefield, BAPA, and, most of all, Blair High School. Thanks for providing the labor that made the shows great, thanks for the enthusiastic support, and thanks for helping me make my dreams and ideas a reality. I hope I gave you rewards in equal measure.

MY SHOWS

In second grade I got to crawl under the multipurpose room stage at Henry Clay Elementary and hook up the microphone cord. I distinctly remember how much fun it was to help set up for a big show (it might have been *The Nutcracker*). So I got the bug early. My buddy Mark (his real name) got me involved with the stage crew at Washington-Lee High School (*Go Generals!*), and ever since I've been a part of something backstage somewhere, and occasionally on stage too. Here's a list of shows and places I've worked since college:

K-2 World Premiere—Arena Stage (all I did was cut Plexi)
Handiwork at The Folger
Technical Theater Assistant at Wakefield High School (I taught there)
Museum Artist (did the stuff inside the Statue of Liberty museum,
    and some Smithsonian)
Starstruck—TOMI Park Royal (NY)
Lights and sound for various comedians, including Dave Werner
    and Glen Steer
Lights and sound for various musicians and open mics, including
    Susan Werner
Pyrotechnics at the Capital Center
Grunt roadie at the Cap Center for some rock shows
Working—Montgomery Players
Frankenstein—Montgomery Players
I Hate Hamlet—Alliance Theater
The Sleep—Lumina Stage
Bass Player on *Turbine Tunes*
House Band at *Bad Habits Grill*
Opening Band for Toy Caldwell and Molly Hatchet
Featured Band at *Zoofari 1992*
Installed (some) television studio equipment at Radford U.
Taught "Soldering for Industry" at Montgomery College

Blair High School
The Sting
Rumors
Fame
Noises Off
The King & I
Tom Jones
The Music Man
A Midsummer Night's Dream
Annie
You Can't Take It With You
Fiddler on the Roof
An Autumn Evening of Theater
Anything Goes
Les Misérables
Into the Woods
Much Ado About Nothing
Hello, Dolly!
A Tale of Two Cities
Guys & Dolls
Charley's Aunt
The Rivals
West Side Story
Pericles
(Many) variety and talent shows
I teach there, too:
    Communications Systems Technology
    Technological Innovations
    Exploring Technological Concepts

The Bethesda Academy of Performing Arts
Annie Jr.
Fiddler on the Roof Jr.
Leader Of the Pack: The Ellie Greenwich Musical
Charlie and the Chocolate Factory

That's about it.

APPENDIX 1

Lighting Plot Cheat Sheet (Sample)

This cheat sheet is a complete fake, but it shows how one would go about the task of patching the lights as described in Cue 10. The big numbered grids represent the electrics, the top numbers represent the socket on the pipe; these sometimes appear in a quasi-random fashion. Some of these can be assigned or changed, so watch out here. The middle numbers represent a dimmer assignment; you'll need these if you have a patch panel. The bottom numbers represent the channel sliders assigned at the lighting control board. The lines represent the cabling, the big boxes are scoops, the rectangles are ellipsoidals—oh, just stare at it long enough and it'll all make sense. This method is at least ten times faster than drawing a real light plot, and you'll be changing the light plot a lot in your first few shows, so use it. I omitted some lights, and I left off the gel color assignments for clarity.

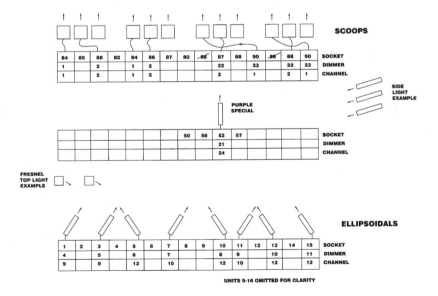

APPENDIX 2

COSTUME CHEAT SHEET

Feel free to copy this cheat sheet into wallet-sized sheets and distribute to the cast. You never know when Steven Spielberg might happen by and select you for a big role because you fit the jacket. We can all dream, can't we? By the way, keep these measurements top secret, especially for women. Lock-and-key secret. Really.

MEN

Jacket: _____

Neck: _____ Sleeve: _____

Waist: _____ Inseam: _____

Shoe size: _____ Hat size: _____ Glove size: _____

Base of neck to waist: _____

Underarm to waist: _____

WOMEN

Bust: _____

Waist: _____

Hips: _____

Waist to floor barefoot: _____

Base of neck to waist: _____

Underarm to waist: _____

Dress size: _____

Shoe size: _____ Hat size: _____ Glove size: _____

APPENDIX 3

STAir RisER HEiqHTs foR 6¾" RisE

You do not *have* to make stairs rise 6¾ inches. I selected this rise because many home improvement centers sell pre-cut stringers with this rise. Whatever you do, design your permanent units all the same for inter-changeability. You can, of course, build a differing size for some special purpose, but remember: any single staircase should have a constant rise, so no one trips. I suppose you could break this rule if you want to design a strange, shrinking, expanding, dramatic staircase with varying steps, but your actors will probably trip and your audience will probably think the crew made a mistake. When we say "break a leg," we don't really mean it.

STEP	¾" TREAD (PLYWOOD)	1" TREAD (REAL TREADS)	1½" TREAD (CUT UP 2 × 12)	HEIGHT AT TOP OF STEP
14	93¾	93½	93	94½
13	87	86¾	86¼	87¾
12	80¼	80	79½	81
11	73½	73¼	72¾	74¼
10	66¾	66½	66	67½
9	60	59¾	59¼	60¾
8	53¼	53	52½	54
7	46½	46¼	45¾	47¼
6	39¾	39½	39	40½
5	33	32¾	32¼	33¾
4	26¼	26	25½	27
3	19½	19¼	18¾	20¼
2	12¾	12½	12	13½
1	6	5¾	5¼	6¾
0	stage floor	stage floor	stage floor	0

INDEX

The smart thing to do is to begin
trusting your intuition
...backstage

Books from Allworth Press

Allworth Press is an imprint of Allworth Communications, Inc. Selected titles are listed below.

TECHNICAL THEATER FOR NONTECHNICAL PEOPLE
by Drew Campbell (paperback, 6 × 9, 256 pages, $18.95)

THE BUSINESS OF THEATRICAL DESIGN
by James L. Moody (paperback, 6 × 9, 288 pages, $19.95)

THE HEALTH AND SAFETY GUIDE FOR FILM, TV AND THEATER
by Monona Rossol (paperback, 6 × 9, 256 pages, $19.95)

BUSINESS AND LEGAL FORMS FOR THEATER
by Charles Grippo (paperback, includes CD-ROM; 8½ × 11, 192 pages, $29.95)

BUILDING THE SUCCESSFUL THEATER COMPANY
by Lisa Mulcahy (paperback, 6 × 9, 240 pages, $19.95)

PRODUCING YOUR OWN SHOWCASE
by Paul Harris (paperback, 6 × 9, 240 pages, $18.95)

BOOKING AND TOUR MANAGEMENT FOR THE PERFORMING ARTS
by Rena Shagan (paperback, 6 × 9, 288 pages, $19.95)

THE STAGE PRODUCER'S BUSINESS AND LEGAL GUIDE
by Charles Grippo (paperback, 6 × 9, 256 pages, $19.95)

MOVEMENT FOR ACTORS
edited by Nicole Potter (paperback, 6 × 9, 288 pages, $19.95)

MASTERING SHAKESPEARE: AN ACTING CLASS IN SEVEN SCENES
by Scott Kaiser (paperback, 6 × 9, 288 pages, $19.95)

CAREER SOLUTIONS FOR CREATIVE PEOPLE
by Dr. Rhonda Ormont (paperback, 6 × 9, 320 pages, $19.95)

Please write to request our free catalog. To order by credit card, call 1-800-491-2808.

To see our complete catalog on the World Wide Web, or to order online, you can find us at *www.allworth.com*.